Oil, Nationalism and British Policy in Iran

Oil, Nationalism and British Policy in Iran

The End of Informal Empire, 1941–53

Jack Taylor

BLOOMSBURY ACADEMIC
LONDON • NEW YORK • OXFORD • NEW DELHI • SYDNEY

BLOOMSBURY ACADEMIC

Bloomsbury Publishing Plc, 50 Bedford Square, London, WC1B 3DP, UK
Bloomsbury Publishing Inc, 1385 Broadway, New York, NY 10018, USA
Bloomsbury Publishing Ireland, 29 Earlsfort Terrace, Dublin 2, D02 AY28, Ireland

BLOOMSBURY, BLOOMSBURY ACADEMIC and the Diana logo are trademarks of Bloomsbury Publishing Plc

First published in Great Britain 2024
This paperback edition published in 2025

Copyright © Jack Taylor, 2024

Jack Taylor has asserted his right under the Copyright, Designs and Patents Act, 1988, to be identified as Author of this work.

For legal purposes the Acknowledgements on p. vii constitute an extension of this copyright page.

Cover image © A portrait of the Shah is carried triumphantly atop an Iranian army tank patrolling the streets of Tehran after the coup that overthrew the regime of Premier Mohammed Mossadegh. Bettmann/Getty.

All rights reserved. No part of this publication may be: i) reproduced or transmitted in any form, electronic or mechanical, including photocopying, recording or by means of any information storage or retrieval system without prior permission in writing from the publishers; or ii) used or reproduced in any way for the training, development or operation of artificial intelligence (AI) technologies, including generative AI technologies. The rights holders expressly reserve this publication from the text and data mining exception as per Article 4(3) of the Digital Single Market Directive (EU) 2019/790.

Bloomsbury Publishing Plc does not have any control over, or responsibility for, any third-party websites referred to or in this book. All internet addresses given in this book were correct at the time of going to press. The author and publisher regret any inconvenience caused if addresses have changed or sites have ceased to exist, but can accept no responsibility for any such changes.

A catalogue record for this book is available from the British Library.

A catalog record for this book is available from the Library of Congress.

ISBN: HB: 978-1-3503-2058-1
PB: 978-1-3503-2117-5
ePDF: 978-1-3503-2119-9
eBook: 978-1-3503-2116-8

Typeset by Deanta Global Publishing Services, Chennai, India

For product safety related questions contact productsafety@bloomsbury.com.

To find out more about our authors and books visit www.bloomsbury.com and sign up for our newsletters.

Contents

List of figures	vi
Acknowledgements	vii
The unresolved coup	1
1 Iran under occupation	13
2 Labour, imperialism and Iran	45
3 Development and division	77
4 Welfare imperialism in crisis	109
5 British responses and British failures	139
6 Countdown to midnight	175
Reflecting on the end of empire in Iran	207
Bibliography	213
Index	223

Figures

0.1	The Abadan Polo Club	7
1.1	Indian troops under British command enter the Abadan refinery, 1941	17
1.2	Mohammad Reza Shah soon after his accession to the throne	19
2.1	Abadan from the air	53
2.2	A drilling crew at work in southern Iran	69
3.1	Ernest Bevin, British foreign secretary and the architect of welfare imperialism	85
3.2	British and Iranian AIOC officials, February 1946	86
3.3	AIOC workers enjoy a performance by the AIOC band at the Labour Cinema, Bahmanshir	92
4.1	Returned to the Majlis in 1950 Mossadegh was immediately invited to meet with the shah	116
5.1	Demonstrators hold aloft a sign torn from the AIOC's offices in Tehran, July 1951	143
5.2	Mossadegh addresses supporters outside the Majlis, October 1951	143
5.3	Mossadegh inspects the Liberty Bell during his visit to the United States	156
5.4	Security forces attempt to disperse crowds that have rallied in Mossadegh's defence, July 1952	172
6.1	With Anglo-American backing, mobs rally in Tehran	204

Acknowledgements

I am indebted to many people for their scholarly advice and generosity of time. Particular thanks must go to Michael Hopkins, Michael Collins and Sarah Snyder for their guidance and encouragement at various points during my studies. Without their support this book would not have been written and my horizons would be much narrower.

I am also hugely appreciative of Orlando Cantell and Ewan Gibbs for their feedback, which was challenging and helpful in equal measure, and for their friendship.

The team at Bloomsbury, particularly Maddie Smith, has been fantastic to work with, and I have valued the advice they have given me from pitching to publication. It would be remiss not to mention the archivists and librarians who have helped me to track down books and uncover interesting sources. Trawling the stacks can sometimes be a lonely endeavour, but with their assistance it can also be inspiring.

Most importantly, I am forever grateful to my wife, Tricia, for her love and patience, concerning both this book and everything else. I cannot thank my parents, Sian and Keith, enough for their encouragement.

This study, like every work of history, is a collective endeavour, but any errors are very much my own.

The unresolved coup

On 19 August 1953 General Fazlollah Zahedi became Iran's thirty-sixth prime minister. The general was ostensibly the beneficiary of a popular revolt against Mohammad Mossadegh, whose perceived republicanism and alleged closeness with left-wing forces brought him into conflict with the country's monarch, Mohammad Reza Shah, and clerical leaders. The British and American governments welcomed Zahedi's premiership as a triumph of the Iranian people, the shah and the army over Mossadegh, a reactionary obsessive who threatened Western interests in Iran and throughout the Middle East.

Three days later the shah returned to Iran from self-imposed exile in Italy and was met at Tehran airport by senior members of Zahedi's government, army officers and the diplomatic corps. Escorted by a convoy of tanks he travelled to his summer palace and addressed the nation, commending the Iranian people for their 'valiant rising in defence of the independence of the country'. According to the Foreign Office, Tehran was gripped by jubilation as the masses celebrated Iran's liberation from Mossadegh and the threat of atheistic communism.[1]

It did not take long for rumours to spread that the official narrative was not the full story and that the British and American governments had contributed to Mossadegh's downfall. On 16 September, *Times of India* correspondent G. K. Reddy ruminated on the 'good many people' who suspected that the recent coup had been inspired 'if not actually engineered' abroad.[2] In the decades that followed, a steady drip feed of information concerning Anglo-American collusion in Iran gave credence to Reddy's analysis including several accounts written by intelligence agents themselves.[3] In 2000 *The New York Times* journalist James Risen published a secret history, written by one of the CIA's

---

[1] Persia: Political Review of the Recent Crisis, 2 September 1953, RG 59 788.00/9-253 (National Security Archives – NSA). Also published in a redacted form as Document 362: British Memorandum, 2 September 1953, *Foreign Relations of the United States: Diplomatic Papers, 1952-1954, Iran, 1951–1954, Vol. X* (Washington DC: United States Government Printing Office, 1989).
[2] G. K. Reddy, 'Iran's Royalist Coup: Foreign Supporters', *The Times of India*, 16 September 1953.
[3] Sam Falle, *My Lucky Life: In War, Revolution, Peace and Diplomacy* (Lewes: Book Guild, 1996); Kermit Roosevelt, *Countercoup: The Struggle for the Control of Iran* (New York: McGraw Hill, 1979); C. M. Woodhouse, *Something Ventured: An Autobiography* (London: Granada, 1982).

senior operatives, which suggested that Mossadegh's removal – codenamed TPAJAX or Operation Ajax in the United States and Boot in Great Britain – was not only directed by American agents but became the blueprint for subsequent Cold War interventions.[4] A number of additional agency histories have since become available.[5]

Recognizing the growing weight of evidence, Secretary of State Madeleine Albright acknowledged American culpability for the coup, a position President Obama endorsed in 2009.[6] Four years later, following a series of leaks, previously classified CIA files were made public and in 2017 the Foreign Relations of the United States' series published over 1,000 documents concerning American activity in Iran, building on an earlier 1989 edition. Updated in 2018, these documents clarify beyond all doubt the depth of American involvement in the planning and execution of operations to remove Mossadegh. Document 306, dated 28 August 1953, for example, makes clear that American agents were 'to be highly commended for laying the groundwork for action and providing the spark which set off the demonstration on 19 August'.[7] Elsewhere the collection outlines the vast network of spies, assets and thugs constructed by British and American agents in great detail. Although historiographical debates rage as to *why* Mossadegh was toppled – to safeguard Iran from communism, to preserve the international oil order or some variation of the two – there is a widespread consensus that the State Department and the CIA played a significant role.

The nature and depth of British involvement, however, is less clear-cut. Unlike their American counterparts, successive British governments have persisted to maintain a veil of secrecy and to deny historians access to key files concerning the operation against Mossadegh. The British Embassy's annual report for 1953 is typical in its focus on the official account of events. Mossadegh, the report suggests, was pushing his country to political and economic breaking point. Against this profligate leadership, the shah galvanized popular and

---

[4] James Risen, 'SECRETS OF HISTORY: The CIA in Iran', *The New York Times*, 16 April 2000; Clandestine Service History: Overthrow of Premier Mossadeq of Iran, November 1952–August 1953, March 1954 (NSA).
[5] Scott A. Koch, *'Zendebad, Shah!' The Central Intelligence Agency and the Fall of Iranian Prime Minister Mohammed Mossadeq, August 1953* (Washington, DC: CIA History Staff, 1998); The Battle for Iran, undated – 1970s (NSA).
[6] 'Remarks before the American-Iranian Council', 17 March 2000, https://1997-2001.state.gov/statements/2000/000317.html; 'Remarks by the President on a New Beginning', 4 June 2009, https://obamawhitehouse.archives.gov/the-press-office/remarks-president-cairo-university-6-04-09.
[7] Document 306: Memorandum From the Chief of Station in Iran to the Chief of the Near East and Africa Division, Directorate of Plans, Central Intelligence Agency, 28 August 1953, *Foreign Relations of the United States: Diplomatic Papers, 1952-1954, Iran, 1951–1954*, Second Edition (Washington DC: United States Government Printing Office, 2018).

military support to save his country.⁸ Following Mossadegh's death in 1967, *The Times* published an obituary that noted his 'many eccentricities of manner and method' and blamed his unyielding negotiating tactics, alignment with the Iranian left and purported republicanism for his downfall. Britain's role was left undiscussed.⁹

In the late 1970s, as State Department historians began to prepare documents for public release, Foreign Office mandarins rushed to limit the publication of information that may contain sensitive or 'very embarrassing things about the British'.¹⁰ In a 1979 message titled 'IRAN: RELEASE OF CONFIDENTIAL RECORDS', officials in London urged their colleagues in the United States to impress upon the American government the importance of suppressing the release of anything concerning the coup that may be damaging to British prestige and interests.¹¹ Keenly aware that the shah was under enormous pressure from Islamist and nationalist factions, concealing sensitive information was framed as vital to defending his regime and national security interests.

Since then, alongside the publication of American materials, senior British operatives working in Iran have given interviews and published books detailing their involvement. In 1984, Britain's ambassador to Iran from 1963 to 1971, Denis Wright admitted that when first posted to the country in 1953 he had been briefed on Britain's hand in the coup.¹² In February 2006, then Foreign Secretary Jack Straw testified before the House of Commons' Select Committee on Foreign Affairs and acknowledged the role that 'elements of British intelligence and the CIA' played in Mossadegh's removal from office.¹³ Straw would later write and speak widely on the Anglo-Iranian relationship, tellingly giving a book on the subject the title *The English Job: Understanding Iran and Why It Distrusts Britain*.¹⁴

Despite widespread acknowledgement that Britain had *some* role in the coup against Mossadegh, the Foreign Office claims that files relating to this operation 'should remain withheld as they fall under FOIA Section 23(1) . . . information

---

[8] Summary of Events in Persia, 1953, FO 416/107 (The National Archives – TNA).
[9] 'Dr Muhammad Moussadek', *The Times*, 6 March 1967.
[10] Summary Record: British-American Planning Talks, 11–12 October 1978; Crowe to Gorham, 12 October 1978; Kerr to Crowe, 24 October 1978, FCO 8/3216 (TNA).
[11] Gorham to Muir, 24 October 1978, FCO 8/3216 (TNA).
[12] Denis Wright: Interview recorded by Habib Ladjevardi, 10 October 1984 (Iranian Oral History Collection – IOHC).
[13] Minutes of Evidence: Foreign Affairs Committee, 8 February 2006 (House of Commons Library).
[14] Jack Straw, *The English Job: Understanding Iran and Why It Distrusts Britain* (London: Biteback Publishing, 2020).

supplied by or relating to, bodies dealing with security matters'.[15] Appeals against this decision continue to be unsuccessful. From the sources available to us, whether through Britain's National Archives, documents released by the US government or those collected by university and private collections, it is clear that the UK undertook a deeply interventionist policy towards Iran well in advance of 1953. This included not only assistance in coup planning and execution but also a broader policy of social, economic and political interventionism that requires careful examination. There is also unambiguous evidence to illustrate that successive British governments attempted to involve the United States in clandestine operations in Iran and used the threat of communism to draw them into action.

Oil and imperialism

The history of Anglo-Iranian relations is based fundamentally on oil and imperialism. The earliest records of contact between Britain and Persia date from 1238, an unsuccessful effort by Henry III to secure an alliance against the Mongols, and relations between the two countries remained distant until the 1500s. Granted a Royal Charter in 1600, the East India Company was key to establishing relations between the two nations, securing two royal firmans from the shah to provide for a permanent residency and trading post. The company's resident became, in the words of Lord Curzon, the Persian Gulf's 'uncrowned king' with oversight over Britain's regional commercial and naval interests.[16]

The British viewed Persia as both a marketplace and a shield to defend India's riches. Wedged between the Russian Caucasus and Britain's Baluchistan Agency, it was at the centre of a geopolitical chess game played in distant capitals. According to Ann Lambton, celebrated Orientalist scholar, wartime press attaché at the British Embassy and regular source of advice to the Foreign Office, the question of political power in Iran was 'not simply an internal matter' but inherently influenced by its position at the intersection of imperial competition.[17]

Alongside proxy wars and diplomatic machinations, investment was crucial to expanding their interests and by the late 1800s the British enjoyed concessions

---

[15] Correspondence between the Foreign, Commonwealth & Development Office Historical Information Rights Team and the author, 2021–2.
[16] George N. Curzon, *Persia and the Persian Question: Vol. II* (London: Longman, Green & Co, 1892), 451.
[17] SOAS Lecture Notes, undated, Ann Lambton Papers – Box 48/6 (Durham University Archives – DUA).

in railway, road and waterway construction, mining, telecommunications and myriad other public utilities. In 1889 a banking concession was granted and the Imperial Bank of Persia established, quickly becoming the country's bank of issue and cementing Britain's deep influence over Persia's economy. With investment came ambitious young men and their cultural exports. They formed cricket, hunting and shooting clubs and the Iranian Football Association, the first president of which was Imperial Bank director James McMurray. More importantly, they established networks of prestige among royal courtesans, politicians, merchants and tribal leaders. Fuelled by favour and corruption, these networks enabled the British to exert ever-greater influence across Persian society.

The expansion of British power in the nineteenth century was piecemeal compared to the granting of a petroleum concession to English gold magnate William Knox D'Arcy in May 1901. The D'Arcy concession included a guarantee that the Persian government would not allow another company to build a pipeline in southern Iran while exploration was ongoing, effectively carving out a British mineral monopoly and blunting Russia's ambitions. However, oil was not immediately forthcoming. Keen to maintain exploration and preserve their brake on Russian expansionism, in 1905 the Admiralty intervened to broker an agreement between D'Arcy and Glasgow's Burmah Oil Company and establish a new syndicate: the Anglo-Persian Oil Company (APOC).

Three years later APOC engineers finally, after innumerable false starts, discovered oil in commercial quantities at Masjid Soleiman. In 1909 APOC became a publicly traded company and within a decade the company was extracting over 1.1 million long tons of oil annually.[18] Rich in sulphur, Persian oil was foul smelling and useless for domestic purposes. It was, however, a highly effective industrial fuel and found a ready market as the Royal Navy transitioned from coal to oil-powered engines. The Admiralty bought a 51 per cent stake in the company, an investment of little over £2 million that one parliamentarian called 'wholly without precedent'.[19] The integration between the company and state's interest had been formalized, but APOC continued to be managed as a private concern.

The company's flagship site was the Abadan refinery on the banks of the Arvand Rud connected to Masjid Soleiman via a 130-mile-long pipeline. The

---

[18] R. W. Ferrier, *The History of the British Petroleum Company Vol. I: The Developing Years, 1901-1932* (Cambridge: Cambridge University Press, 2000), 271.
[19] Timothy Mitchell, *Carbon Democracy: Political Power in the Age of Oil* (London: Verso, 2013), 59–61; House of Commons Debate, 29 June 1914, *Hansard*, vol. 64 cc 54.

refinery's construction began in 1910 and ended two years later. Built on alluvial, salt-rich land that seemed incapable of supporting much beyond a few peasant hamlets, Abadan became one of the empire's single largest asset and a totem of British wealth and power. In 1913 the refinery had a capacity of 120,000 tons, rising to 1,000,000 tons in 1925 and 5,000,000 tons by 1930. Within less than a decade this figure had doubled.[20] Investment in a network of pipelines, roads and railways increased output, and profitability remained buoyant throughout the 1920s. It is notable, however, that while APOC profits topped £20.88 million in the five fiscal years between 1923/4 and 1927/8, royalties paid to the Iranian government were barely a fifth of this and in some years were less than 12 per cent of total profits.[21]

Abadan was not merely an industrial hub but a city built and sustained by British interests. The oil company provided everything from infrastructure, drinking water, electricity and sewage facilities to recreation and housing. In turn, APOC presented themselves as a model employer and a model of progressive workforce planning. In truth, the standard of living enjoyed by most Iranian workers was poor. This accommodation was often squalid, their wages low and their at-work safety minimal. Deprived of coal in the winter and ice in the summer, workers were regularly consumed by preventable ailments like pneumonia and sunstroke.[22] Manucher Farmanfarmaian, a future director of the National Iranian Oil Company, recalled later that 'wages were fifty cents a day. There was no vacation pay, no sick leave, no disability compensation.'[23] Recalling his time in Abadan and the company's use of child labour in particular, Israeli journalist Gad Sella suggested that Iranian oil workers were among 'the poorest creatures on earth'.[24] Although APOC employees could make representations to the government regarding their treatment, trade union organization was suppressed.

In contrast to their Iranian counterparts, British staff – managers and technicians – lived lives of ease. They could enjoy Abadan's polo, tennis and golf clubs, contemporary housing ringed by manicured gardens, access to an army of servants and almost total segregation from the poverty that surrounded

---

[20] Memorial Submitted by the Government of the United Kingdom of Great Britain and Northern Ireland, 10 October 1951, Anglo-Iranian Oil Co. Written Proceedings (International Court of Justice Library).
[21] Mostafa Elm, *Oil, Power, and Principle: Iran's Oil Nationalization and Its Aftermath* (Syracuse: Syracuse University Press, 1994), 18.
[22] Touraj Atabaki, Elisabetta Bini and Kaveh Ehsani, eds, *Working for Oil: Comparative Social Histories of Labor in the Global Oil Industry* (Cham: Springer International, 2018), 209; Reports of Parliamentary Delegation to Persia, 10 July 1946, FO 371/52718 (TNA).
[23] Stephen Kinzer, *All the Shah's Men: An American Coup and the Roots of Middle East Terror* (Hoboken: J. Wiley & Sons, 2003), 67.
[24] Gad Sella, 'AIOC's Primitive Labour', *The Jerusalem Post*, 6 July 1951.

Figure 0.1 The Abadan Polo Club – just one of the facilities available to British staff in Iran. Courtesy of the BP Archive © BP plc.

them.[25] Styled along European lines, the company built modern suburbs to be enjoyed solely by their white, European populace. Visiting in 1951, Welsh poet Dylan Thomas was struck by Iranian society's divisions. Nowhere were these more striking than in Abadan, a city that was simultaneously 'evergreen, gardened, cypressed, cinema'd, oil-tanked, (and) boulevarded' and the 'armpit cradle of Persian culture'.[26]

The British protected their favoured status by constructing, through bribes and favour, a network of friendly newspapers, politicians, spies and tribal forces across Persia backed up by the company's security forces and, if required, the might of Britain's combined army and navy. Though still a nominally independent nation, this was an informal imperialism and the Persian people came to see Britain's hand in every cruelty and misdeed. Stories of pernicious deeds perpetrated by greedy oilmen and devious bankers were widespread with some conspiracies containing more than a grain of truth. When Reza Khan became shah in 1921, for example, he did so in part thanks to the intervention of Edmund Ironside, head of a British military mission, who saw in Khan the

---

[25] Transcript: Interview with Sir Donald Logan; Transcript: Interview with Nasrollah Fatemi, 'Iran', *End of Empire* (Granada Television, Manchester, 1985).
[26] Dylan Thomas and Paul Ferris, *The Collected Letters* (London: J. M. Dent, 2000), 876–7.

kind of strong leader needed to stand up to Bolshevism.[27] Even decades later whispers persisted that Britain's representative to Tehran, Herman Norman, was the midwife of Khan's rise to power.[28]

A fervent nationalist, the new shah was desperate to modernize Iran and liberate it from foreign influence. He believed that the D'Arcy concession was fundamentally unbalanced and the annual fluctuation in royalties his treasury received most unsatisfactory. In November 1932, the Persian government informed APOC that its concession had been terminated, a decision that was widely celebrated in Iran.[29] Local newspapers captured the anger towards the oil company and the British people more generally, describing them as duplicitous, immoral and 'the most bigoted people in the whole world because they are the most selfish people'.[30] The D'Arcy concession, meanwhile, was dismissed as a mere 'scrap of paper'.[31]

Demonstrating the commonality between company and state, the British government intervened and referred the cancellation to the council of the League of Nations. The League, however, found that the issue was one of commerce, not diplomacy, and negotiations to mediate a solution between APOC and the shah opened in April 1933. These concluded barely a month later with the signing of a new concession that significantly reduced the size of area under APOC control and guaranteed royalty payments of at least £750,000 – or 20 per cent of net profits – per annum. It also included a one-off payment of £1 million and promised to 'Iranize' the company. In turn, however, APOC's concession in Iran was extended to 1993 and a clause preventing any alteration unless discussions were called for by the company inserted.[32] When Persia became Iran in 1935 APOC followed suit and was rechristened the Anglo-Iranian Oil Company (AIOC).

World War, Cold War and imperialism in Iran

The greatest source of British power and influence in Iran, but loathed by the Iranian people, the oil company described its operations as 'one of the great

---

[27] Mehran Kamrava, *A Dynastic History of Iran: From the Qajars to the Pahlavis* (Cambridge: Cambridge University Press, 2022), 99.
[28] Michael P. Zirinsky, 'Imperial Power and Dictatorship: Britain and the Rise of Reza Shah, 1921–1926', *International Journal of Middle East Studies* 24, no. 4 (November 1992), 645–6; Pyman Minutes, 7 November 1950, FO 248/1509 (TNA).
[29] Tehran to Ahwaz, 28 November 1932, IOR/R/15/1/635; (British Library – BL).
[30] Extract from *Shafaq-i-Surkh*, 23 January 1933; Press Summary, 28 January 1933, IOR/R/15/1/636 (BL).
[31] Ibid.
[32] Anglo-Persian Oil Company Ltd. Persian Concession, 1933, 22 April 1933, 70223; *The Company's Interest in Iran*, 2 July 1951, 9233 (BP Archive – BPA).

romances of our age' and credited British ingenuity alone for creating something of value in an otherwise barren backwater.[33] In reality, the AIOC was a relentless extractive force, which directed capital to preserve Britain's informal empire on the Persian Gulf in the pursuit of ever-greater profits. Iran's occupation by British and Soviet forces during the Second World War provided a break in this arrangement and set off a chain of events that eventually led to the collapse of Britain's informal empire in Iran. The purpose of this study is to understand why.

It provides a longer-term analysis of Britain's changing policy and priorities towards Iran and demonstrates the textures of imperialism there. British hegemony was advanced through a diversity of soft and hard methods ranging from political, cultural and media manipulation directed by the British Embassy and supplemented by the AIOC to outright acts of espionage. Although historians tend to recognize the CIA's role as the executor of the coup against Mossadegh, the operative network built by Britain was critical to its success. Figures like Robin Zaehner, Sam Falle, Monty Woodhouse and Norman Darbyshire worked with Iranian assets to develop webs of influence across Iranian society and politics, which spanned from Tehran's *zurkhaneh* gyms to the royal court. The street thugs recruited in the former would prove crucial for the fortunes of the latter.

Although the broad pattern of British imperialism was largely unchanged regardless of who occupied 10 Downing Street, its details were subject to variation. Most notably, the 1945–51 Labour government attempted to use welfare imperialism to safeguard their interests. The company was critical to Britain's post-war reconstruction but recognized as a poor employer and source of political tension. Through the export of British expertise, particularly in labour relations, and improvements in workers' material conditions, Foreign Secretary Ernest Bevin hoped to develop a new consensus and dampen growing Iranian criticism of their unbalanced relationship. These efforts were undermined by not only a misunderstanding of the impulses that drove and shaped Iranian politics but also domestic economic challenges and divergent interests between state and company. Although the Second World War saw the total alignment of business and state goals, this relationship was to prove temporary. It was clear that while British imperialism in Iran was maintained primarily by the AIOC, its reliability as a partner was secondary to impulsive profit seeking. Reflecting later, Donald Logan, a former commercial advisor at the Tehran Embassy, wondered whether Bevin and Prime Minister Clement Attlee simply had 'limited scope' in

---

[33] Persian Oil, undated, 9233 (BPA).

managing the government's relationship with such a large and well-entrenched imperial concern.[34]

The 1941 transition from Reza Shah's rule to that of his son, Mohammad Reza Pahlavi, injected new energy into Iranian politics, media, culture and civil society. Freed from autocracy, diverse political movements were able to flourish. Particularly important were French-influenced liberal nationalism, socialism expressed through both political parties and trade unionism, and Islamism. These were dynamic, adaptable strains of thought that ebbed and flowed in their contribution to Iran's national life. Though they sometimes drew on European influences, Iran's nascent political movements were not necessarily guided by them.

The bulk of British officials, however, ignored the nuances of Iranian politics choosing instead to patronize or scold. In their collective imagination, Iran was a land of avaricious politicians who led easily corruptible peasants. Firmly rooted in Britain's experiences of the nineteenth and early twentieth centuries, this analysis was as orientalized as it was counterproductive. Diplomats and AIOC officials treated the nationalization of Iran's oil as a transient emotional spasm rather than the culmination of decades of material exploitation and an active, autonomous political culture. Their conduct towards Mohammad Mossadegh was the clearest example of this. Acknowledged by British Embassy staff to be among Iran's finest political mind, they nevertheless regarded the prime minister a pyjama-clad idiot savant capable only of leading his country to destruction.[35] Simultaneously he was a naive, confused fool and a scheming demagogue.

Underscoring Anglo-Iranian relations was Iran's place in the post-Second World War geopolitical order and the emerging Cold War. Anglo-American perceptions of and reactions to Iranian nationalism were not analogous. While the British immediately saw it primarily as a threat to their economic interests, the United States was not instinctively unsympathetic to Mossadegh or the movement he led. Aware of the lopsided nature of the Anglo-Iranian concession, State Department officials believed that rapprochement required compromise from the British side, even a concession to the 'principle of nationalisation'.[36]

---

[34] Sir Donald Logan: Interview recorded by the British Diplomatic Oral History Programme, 2002 (Cambridge University, Churchill Archives Centre – CAC).
[35] Middleton to Foreign Office, 21 November 1951, FO 371/91465 (TNA).
[36] Franks to Foreign Office, 12 May 1951, FO 371/91533 (TNA); House of Commons Debate, 20 June 1951, *Hansard*, vol. 489 cc 519–20; Document 61: Grady to the Embassy in the United Kingdom, 29 July 1951 *FRUS, 1952-1954, Iran – Vol. X*.

As Britain and Iran proved themselves to be poles apart and fruitful negotiations, let alone an agreement, unforthcoming, the United States retreated to a position that prioritized stability, both diplomatic and economic. Iranian nationalism was increasingly identified as a threat to American interests by the CIA, which warned that it could deepen socio-economic dislocation and open the door to communism. In nationalizing a foreign asset, Mossadegh had also set a dangerous precedent that could undermine confidence in Western investments in the Middle East and beyond. General Dwight Eisenhower's election as president and the hardening of the American foreign security apparatus under the Dulles brothers served to complete the American transition from self-styled honest broker in Iran to lead participant in the coup against Mossadegh after he threatened to introduce cut-price oil to the international market. It is not without irony that having urged greater American participation in Iran, the British found themselves displaced, their informal empire shattered.

A partial truth

Although Mossadegh was a beloved figure among many Iranians after the coup, since Iran's theocratic revolution in 1979 the former prime minister, a secular and liberal nationalist, has officially become something of a non-person. There are no public markers of his legacy and his home lies abandoned. Meanwhile in Britain, the legacy of imperialism in Iran has been afforded little to no public consideration. Never coloured pink on imperial maps, Britain's informal empire and its effects remain underappreciated. However, while the letters AIOC are generally meaningless, the company's successor BP remains among Britain's most recognizable brands and a global behemoth.

This study is not the final word concerning British policy in Iran before 1953 or anything close to it, and until British documents concerning the operation against Mossadegh are released this study will be partial in nature. It serves instead as a synthesis of the primary materials and research available to us and contribution to a wider canon of historiography from a firmly British perspective. In identifying Iran as an explicitly imperial concern, it hopes to add to our collective understanding of empire, its diversity and its deep effects. Similarly, it hopes to contribute, even in a small way, to a better understanding of Anglo-Iranian relations and their complex lineage. Even in recent years chants of 'death to England' outside the British Embassy, Tehran, have not been particularly unusual, and the 'little Satan' is still eyed with at least some suspicion.[37] Such epithets owe much to later revolutions in Iranian society. However, the effects of Mossadegh's defenestration and the years that preceded it should not be ignored but instead sought to be understood.

---

[37] Karl Vick, 'For Old Times' Sake: Iranians Briefly Sack the Embassy of Their Once and Future Satan—Britain', *Time*, 29 November 2011; Patrick Wintour, 'UK Denounces Iran's Arrest of Ambassador Amid Protest Row', *The Guardian*, 12 January 2020.

1

Iran under occupation

At dawn on 25 August 1941, the people of Iran woke to the invasion of their country by British and Soviet forces. The operation, codenamed Countenance, was swift and within three weeks Tehran had fallen under foreign occupation for the first time in its history. Deposed from power, Reza Shah left Iran on a British ship bound for Mauritius and was replaced by his 21-year-old son, Mohammad Reza.

Reza Shah's deposition ushered in a quiet revolution in Iranian politics as autocracy gave way to constitutionalism. Alongside political parties and newspapers came an atmosphere of pluralism and new opportunities for dissent. The new settlement was restless and Iran's parliament, the Majlis, struggled to reconcile its innate conservatism with new political forms or the realities of occupation. Class politics, contested nationalisms and material deprivation collided to create an unstable political environment that the British struggled to understand or fully reconcile.

This chapter explores the events that led to Iran's occupation, its fallout and the changing nature of Anglo-Iranian relations. In doing so it illustrates that occupation created a paradoxical situation in which foreign forces helped to reignite participatory politics, creating ripples in public consciousness that would eventually become a nationalist wave.

Justifying occupation

The primary reason for Iran's occupation was Germany's oversized influence there and the threat it posed to the Allied war effort. Strategically located between Europe, India and the Soviet Union and home to significant oil reserves, Iran was readily identified as a key defensive staging post and essential for Britain's survival.¹ This importance was well understood by Nazi leaders. In the early 1930s, a slew of racist magazines and periodicals were published by Siemens-Schuckert and the German Propaganda Ministry to glorify Hitler and Reza Shah as shining examples of the 'Fuhrer principle' and obsess over the genetic differences between Aryan Iranians and their Arab, Turkish and Jewish neighbours.² Europe's rising power and a beacon of a certain kind of modernity, Nazi sympathies readily found an audience among Iran's urban elite and Iranians were subsequently exempted from the Nuremberg Racial Laws.

Cultural and political ties were supplemented by shared economic interests. In 1936, German finance minister and president of the Reichsbank Dr Hjalmar Schacht visited Reza Shah in Tehran and a trade deal was signed between the two countries enabling the exchange of German industrial goods for Iranian wheat, rice and other agricultural products.³ Within five years, Germany accounted for over 40 per cent of Iran's foreign trade purchasing 60 per cent of its cotton and 90 per cent of its wool.⁴ German engineering support was vital in the construction of the Trans-Iranian Railway and the Junker aircraft company was awarded a five-year contract to deliver air postal services across Iran. Registered as Junkers Luftverkehr Persien, the company became Iran's sole provider of commercial and civilian aviation.⁵ Visitors to Tehran railway station would only need to look up to understand the strength of Germany's influence: its ceiling was embellished with several swastikas.⁶ Among the growing colony of several thousand Germans in Iran were a significant number of Abwehr intelligence agents who not only reported on Soviet military activity in the Caucasus and the AIOC's vast operations but also contributed to growing propaganda networks.⁷

---

¹ Arthur Bryant, *The Turn of the Tide: A History of the War Years Based on the Diaries of Field Marshall Lord Alan Brooke, Chief of the Imperial General Staff* (New York: Doubleday & Company, 1957), 262.
² Mehdi Parvizi Amineh and Mehdi Parvizi Amineh, *Die Globale Kapitalistische Expansion Und Iran: Eine Studie Der Iranischen Politischen Ökonomie, 1500 - 1980*, (Münster: Lit, 1999), 200; Miron Rezun, *The Iranian Crisis of 1941: The Actors, Britain, Germany, and the Soviet Union* (Cologne: Böhlau, 1982), 29.
³ A. Asgharzadeh, *Iran and the Challenge of Diversity: Islamic Fundamentalism, Aryanist Racism, and Democratic Struggles* (New York: Palgrave Macmillan, 2007), 91–2; Persia Annual Report, 1936, 30 January 1937, IOR/L/PS/12/3472A (BL).
⁴ Ahmad Ghoreichi, *The External Relations of Iran Under Reza Shah* (Berkeley: University of California Press, 1960), 122–3; Bullard to Foreign Office, 1 July 1941, IOR/L/PS/12/3513 (BL).
⁵ Parviz Tarikhi, *The Iranian Space Endeavor: Ambitions and Reality* (New York: Springer, 2014), 15–16.
⁶ Homa Katouzian, *Musaddiq and the Struggle for Power in Iran* (London: I.B. Tauris, 2009), 37.
⁷ Melzig to Knatchbull-Hugessen, 14 November 1939; Bullard to Foreign Office, 1 July 1941, IOR/L/PS/12/3513; Persia: Annual Report 1941, 17 June 1942, IOR/L/PS/12/3472A (BL); Bullard to Foreign Office, 9 August 1941, FO 371/27152 (TNA); Document 382: Dreyfus to the Secretary of State, 21 August 1941, *Foreign Relations of the United States: Diplomatic Papers, 1941, The British Commonwealth; The Near East and Africa* Vol. III (Washington DC: United States Government Printing Office, 1959).

Following the outbreak of conflict in Europe, British Minister at Tehran Reader Bullard described the Iranian government's position as one of 'frantic neutrality', but fears persisted that Nazi agents could undermine British interests.[8] Early German successes saw new Iranian overtures to Berlin and, much to London's chagrin, the Iranian government chose to circumvent barriers on the export of goods to Germany by sending them via Turkey and the Soviet Union.[9] The fall of France helped raise German prestige to new heights and the British Legation's efforts to drum up support in the Iranian press had little effect.[10] To the Iranian government and public, Britain appeared increasingly isolated and at risk of military defeat. The Wehrmacht's march through Europe had also opened a potential corridor to the Middle East through French Syria, necessitating its occupation by already overstretched Commonwealth forces. Subsequently, in April 1941, a Nazi-backed coup in Iraq succeeded in removing the nominally pro-British government led by Prince Abdulilah and replacing him with the nationalist Rashid Ali al-Gaylani. In turn, the Iraq Petroleum Company's plants were sequestered and the Grand Mufti of Jerusalem issued a fatwa in support of the struggle against the British. Commonwealth soldiers were called upon to help return Prince Abdulilah to power and in subsequent de-Nazification operations scores of Nazi operatives, along with al-Gaylani himself, crossed into Iran, cementing its reputation among British intelligence staff as the 'centre of German intrigue in Asia'.[11]

Although threatened by the Nazi presence in Iran, the British were in no position to demand Iran move from its position of ostensible neutrality. Alongside the threat posed by Nazi agents and supporters, the 1939 Molotov-Ribbentrop pact between Germany and the Soviet Union had legitimized British fears that Berlin and Moscow may agree to split their assets.[12] As late as spring 1941, Bullard described Soviet policy in Iran as 'incalculable' and actively dissuaded Whitehall from overcommitting military resources lest it provoke a response.[13] The Nazi invasion of the USSR in June 1941 changed

---

[8] Military Attaché Tehran to the War Office, 23 September 1939, IOR/L/PS/12/3513; Political Review of the Year 1939 in Iran, 10 February 1940, IOR/L/PS/12/3472A; General Distribution from Iran, 2 March 1940, IOR/L/PS/12/87 (BL).
[9] General Distribution from Iran, 2 March 1940, IOR/L/PS/12/87; Annual Report for 1940, 7 May 1941, IOR/L/PS/12/3472A (BL).
[10] Persia: Annual Report 1941, 17 June 1942, IOR/L/PS/12/3472A (BL); Bullard to Eden, 27 December 1940, FO 371/27183 (TNA).
[11] Tehran Intelligence Summary #10, 17 May 1941; Tehran Intelligence Summary #11, 31 May 1941, FO 371/27188 (TNA); Persia: Annual Report 1941, 17 June 1942, IOR/L/PS/12/3472A (BL).
[12] Foreign Office to Tehran, 17 May 1941, FO 371/27149 (TNA); Bullard to Foreign Office, 7 May 1941, IOR/L/PS/12/3489; Bullard to Foreign Office, 18 May 1941, IOR/L/PS/12/3513 (BL).
[13] Bullard to Foreign Office, 12 May 1941, FO 371/27149 (TNA).

the situation completely, forcing the British and Soviets together as allies of convenience to defeat Hitler.[14] Concurrently, the invasion stoked new fears that Germany's deeply integrated operative network in Iran would spring into life. Singled out as particularly vulnerable, Secretary of State for India Leo Amery warned that Iran was in 'immediate danger' of falling to the Nazis.[15] Commander-in-Chief in India Archibald Wavell agreed, describing the removal of German agents from Iran as nothing less than 'essential to the defence of India'.[16] Amery and Wavell found an ally in no less than Joseph Stalin who British Ambassador Stafford Cripps reported was convinced that immediate, joint action was required to tackle the Nazi threat.[17] The War Cabinet agreed and final representations were made to the shah stressing the 'alarmingly high proportion of notorious agents' operating across Iran. Whether unwilling to be dictated to or paralysed by uncertainty, Reza Shah ignored these appeals.[18] It was now evident, Bullard suggested, that the Iranians 'attached greater importance to retaining these German nationals in Persia than they attach to meeting the wishes of His Majesty's Government' and would have to bear responsibility for the consequences.[19]

At 04.45 on 25 August 1941, British naval and military forces struck at Abadan and Khorramshahr, and Kermanshah, while two Soviet groups advanced into northern Iran. Although the shah had bestowed upon the military a wealth of resources their morale was low and resistance limited. Rather than fighting back many undernourished soldiers chose to lay down their arms and return home. Despite pleas to President Franklin D. Roosevelt for the United States to intervene, Reza Shah was unable to halt the invasion and with Anglo-Soviet forces just twenty miles from Tehran he surrendered his throne.[20] Two zones of occupation were established: the British claimed a band of territory surrounding the AIOC's assets in south-western Iran while the

---

[14] Cripps to Foreign Office, 20 July 1941, IOR/L/PS/12/551 (BL).
[15] Secretary of State to Government of India to H. M. Minister Kabul, 25 June 1941, IOR/L/PS/12/551 (BL).
[16] Winston Churchill, *The Grand Alliance*, The Second World War Vol. III (Boston: Houghton Mifflin, 1986), 424.
[17] Cripps to Foreign Office, 9 July 1946, FO 371/27230; War Cabinet Conclusions, 17 July 1941, CAB 65/19 (TNA).
[18] War Cabinet Conclusions, 28 July 1941; War Cabinet Conclusions, 31 July 1941; War Cabinet Conclusions, 18 August 1941, CAB 65/19 (TNA); Persia: Annual Report 1941, 17 June 1942, IOR/L/PS/12/3472A; Foreign Office to Tehran, 9 August 1941, IOR/L/PS/12/551 (BL).
[19] Ibid.
[20] Bullard to Eden, 11 October 1941, FO 371/27224 (TNA); Ashley Jackson, *Persian Gulf Command: A History of the Second World War in Iran and Iraq* (New Haven: Yale University Press, 2018), 150–71; Churchill, *The Grand Alliance*, 481.

Figure 1.1 Indian troops under British command enter the Abadan refinery, 1941. Courtesy of Getty Images Keystone-France/Contributor.

northern territories from Azerbaijan to Mazandaran fell under Soviet control. Tehran was not officially occupied, but British, Soviet and later American troops became a common presence there.[21]

Retrospectively described by the American Ambassador Wallace Murray, as 'a brutal, avaricious, and inscrutable despot in his later years', few outside the royal inner circle regretted Reza Shah's fall from power or subsequent exile.[22] In supressing class, religious and ethnic opposition, the shah had created a culture of simmering resentment with few channels for dissent. Even before occupation there was growing speculation as to whether social unrest was inevitable given the tensions within Iranian society.[23] The British Legation warned that Iran's non-Persian minorities harboured 'long-standing grievances' against the central government and that the seeds of social foment may eventually lead to civil unrest and perhaps even Bolshevism.[24] In a candid note for Bullard, Ann

---

[21] F. Eshraghi, 'The Immediate Aftermath of Anglo-Soviet Occupation of Iran in August 1941', *Middle Eastern Studies* 20, no. 3 (1984), 326–30.
[22] Document 349: The Ambassador in Iran (Murray) to the Secretary of State, 26 June 1945, *Foreign Relations of the United States: Diplomatic Papers, 1945, The Near East and Africa Vol. VIII* (Washington DC: United States Government Printing Office, 1969).
[23] Ervand Abrahamian, *Iran Between Two Revolutions*, Princeton Studies on the Near East (Princeton: Princeton University Press, 1983), 164.
[24] Bullard to Eden, 26 September 1941, FO 371/27188 (TNA).

Lambton, the Tehran Legation's press attaché and a decorated Orientalist scholar, summarized the challenge facing Britain in Iran. She suggested that the majority of Iranians hated the regime and welcomed occupation as 'the only way in which the removal of the shah can be secured'.[25] However, she also warned that the British were not viewed as liberators. Instead, occupation underscored Iranian resentment towards long-standing foreign interference and a collective sense that the country was not truly independent.[26] Reflecting on the atmosphere that followed occupation, Bullard acknowledged that a general sense of 'panic, defeatism and despair' had set in among the Iranian people.[27] Although Reza Shah had been removed from office, the indignity of conquest was palpable and there were few certainties as to what may follow.

Determined to preserve the state apparatus and prevent a power vacuum from emerging, the occupying forces moved quickly to replace Reza Shah and concluded that his son, Mohammad Reza, should take the throne. Barely twenty-one, the young shah had grown up in his father's shadow and was reputed for political naivety and personal timidity. Despite rumours that he harboured pro-German sympathies, the British were unable to identify a suitable alternative and the Foreign Office relented to his appointment on the understanding that his authority was incumbent on his 'good behaviour'.[28] In a break from his father's rule, the young monarch publicly committed to uphold Iran's constitution and offered assurances that he would respect the Majlis' sovereignty.[29] Satisfied that the shah would not threaten Allied interests, a tripartite treaty of alliance was agreed. This included both a recognition of Iran's territorial integrity and independence and a commitment that Allied forces would withdraw from the country within six months once the war had ended.[30]

The invasion of Iran coincided with legislative elections and a new Majlis term was due to begin on 13 November. Although the British Legation reported that 'all the candidates were nominees of Reza Shah' there was little appetite to demand fresh elections and Bullard hoped that new deputies may show an independence of mind under Mohammad Reza.[31] These were

---

[25] Lambton to Bullard, 1 May 1941, IOR/L/PS/12/3405 (BL).
[26] Ibid.
[27] Persia: Annual Report 1941, IOR/L/PS/12/3472A (BL).
[28] Ibid.; Foreign Office to Tehran, 28 August 1941, IOR/L/PS/12/551 (BL); Foreign Office to Tehran, 17 September 1941, FO 371/27217 (TNA).
[29] Bullard to Foreign Office, 18 September 1941, FO 371/27218 (TNA)
[30] Treaty of Alliance between the United Kingdom and the Soviet Union and Iran, 29 January 1942, 271 (United Nations Treaty Collection); Bullard to Foreign Office, 29 January 1942, IOR/L/PS/12/3520 (BL).
[31] Persia: Annual Report 1941, IOR/L/PS/12/3472A (BL).

Figure 1.2 Mohammad Reza Shah soon after his accession to the throne, age twenty-one. Courtesy of Getty Images, Pictures from History/Contributor.

uncharted waters for Iranian legislators who, with autocracy ruptured, were afforded greater autonomy. Following the new shah's lead, the Majlis legislated for a programme of reform: property seized by Reza Shah was returned to its previous owners, onerous taxes reduced and unpopular curbs on religious freedom, including the 1935 Forced Unveiling Act, repealed. The Majlis also rolled back restrictions on political organizing, relaxed press regulations and declared an amnesty for political prisoners, more than 1,250 of whom were released. According to Ann Lambton it was widely assumed among the Iranian public that 'constitutional democracy would automatically replace the hated dictatorship'.[32] In some respects this optimistic suggestion was correct as a series of new parties and political movements rapidly developed. However, Iran's democratic explosion did little to reconcile parliamentary fragmentation as coalitions emerged and collapsed in rapid succession. By the end of 1945, there had been nine different governments under eight prime ministers creating a state of perpetual unrest. For their part, the British did little to ease political dislocation and were in fact responsible for exacerbating it. Although Iran's sovereignty was guaranteed, they nonetheless attempted to

---

[32] A. K. S. Lambton, 'Some of the Problems Facing Persia', *International Affairs* 22, no. 2 (1946), 266.

influence the country's emerging political settlement, justifying attempts to do so on the basis that Iranian legislators were simply incapable of responsible government.

Factionalism and crisis during the thirteenth Majlis

The first prime minister to govern under occupation was Mohammad Ali Foroughi, who held office between August 1941 and March 1942. A former dean of the Tehran School of Political Science and president of Iran's Supreme Court, Foroughi had briefly served as prime minister on two previous occasions and was described by Bullard as one of the few Iranian politicians 'who was trusted for his honesty'.[33] However, having overseen Iran's entry into the Tripartite Treaty of Alliance, Foroughi found himself unable to deal with the immediate realities of occupation. The Allied invasion had taken place during the Iranian harvest, damaging the production and distribution of crops and leading to nationwide shortages. Maladroit in the face of crisis, the prime minister's authority rapidly ebbed and by the spring of 1942, rebellious deputies were openly plotting against him.

Bullard hoped that the prime minister's difficulties could be engineered to Britain's advantage and called for Sayyid Hasan Taqizadeh to take office.[34] A former SOAS and Cambridge University lecturer, Taqizadeh had recently been appointed Iranian minister to London, a post he was loath to resign so quickly. Aware of the unenviable parliamentary arithmetic he would face, Taqizadeh privately professed his unwillingness to place himself 'at the mercy of irresponsible deputies'.[35] The beneficiary of Taqizadeh's hesitancy was Ali Soheily who Bullard regarded as the most acceptable alternative. A member of the technocratic Justice Caucus but regarded as having a limited personal following, Soheily sought to broaden his appeal by styling himself the 'shah's candidate' and encouraged royal supporters to lobby deputies on his behalf. There were also reports that he used police officers to intimidate his parliamentary opposition.[36] This pressure paid dividends and Soheily was able to win the confidence of over 100 deputies with just 2 actively opposing him.[37] However,

---

[33] Persia: Annual Report 1941, IOR/L/PS/12/3472A (BL).
[34] Bullard to Foreign Office, 2 February 1942, FO 371/31385 (TNA).
[35] Bullard to Eden, 18 March 1942, IOR/L/PS/12/554 (BL).
[36] Ibid.; Bullard to Foreign Office, 2 February 1942, FO 371/31385 (TNA); Abrahamian, *Iran Between Two Revolutions*, 181–2.
[37] Bullard to Foreign Office, 14 March 1942, FO 371/31385 (TNA).

while his support was broad it was also shallow and Soheily had reportedly won the backing of fewer than fifty deputies when the Majlis first convened to choose Foroughi's successor. Recognizing the fragility of his power and growing food shortage, Soheily attempted to curry favour with the British. Having pledged to arrest Nazi agents and close the Japanese mission in Tehran, the prime minister hoped London would take steps to increase grain imports, having failed to fulfil previous orders.[38] However, he was able to secure just 70,000 tons of wheat, little more than one-fifth of Iran's annual consumption. The prospect of famine hardened anti-British resolve and fuelled rumours that bread, sugar and other necessities were being withheld.[39] Sensing rising public enmity, Bullard warned that there were 'many Persians who would be glad to see the Germans come and put an end to the presence of Russian and British troops on Persian soil'.[40]

In speeches given to celebrate the Iranian New Year a matter of days after his appointment in March, Soheily and the shah had exhorted the value of 'unity' and 'self-sacrifice' in deference to the public good.[41] Such rhetoric, however noble, could not disguise the maladies facing Iran or the prime minister's limited parliamentary backing. By the end of July a series of bread riots had broken out and Soheily faced an increasingly organized challenge in the Majlis.[42] Unwilling to cede political capital in support of a 'discredited' figure, Bullard refused to intervene and Soheily's government collapsed.[43]

Even before the prime minister's resignation, British officials had discussed alternative candidates for office considering also whether the Majlis' dissolution and the holding of new elections may lead to a less fractious parliament.[44] Unwilling to intervene so explicitly in Iranian affairs, the British instead lent their support to Ahmad Qavam who had served as prime minister twice between 1921 and 1923 before being exiled by Reza Shah. An aristocratic Qajar with a power base in northern Iran, Qavam's parliamentary faction, the Azerbaijan Caucus, had formed a coalition of convenience with their Soviet occupiers. Nicknamed 'the old fox', Qavam was a political shapeshifter who was respected

---

[38] Document 141: The Minister in Iran (Dreyfus) to the Secretary of State, 6 April 1942, *Foreign Relations of the United States: Diplomatic Papers, 1942, The Near East and Africa Vol. IV* (Washington DC: United States Government Printing Office, 1963).
[39] Bullard to Eden, 28 July 1942, FO 371/31443 (TNA).
[40] Document 138: The Chief of the Iranian Trade and Economic Commission (Saleh) to the Chief of the Division of Near Eastern Affairs (Murray), 24 February 1942, *FRUS 1942 Vol. IV*; Bullard to Eden, 28 July 1942, FO 371/31443 (TNA).
[41] Fakhreddin Azimi, *Iran: The Crisis of Democracy* (London: I.B. Tauris, 1989), 61.
[42] Bullard to Foreign Office, 28 July 1942, FO 371/31385 (TNA).
[43] Foreign Office to Bullard, 15 July 1942; Bullard to Foreign Office, 31 July 1942, IOR/L/PS/12/556 (BL).
[44] Holman to Foreign Office, 8 July 1942, FO 371/31385 (TNA).

and loathed in equal measure.⁴⁵ A constant feature of his politics was animosity towards the shah, whose father had forced him into exile. While acknowledging his rivalry with the royal court and Qavam's relationship with the USSR, Bullard found little to object to in his appointment and noted that he was one of the few Iranian politicians 'who could hope to make some headway' in the otherwise gridlocked Majlis.⁴⁶ American Minister Louis Dreyfus concurred, suggesting that Qavam was capable of assembling a sustainable government and working collaboratively with the Allied occupiers.⁴⁷

Dreyfus and Bullard's shared optimism failed to acknowledge the depth of the socio-economic crisis or challenging parliamentary arithmetic Qavam faced when he took office in August 1942. Iran's price index had risen from a base rate of 100 in 1937 to 193 in August 1941 and 331 in September 1942. Concurrently, the cost-of-living index had increased from 100 to 418.⁴⁸ Post-occupation inflationary pressure saw the number of rials in circulation more than double in less than six months. Food was particularly affected and prices increased by an average of 555 per cent between 1939 and 1943.⁴⁹ To improve Iran's deteriorating finances, Qavam nominated Dr Arthur Millspaugh as Administrator General of Finances, a role similar to that which the American economist had performed some twenty years prior.⁵⁰ Winning the Majlis' endorsement for Millspaugh's appointment was, however, one of few tangible successes, and Qavam, like his predecessors, struggled to piece together a coherent legislative agenda. Without a sustainable parliamentary majority, Bullard reported that Qavam had grown 'very depressed'.⁵¹ Increasingly Majlis sessions were held in private as the prime minister faced riotous and occasionally violent opposition. In a last-ditch attempt to pass much-needed legislation on currency reform and food hoarding, Qavam formally asked the Majlis for emergency powers, a suggestion that evoked charges of despotism from monarchist deputies who were keenly aware of his antagonism towards the shah.⁵²

---

[45] Katouzian, *Musaddiq and the Struggle for Power in Iran*, 46.
[46] Bullard to Foreign Office, 28 July 1942, FO 371/31385 (TNA).
[47] Document 168: The Minister in Iran (Dreyfus) to the Secretary of State, 5 August 1942, *FRUS 1942 Vol. IV*.
[48] Ibid.; Document 211: The Minister in Iran (Dreyfus) to the Secretary of State, 18 November 1942.
[49] Stephen L. McFarland, 'Anatomy of an Iranian Political Crowd: The Tehran Bread Riot of December 1942', *International Journal of Middle East Studies* 17, no. 1 (1985), 53.
[50] Persia During World War Two, undated, Ann Lambton Papers – Box 57/5 (DUA).
[51] Bullard to Foreign Office, 7 October 1942, FO 371/31386 (TNA).
[52] Report on Political Events of 1942, IOR/L/PS/12/3472A (BL).

British officials saw Qavam's failure as evidence that the Majlis needed to be dissolved and new elections held. Brushing off suggestions that this might violate Iran's constitution, Bullard argued that 'attachment to the letter of the law (is) not a feature of the Persian character' and inferred that the prime minister's critics would respond only to a firm hand.[53] While acknowledging that dissolution would be seized upon as evidence of British meddling in Iranian affairs and 'furnish material for Axis propaganda', Bullard nonetheless recommended this course of action indicating that constitutional norms should be upended in the pursuit of strong government.[54] Majlis deputies were increasingly portrayed as simultaneously corrupt, naïve and possessing 'only a thin veneer of civilisation'.[55] No less critical, Ann Lambton wondered whether the experience of constitutional democracy after Reza Shah's fall demonstrated that Iranians lacked the restraint and responsibility to effectively govern themselves.[56] The obvious corrective to such political immaturity was strong leadership with London's oversight.

The supply of food continued to dwindle and, following a further cut in bread rations, Iranians took to Tehran's streets in protest. With less than a day's wheat remaining in silos, crowds of women and children gathered in front of the Majlis, crying, 'you may kill us, but we must have bread!'[57] On 8 December, peaceful protests turned violent and the Iranian army opened fire on students marching to parliament. In the chaos that followed it was reported that more than 20 people were killed, some 700 wounded and at least 150 properties looted and burned.[58] Rumours spread that the royal court had orchestrated the disorder on Britain's instruction to provide the pretext for a crackdown on civil liberties.[59] Immediately scotched by the Foreign Office the persistence of such rumours illustrates the depth of perceived British machinations and the fine margins that existed between influencing events and deciding their conclusions.[60] Privately, Bullard had made light of the persistent shortages, joking that 'the Persians

---

[53] Bullard to Foreign Office, 2 September 1942, IOR/L/PS/12/556; Report on Political Events of 1942, IOR/L/PS/12/3472A (BL).
[54] Bullard to Foreign Office, 7 October 1942, FO 371/31386 (TNA).
[55] Louise L'Estrange Fawcett, *Iran and the Cold War: The Azerbaijan Crisis of 1946* (Cambridge: Cambridge University Press, 2009), 145.
[56] Lambton, 'Some of the Problems Facing Persia', 266.
[57] Document 222: The Minister in Iran (Dreyfus) to the Secretary of State, 8 December 1942; Document 227: The Secretary of State to the Ambassador in the United Kingdom (Winant), 9 December 1942, *FRUS 1942 Vol. IV*.
[58] McFarland, 'Anatomy of an Iranian Political Crowd', 51.
[59] Habib Ladjevardi, *Labor Unions and Autocracy in Iran* (Syracuse: Syracuse University Press, 1985), 71.
[60] Foreign Office to Bullard, 9 December 1942, FO 371/31387 (TNA).

are used to the wheat problems – they are bred on it!'[61] Such quips led to an intervention by Prime Minister Winston Churchill who chastised his minister on the basis that such contempt for the Iranian people, 'however natural', may obscure his judgement and damage Britain's immediate interests.[62] In a damning note for Secretary of State Cordell Hull, Dreyfus indicated British culpability for the unrest suggesting that although they had not 'incited disturbances or connived at deterioration of (the) situation', they had done nothing to correct long-running and widely understood challenges.[63] In essence, Britain's interventions in Iran were mismanaged and failed to understand the growing weight of public opposition towards them.

Under pressure, Qavam shuffled his cabinet in early January, pledged to undertake new economic reforms and tabled a bill that would enable the Majlis to veto nominations for the head of the Iran's National Bank. This tinkering was momentarily successful and the prime minister survived a vote of confidence by sixty-four votes to forty-two, a fine margin compared to the 109 votes (of 116) that had taken him into office. On 13 February, however, a second confidence vote was lost and Qavam resigned.[64] Scornful towards Iran's irresponsible parliamentarians, Bullard expressed sympathy for the 'hopeless' conditions Qavam had endured and subsequently reiterated his belief that firm leadership was essential in quelling political unrest.[65] Qavam's departure saw Ali Soheily return to office, again relying on a shallow coalition of convenience. Dismissed by Bullard as a 'futility' prime minister, Soheily's second stint as prime minister is most notable for coinciding with Arthur Millspaugh's arrival in Iran and for codifying the Millspaugh mission's authority over extensive parts of the economy.[66] To stabilize prices and reduce Iran's burgeoning deficit, Millspaugh drew up a new income tax bill, which passed the Majlis only after an intervention by the shah. Although a brake on inflation, the bill enraged merchants and landowners by driving up their liabilities and provided succour for rising dissent towards the occupation.[67]

---

[61] Jackson, *Persian Gulf Command*, 243.
[62] Reader Bullard and E. C. Hodgkin, *Letters from Tehran: A British Ambassador in World War II, Persia* (London: I.B. Tauris, 1991), 187.
[63] Document 225: The Minister in Iran (Dreyfus) to the Secretary of State, 9 December 1942, *FRUS 1942 Vol. IV*.
[64] Azimi, *Iran*, 75–7.
[65] Report on the Political Events of 1943, IOR/L/PS/12/3472A; Bullard to Foreign Office, 17 April 1943, IOR/L/PS/12/559 (BL); Bullard to Eden, 25 February 1943, FO 371/35070 (TNA).
[66] Bullard to Foreign Office, 17 April 1943, IOR/L/PS/12/559 (BL).
[67] Bullard to Foreign Office, 31 August 1943, FO 371/35075; Bullard to Eden, 7 September 1943, FO 371/35110 (TNA); Chatham House Lecture Notes, undated – 1945, Ann Lambton Papers – Box 57/10 (DUA).

The thirteenth Majlis concluded on 22 November guaranteeing Soheily's position for four months while new elections took place. Shaped by factionalism and instability, Iran's first experiment with constitutional democracy had doomed a succession of prime ministers to failure. Parliament's dislocation underlined not only the limitations of politics as an exercise in deal-making between volatile factions but also the British government's preferred method of using strong leadership to overcome parliamentary arithmetic. Beyond the Majlis, however, an undeniable democratic renewal was taking place. Liberal nationalism, manifested through Mohammad Mossadegh's return to politics, and socialism, expressed through the Tudeh and the labour movement, were suppressed by Reza Shah but were now able to flourish reshaping Iran's political culture and relationship with the occupying powers.

Political renewal

Mohammad Mossadegh, the Iran Party and liberal nationalism

Born in 1882, Mohammad Mossadegh was very much a child of Iran's elite: his father was a finance minister and his mother a Qajar princess. He was educated at the prestigious *Institut d'études Politiques de Paris* and at the University of Neuchatel in Switzerland where he received a doctorate in law, the first Iranian to do so at a European university. It is notable in retrospect that Mossadegh's doctoral thesis both championed the modernization of Islamic law and railed against 'imposition' of European institutions on Iran.[68] He accepted a post at the Tehran School of Political Science before serving in government as justice, finance and foreign minister and governor of Fars and Azerbaijan. Mossadegh was a polarizing figure. Deeply patriotic and prone to moralizing, he was a leading opponent of colonial overreach, political impropriety and corruption. Although briefly a member of the Democratic Party he remained resolutely independent throughout his career, drawing support and occasional patronage from the urban middle class and the traders of Tehran's Grand Bazaar.

In 1925 he was one of just four Majlis deputies to speak out against Reza Shah seizing power and it appeared his political career was over. He retired to his estate at Ahmad-Abad in 1928, unable to speak out against the hardening of Iranian autocracy or the unfavourable conditions of the 1933 oil concession: 'I longed

---

[68] Christopher De Bellaigue, *Patriot of Persia: Muhammad Mossadegh and a Very British Coup* (London: Vintage, 2013), 42.

to warn people about the harmful effects of [the concession's] renewal, but the circumstances didn't permit this, and it was impossible for anyone to utter a word in defence of the nation's interests.'[69] In July 1940, Mossadegh was arrested and sent to Birjand prison. Transferred back to Ahmad-Abad in November he expected to remain under house arrest until his death. His sentence ended in September 1941 when, following the Anglo-Soviet occupation, he was released under the terms of Mohammad Reza Shah's assumption of power. Mossadegh carried the experience of imprisonment with him to the end, not only in a visible limp but also a righteous fury at his ill-treatment.

A political iconoclast, Mossadegh's ideology was broadly liberal nationalist. Although at times religiously minded, certainly in manner, the tenets of Islam were secondary to his fundamentalist commitment to Iranian democracy and autonomy. His campaign for the fourteenth Majlis was typical in its focus on securing civilian control of the military, diluting the influence of landowners in parliament and reducing foreign interference. Mossadegh argued that Iran's past and present were defined by what he dubbed 'equilibrium' or the nature of its relationship with foreign powers. In the past, the country had pursued a strategy of positive equilibrium by actively trying to balance British and Russian influence, even appealing to third countries like Germany and the United States to do so. As a result, successive leaders had surrendered Iran's dignity and wealth and turned their country into a de facto client state. Rather than appealing for foreign investment, Mossadegh argued that Iran should pursue a policy of negative equilibrium or total non-alignment and the outright rejection of foreign influence where possible.[70]

Mossadegh's domestic objectives were, he believed, essential to preserving Iranian democracy. He argued that militarism had sustained Reza Shah, and only parliamentary control of the armed forces could prevent a similar situation arising in future. The Majlis, though fraught with infighting and factionalism, provided a degree of accountability that the royal court was unable to match. Similarly, Mossadegh believed that social and economic inertia was the result of the landed gentry's monopoly on political power. Rural poverty, illiteracy and religious dogmatism had created a docile population that avaricious

---

[69] Ibid., 98.
[70] James L. Gelvin, *The Modern Middle East: A History* (Oxford: Oxford University Press, 2005), 279; Sepehr Zabih, *The Mossadegh Era: Roots of the Iranian Revolution* (Chicago: Lake View Press, 1982), 88; Donald Wilber, *Iran, Past and Present: From Monarchy to Islamic Republic* (Princeton: Princeton University Press, 2014), 142; James A. Bill, *The Eagle and the Lion: The Tragedy of American-Iranian Relations* (New Haven: Yale University Press, 1988), 26–7.

deputies exploited. Education and an independent parliament were essential to overcoming this.

Although not a member, Mossadegh was supported by the Iran Party, which won five seats in the fourteenth Majlis. Formed in 1941 by members of the Engineering Association, the Iran Party's leadership were, like Mossadegh, Western-educated members of the liberal intelligentsia and adopted politics not dissimilar to the British Fabian Society. Rather than active class struggle, they hoped to achieve a gradual transition of power guided by domestic, technocratic expertise. Instead of focusing on the differences between the petit bourgeois and peasantry or internecine regional squabbles, Mossadegh and the Iran Party argued that the real social conflict in Iran was the result of national exploitation, which necessitated that the Iranian people, through the state, should take ownership of the country's profitable resources and industries. The current system, they argued, concentrated power 'in the hands of a few illiterate robber-barons who not only exploit the masses but also have little respect for skilled professionals and technicians'.[71]

Like Mossadegh, the Iran Party was critical of foreign intervention in Iran and rejected the notion that the country required overseas expertise to support and shape its development. Whether British, German or, latterly, American, foreign advice came with the tacit assumption that Iranians required assistance, if not guidance, in managing their own affairs. According to the Iran Party, the expertise of 'noble patriots' should be prioritized over profit-seeking foreign mercenaries who sought only to exploit Iran and its resources.[72] Mossadegh became the Millspaugh mission's leading critic in parliament. He attacked its mishandling of food supply and distribution and flayed the government for appointing foreign experts with no stake in Iran's success, demanding that their performance should be guaranteed by the American government.[73] Although the American Chargé d'Affaires Richard Ford suggested such complaints demonstrated 'an amazing lack of knowledge', he grudgingly acknowledged that their sentiment had wide popular appeal and influence.[74] Reflecting on his time in Iran, Millspaugh echoed complains made by Reader Bullard and Ann Lambton concerning the character and rationality of the Iranian people, suggesting: 'the Persian . . . is not a man of reason. He falls short of intellectual

---

[71] Abrahamian, *Iran Between Two Revolutions*, 190–2.
[72] Azimi, *Iran*, 87.
[73] Document 405: The Chargé in Iran (Ford) to the Secretary of State, 25 April 1944, *Foreign Relations of the United States: Diplomatic Papers, 1944, The Near East, South Asia, and Africa, The Far East Vol. V* (Washington DC: United States Government Printing Office, 1965).
[74] Ibid.

maturity. He generally and substantially lacks the apparatus that more advanced peoples developed to solve problems and engineer progress.' Justifying his analysis of the 'immature people', he added:

> A keen American, who was long in a peculiarly favourable position to observe the mentality of this people, remarked to me that Persians were 'children', with a mental age of about eleven years. I am sure he did not mean to say that Persians were mentally deficient; he was referring, rather, to their undeveloped or unused reasoning faculties; and I imagine he had in mind their emotional as well as their mental age.[75]

Against such condescension it is unsurprising that Mossadegh opposed foreign intervention in Iran quite so vociferously. Mossadegh's return to politics and the Iran Party's formation were important developments, marking a break with autocracy and the style of parliamentarism represented during the thirteenth Majlis. Numerically small, their political influence belied their size and within a decade liberal nationalism had become Iran's leading ideology. However, in the mid-1940s the fastest-growing vehicle for populist politics was the Tudeh Party and associated labour movement.

The party of the masses

In 1937, fifty-three Iranian communists were arrested, put on trial and jailed for their opposition to Reza Shah. Following his deposition, twenty-seven members of the group were released in September 1941 and, alongside thirteen comrades, launched the Tudeh (Masses) Party with Soleiman Mirza Eskandari as its chair. In little more than a year the Tudeh had recruited over 4,000 members, growing to more than 25,000 by 1944.[76] According to British reports, it was the only party with any established machinery or functioning provisional branches and was unique in a period of political fragmentation for developing a stable support base.[77]

The Tudeh's ambitions and programme are contested. Characterized by opponents as a Soviet puppet, the party's membership was more diverse than is sometimes reported. In October 1942, for example, the Tehran Provincial Committee, which functioned as the executive until an all-party congress took place, included eight followers of Dr Taqi Arani, a Marxist academic and the

---

[75] Arthur C. Millspaugh, *Americans in Persia* (Washington, DC: The Brookings Institute, 1946), 74.
[76] Ladjevardi, *Labor Unions and Autocracy in Iran*, 29.
[77] British Legation to Eden, 28 May 1943, FO 371/35071 (TNA).

intellectual driving force behind the fifty-three group who had died in prison in 1940, four trades unionists, two social democrats and an independent. A devout Muslim, Eskandari was himself reportedly more influenced by Islamic scripture than Marxist doctrine.[78] The party's early platform was broad and populist, including demands for greater democratization, freedom of the press and workers' protections.[79] It is notable that the Tudeh sought to achieve these ambitions within the existing constitutional framework and, whether for reasons of pragmatism or ideology, was not yet a revolutionary party. Indeed, its first conference, held in Tehran in autumn 1942, explicitly agreed to attract Marxists and non-Marxists alike and to avoid the alienating anti-clericalism that had dogged Iranian socialism in the past.[80]

Iran's limited organized working class was viewed as an immediate challenge and, in turn, supporting labour struggles became integral to party strategy. In autumn 1941 the Trade Union of the Workers of Iran, popularly known as the Central Committee, was established by Tudeh members, most of them communist. It was quickly dissolved having faced criticism for being too close to the party's leadership. The Central Committee was reconstituted the following year on the explicit basis that the union would be open to workers alone with the party including members of all classes. Though not formally linked, there would, according to *Razm*, one of several Tudeh newspapers, exist a 'cooperative relationship' between the Central Committee and those parties committed to 'the struggle against the enemies of the working class and to the betterment of the living standards of the workers'. Party dues were capped at 1 per cent of a member's monthly income for those earning less than 1,000 rials; 2 per cent for those earning 1–2,000 rials; and 3 per cent for those earning about 3,000 rials. Membership income was split equitably between the Committee's central council and members' branches. By August 1943, the Central Committee boasted more than 10,000 members with a further 10,000 believed to be sympathetic to it.[81] In comparison to their European and North American equivalents these numbers were small, but they nonetheless illustrate significant growth; in 1941 Iran's trade unions were so weak that industrial action was limited to just three strikes involving fifty workers.[82] The Central Committee benefited from relatively strong

---

[78] Cosroe Chaqueri, 'Eskandari Solayman Mirza', Encyclopaedia Iranica, 1997, https://www.iranicaonline.org/articles/eskandari-solayman-mohsen-mirza.
[79] Ervand Abrahamian, *Tortured Confessions: Prisons and Public Recantations in Modern Iran* (Berkeley: University of California Press, 1999), 76–7 and 80–1.
[80] Abdolrahim Javadzadeh, 'Marxists Into Muslims: An Iranian Irony' (Miami: Florida International University, 2007), 164.
[81] Ladjevardi, *Labor Unions and Autocracy in Iran*, 31–2.
[82] Javadzadeh, 'Marxists Into Muslims', 168.

density in the Soviet-occupied regions Azerbaijan, Gilan, Mazandaran and Khorasan as well as in factory towns like Qom and Tehran itself. Organization in those areas under British occupation, and the Khuzestan oil fields, was, for the moment, limited.

The Tudeh and Central Committee's attitude towards industrial action during the war years was complex. Focusing on the importance of defeating Nazi Germany, party newspaper *Rahbar* argued that 'international fascism and internal reaction do not allow us to utilize certain methods of struggle at this time. Our government is fighting against fascism. Our factories are operating for war and for the joint victory of our allies. Any action, at this time, that may interrupt production is wrong.' Strikes were not ruled out altogether but required careful consideration and needed to be weighed alongside the international working class' broader goals. Tudeh propaganda increasingly focused its ire towards the Iranian state, rather than individual employers, and attacked institutions, including the Ministry of Commerce and the police, as the working class' 'real enemies' for safeguarding the country's conservative order.[83] The necessity of a dual political and industrial strategy to achieve national liberation was made clear in the principles agreed at the party's first congress and subsequently circulated through its local and national newspapers. Without an industrial working-class majority from which to draw support, the Tudeh's primary objective was to mobilize not only workers but 'peasants, progressive intellectuals, merchants, and artisans of Iran'. In turn, the country's social and class structures could be upended and a broad coalition to fight against despotism and imperialism achieved.[84]

The Tudeh consolidated its influence over Iran's labour movement in early 1944 by unifying several independent unions under the Central Council's leadership and launching the Central United Council of the Trade Union of Workers and Toilers of Iran (CUC) on May Day. Membership numbers vary with the CUC itself claiming over 200,000 members and the American Military Attaché arriving at a more conservative 69,000 of whom around two-thirds were active in the Soviet zone of occupation.[85] At the same time, eight deputies were elected to the fourteenth Majlis. In a matter of years, the Tudeh, largely through industrial organization, had established itself as a vibrant, growing movement with a broad base of support among Iran's urban working and intellectual classes.

---

[83] Ladjevardi, *Labor Unions and Autocracy in Iran*, 36–7.
[84] Javadzadeh, 'Marxists Into Muslims', 167.
[85] Cosroe Chaqueri, *The Left in Iran: 1941-1957* (London: Merlin Press, 2011), 20.

Britain responds

Perhaps surprisingly given events to come, Bullard was initially sympathetic towards the Tudeh and wrote favourably about its organizing capacities and leadership. The latter, he suggested, was preferable to many of the 'reactionary' old guard that dominated Iranian politics and which were proving incapable of governing successfully. Though left wing, the minister did not feel that this alone should preclude the Tudeh from participating in the Majlis and he hoped that they would provide a 'much-needed reforming element' to Iranian politics.[86] In correspondence with London, Bullard acknowledged both the depth of Iran's material privations and the Majlis' poverty of political vision. For Iran to be successful, he felt that its institutions and leadership needed to be reformed and the energy represented by groups like the Tudeh fully incorporated into democratic processes. Within the Foreign Office discussions took place concerning the minister's reports and the establishment of a popular front to restrain the Tudeh's less ideologically palatable elements.[87]

Despite media attacks on conservative politicians aligned to Britain and the AIOC in the left-wing press, the Foreign Office's attitudes towards the Tudeh remained tolerant until 1944 corresponding with the party's leadership transitioning to a younger, more militant strain of socialism and growing concern regarding the Soviet Union's influence in Iran.[88] A strike by mill workers in Isfahan who opposed employer efforts to decouple unions from the Tudeh's influence had led to the seizure of goods in lieu of wages and was widely used as evidence of the Tudeh's disrespect for private property.[89] Meanwhile, CUC chairman Ebrahim Mahzari was forced to share responsibilities with Reza Ebrahimzadeh, a communist who had lived and organized in Soviet Azerbaijan before being imprisoned by Reza Shah.[90] The CUC was reorganized and power transferred from individual branches to the executive. This act of centralization meant that consent was required for all decisions concerning industrial action. The Tudeh's change in direction was sealed in August 1944 when, at the first national congress, an avowed Marxist slate of candidates won the party's leadership.

---

[86] Lascelles to Eden 28 May 1943; Bullard to All Consuls in Persia, 6 June 1943, FO 371/35071 (TNA).
[87] Foreign Office Minutes, 8–9 June 1943, FO 371/35071 (TNA).
[88] Bullard to Baxter, 18 June 1943, FO 371/35072 (TNA).
[89] Azimi, *Iran*, 101–2.
[90] Ladjevardi, *Labor Unions and Autocracy in Iran*, 51.

To the Foreign Office the Tudeh now posed two threats to British interests. First, the growing movement had the potential to ignite a 'revolution resulting in a change of Dynasty'. Second, they worried that the shah, fearful for his own position, may rally the forces of conservatism and the military in opposition to Iranian socialism and become a kind of 'benevolent autocrat'.[91] Calls for the shah to head up a 'mild dictatorship' were long-standing in the Foreign Office; however, pursuing this was likely to risk social foment and a countermovement in defence of Iran's constitutional democracy.[92] Officials instead employed a strategy to maintain order and suppress political movements deemed unfavourable to British interests. This included propaganda to ameliorate social unrest and the sponsorship of regressive forces to oppose the Tudeh directly.[93]

Britain's focus on preserving stability reflected Iran's growing importance to the Allied war effort.[94] As early as July 1942, a report for the Chiefs of Staff and War Cabinet by the Oil Control Board stressed the importance of Iranian oil and suggested that the loss of Abadan would be 'irreplaceable'.[95] Several major expansions took place at Abadan and between 1941 and 1944 crude production more than doubled. The refinery also became a critical producer of 100-octane aviation spirit: from just 67,000 tons in 1941 to 858,000 tons in 1944.[96] In a visible manifestation of Iran's importance to the war effort, a pipeline capable of carrying 192,000 gallons of oil a day was built between Abadan and Basra and the refinery's operational capacity more than doubled by the end of the war.[97] In turn, the number of Iranians employed by the AIOC rose by a quarter from 48,000 in 1939 to 60,000 by 1945.[98] It is notable that while taxes and royalties received by the Iranian government during this period grew, they did so at a far slower rate than those accrued by the British government, rising by £1.35 million to £5.62 million compared to a £12.31 million increase to £15.63 million.[99] Iran's vast oil wealth was supplemented by its growing role as a corridor for Lend-Lease goods between the Indian Ocean and the Soviet Union. Between 1942 and

---

[91] Foreign Office to Tehran, 1 August 1943, FO 371/35072 (TNA).
[92] Bullard to Eden, 6 October 1942, FO 371/31400; Bullard to Foreign Office, 27 May 1943, FO 371/35071; Bullard to Foreign Office, 29 June 1943; Hankey Minutes, 3 July 1943; Pink Minutes, 24 July 1943, FO 371/35072 (TNA).
[93] Bullard to Eden, 12 March 1943, FO 371/25069; Bullard to Eden, 23 June 1943, FO 371/35072 (TNA).
[94] Chatham House Lecture Notes, undated – 1945, Ann Lambton Papers – Box 57/10 (DUA).
[95] Jackson, *Persian Gulf Command*, 257.
[96] J. H. Bamberg, *The History of the British Petroleum Company Vol. II: The Anglo-Iranian Years, 1928-1954* (Cambridge: Cambridge University Press, 2000), 242–6.
[97] Thomas Hubbard Vail Motter, *The Persian Corridor and Aid to Russia* (Washington, DC: Office of the Chief of Military History, Department of the Army, 1952), 291.
[98] Jackson, *Persian Gulf Command*, 258.
[99] Bamberg, *The History of the British Petroleum Company Vol. II*, 325.

1945, 45 per cent of the trucks, aircraft, weapons and ammunition despatched to the Soviets were channelled through Iran under the watchful eye of the British Persia and Iraq Command and American Persian Gulf Command.[100]

The infrastructure required to maintain oil operations and the corridor to the USSR was vast and led to deep intervention in Iran's economy. In 1940 the United Kingdom Commercial Corporation was established to manage the purchase and sale of goods from neutral countries, including Spain, Turkey and Iran, and prevent them from reaching Nazi Germany. In April 1941 this was supplemented by the Middle East Supply Centre, an Anglo-American operation to rationalize the supply of civilian goods in the region. These bodies effectively took control of Iran's foreign trade, operating to meet Allied war, rather than civilian, priorities, effectively undermining Iranian sovereignty.

According to President Roosevelt's Personal Representative in Iran Major General Patrick Hurley, the British had 'to a considerable degree, succeeding in establishing a complete trade monopoly in Iran'.[101] To support the movement of war goods Iran's railways and roads were commandeered and reconstructed to allow for use by haulage vehicles. Similarly, the British oversaw the deployment of local tyre stocks for military purposes leading to around 1,500 of Iran's 4,000 trucks being taken off the road. The result, Hurley suggested, was that 'the Iranian officials and indeed of all the Iranian people who are in a position to appraise conditions, is one of intense bitterness toward Great Britain'.[102] Any suggestion of wrongdoing was rejected by President of the Board of Trade Hugh Dalton who argued that the Commercial Corporation was 'an indispensable instrument' in the British war effort and 'ordinary commercial considerations cannot apply to the Middle East at the present time'.[103]

Economic disruption was matched by a propaganda and deep interference in the media. According to a paper prepared by the Ministry of Information and the Foreign Office through the Overseas Planning Committee, the aim of British propaganda in Iran 'must be to obtain the friendly cooperation of the Persians' to allow for the swift transmission of soldiers, materials and communications. Crucially, the document also stressed that: 'Parallel with this British propaganda should aim to create conditions for the emergence, after the war, of an

---

[100] Steven R. Ward, *Immortal: A Military History of Iran and Its Armed Forces* (Washington, DC: Georgetown University Press, 2014), 176.
[101] Ibid.
[102] Document 389: General Patrick J. Hurley to the President, 13 May 1943, *FRUS 1943 Vol. IV.*
[103] House of Commons Debate, 2 February 1943, *Hansard*, vol. 386 cc 728–30.

independent Persia which will be pro-British.'[104] Propaganda had a dual focus aimed at maintaining internal security and ensuring local cooperation. This would be achieved by demonstrating the value of international partnership and promoting confidence in the Iranian state. The British Legation established the Public Relations Bureau led by Ann Lambton which, despite an initial staff shortage, quickly became central to British strategy in Iran.[105]

Propaganda was diverse and spanned a range of mediums. Thousands of copies of pamphlets with titles like 'Battle of Production' and 'Workers Under Hitler's Heel' were imported from India and Egypt to supplement weekly news commentary. Meanwhile, articles drafted in English were translated and sent to friendly Iranian newspapers for publication.[106] According to Lambton, the most effective propaganda was not directed from 'behind the scenes' but was reproduced and circulated by local outlets and consumed by the public organically.[107] News reels and films were also translated for screenings in local cinemas; however, these were often interrupted by 'old and worn-out' equipment.[108] More reliable was radio, which, in a country that suffered from widespread illiteracy, was believed to be a key information battleground having been used to some effect by Nazi Germany before the Anglo-Soviet occupation. Although there were a relatively limited number – approximately 7,000 – of radio sets in Iran, communal listening in cafes and workplaces was common and public broadcasts could be used to 'steady public opinion'.[109] Major local stations, including Radio Tehran, were taken under British supervision and transmissions by broadcasts from as far afield as Delhi, Cairo, Kabul, Moscow and Baku.[110] Launched in late 1940, the BBC's Persian Service grew in importance during the occupation providing daily transmissions developed with the British Legation's guidance and supervision.[111]

---

[104] Overseas Planning Committee: Plan of Propaganda in Persia, 12 January 1943, FO 371/31400 (TNA).
[105] Lytleton to Eden, 15 February 1942, FO 371/31385; Foreign Office to Bullard, 26 March 1942, FO 371/31400 (TNA).
[106] Graves Law to Monroe, 3 March 1942, 371/31400 (TNA).
[107] Lambton to Lady Chelwood, 21 April 1942, Ann Lambton Papers – Box 52/4 (DUA).
[108] Kermanshah Diary for July 1942, 1 August 1942, IOR/L/PS/12/3522 (BL).
[109] Kerman Diary for the Second Half of September 1942, undated, IOR/L/PS/12/3530 (BL).
[110] Overseas Planning Committee: Plan of Propaganda in Persia: Channels, 27 January 1943, FO 371/31400 (TNA).
[111] Annabelle Sreberny and Massoumeh Torfeh, *Persian Service: The BBC and British Interests in Iran* (London: I.B. Tauris, 2014), 31–48; Annabelle Sreberny and Massoumeh Torfeh, 'The BBC Persian Service, 1941-1979', *Historical Journal of Film, Radio and Television* 28, no. 4 (October 2008), 519–21.

In some cases, publicity materials were given a uniquely Iranian twist. Written in 1010, the *Shahnameh* – Book of Kings – tells Iran's history through 55,000 rhyming couplets, expressing many of the stories at the heart of Persian culture. British propagandists employed scholar Mojtaba Minovi to retell the epic through a series of postcards that depicted Hitler as the tyrant Zahhak and Churchill, Roosevelt and Stalin as the brave warriors who caused his demise, leading to the people's liberation.[112] Such creativity was matched by officials' efforts to shape the media landscape. Wartime rationing led to paper shortages, which allowed the British some control over which outlets could and could not go to press. Meanwhile, members of the Public Relations Bureau hoped to curry favour and place positive stories by courting newspaper editors.[113] Among British officials there was an overriding belief that 'all Persian papers can probably be bought', the only question being whether this was best achieved through 'entertainment' by diplomatic staff or direct bribery.[114]

The legation's efforts were supplemented by the British Council, which was made available to promote British interests through a cultural programme that included the establishment of Anglophile societies, English language classes and public lectures.[115] In recognition of radio's effectiveness as a medium, the Council was given Treasury permission to purchase additional local broadcast programming.[116] The information disseminated by the Council was purposefully high-minded and designed to raise awareness and understanding of enlightened British thinking. While this approach won support from the Anglo-Iranian Oil Company, which advocated for more activity in southern Iran, the British Council itself acknowledged that the 'contrast between the mass of people living a very low standard of life and the performance of Shakespeare plays' was undeniable and a limit on its effectiveness.[117] As early as spring 1943, the British consul at Kermanshah warned against overly intellectual programming, reporting that the Iranian public 'would like to see British propaganda descending from its pedestal' and make more effort to appeal to popular taste.[118]

---

[112] Postcards produced by the Ministry of information, undated, COI/PP/13/9L (BL).
[113] Bullard to Foreign Office, 31 May 1943, FO 371/35071 (TNA).
[114] Ibid.; Foreign Office to Tehran, 10 May 1943, FO 371/35071 (TNA).
[115] Plan for British Council Development in Iran, undated; Bingley to Blake, 20 April 1944, BW 49/1 (TNA).
[116] White to Bingley, 23 February 1944, BW 49/1 (TNA).
[117] AIOC and Institutes in Persia, 4 August 1944; British Council Work in the Middle East, 14 August 1945, BW 49/1 (TNA).
[118] Kermanshah Monthly Diary for March 1943, 14 May 1943, IOR/L/PS/12/3522 (BL).

To supplement media manipulation and public relations, the Anglo-Iranian Relief Fund was established in August 1943 on the recommendation of Public Relations Bureau director Stephen Childs. Ostensibly launched for the purposes 'of bringing together British and Iranians in a common endeavour to improve the conditions of the poor in Iran', the fund was used to provide charitable relief to Iran's poor, which in turn created 'useful material' for British propaganda.[119] In a note for Foreign Secretary Anthony Eden, Bullard commented positively on the 'direct propaganda effect of the fund', adding that it had been lauded in the Majlis by Dr Hadi Taheri, a multimillionaire silk trader from Yazd and senior member of the pro-British Patriotic Caucus. In spring 1943, the committee's activity enjoyed, thanks to the work of the Public Relations Bureau, widespread coverage in the Persian press and broadcasts on Radio Tehran.[120] However, its material successes were limited. Although the committee provided a means of facilitating and publicizing regular donations by the British government and AIOC, these were piecemeal and did nothing to improve the significant socio-economic challenges facing Iran.

In the nationalist and left-wing press, the cosy relationship between British officials and their media allies was attacked as an indication of deeper meddling in Iranian affairs.[121] Such complaints were far from unmerited. Although Britain had committed through the Tripartite Treaty of Alliance to recognize Iranian sovereignty, propaganda was supplemented by efforts to actively influence Iranian politics, particularly through the sponsorship of reactionary forces. Iranian Minister to Britain Sayyid Hasan Taqizadeh recorded that 'the worst consequence of the temporary foreign domination is the pervasiveness of the great degeneracy of our own people appealing to and ingratiating themselves to foreigners.'[122] Taqizadeh's barbed remarks were aimed at Britain's growing network of political influence, which included not only the newspaper editors who republished their propaganda but also politicians in thrall to London's influence, particularly Sayyid Zia.

A journalist and editor of several daily newspapers, Zia was an Anglophile critic of the Qajar dynasty and strident anti-communist. He first came to prominence as the architect of the 1921 military coup d'état against Ahmad Shah Qajar,

---

[119] Propaganda Through Relief Work, Feeding and Charitable Donations, 28 April 1942, FO 371/31400 (TNA); Publicity Given to the Working of the Anglo-Iranian Relief Fund During the Quarter Ending 31 March 1943, undated, IOR/L/PS/12/824 (BL).
[120] Ibid.
[121] Coverley Price to Caccia, 19 May 1943, FO 371/35071 (TNA).
[122] Fakhreddin Azimi, 'British Influence in Persia, 1941-47', Encyclopaedia Iranica, 2003, https://www.iranicaonline.org/articles/great-britain-vi.

which saw him become prime minister and his ally, Reza Khan, commander of the army. To consolidate his power, Zia imposed martial law on Tehran, banned public gatherings, suspended the free press and replaced provincial governors with military officers. Although the British government denied involvement in the coup, there were widespread rumours that they supplied equipment, arms and money to support the operation. Zia's time in power was short. His modernization and property reforms proved immediately unpopular, and a crude ploy to raise revenue by arresting irreconcilable landowners provided an opportunity for his enemies and ambitious allies alike. In May, Reza Shah forced Zia from office and into exile, first in Europe and subsequently in Palestine.

Even before his return to Iran in 1943, Bullard had suggested 'making use' of Zia who, as a favourite of the Patriotic Caucus, was identified as a viable candidate for office.[123] On his return from exile, British consular officials organized welcoming committees for him in towns along the way and placed effusive stories in friendly newspapers. Zia was particularly embraced by Iran's propertied elite as a counterbalance to 'the violence of the Tudeh', and unnamed 'wealthy friends' donated over £30,000 for his new political headquarters.[124] He launched *Hezb-e Watan* – the Fatherland Party (later renamed *Hezb-e Erada-ye Melli* – National Will) – alongside *Ra'ad-i Emrus* (Today's Thunder), a newspaper that railed against the threat posed by 'atheistic communism' and advocated instead for a revanchist programme to entrench patriotism and Islam across society.[125] As a consequence, Zia became a hate figure in the Tudeh press, which painted him as a reactionary tool of imperialism.[126] In correspondence with Washington, American diplomats did not refute this claim and hinted that Bullard had played an active role in his return.[127] Arthur Millspaugh went further and suggested that while Zia was 'pro-British and anti-Russian, (and) linked to the merchants and capitalists' his supporters had innately anti-democratic tendencies and could upset Iran's fragile political settlement.[128]

Aware of the role his father had played in Zia's exile, the shah had similar concerns and feared that supporters of the Fatherland Party may even attempt to dethrone him.[129] To ameliorate his suspicions, British diplomats attempted

---

[123] Bullard to Foreign Office, 6 October 1942, FO 371/31400 (TNA); Azimi, *Iran*, 51.
[124] Bullard to Foreign Office, 9 May 1944, FO 371/40186 (TNA).
[125] Abrahamian, *Iran Between Two Revolutions*, 107.
[126] Bullard to Baxter, 18 June 1943, FO 371/35072 (TNA).
[127] Document 405: The Chargé in Iran (Ford) to the Secretary of State, 25 April 1944, *FRUS 1944 Vol. V*.
[128] Millspaugh, *Americans in Persia*, 78.
[129] Bullard to Foreign Office, 27 May 1943, FO 371/35071; Bullard to Foreign Office, 30 May 1944, FO 371/40187 (TNA); Document 501: The Ambassador in Iran (Morris) to the Secretary of State, 8 November 1944, *FRUS 1944 Vol. V*.

to engineer a rapprochement with Zia on the basis of a shared hostility to communism.[130] Zia, they argued, was a counterbalancing political force to the insurgent Tudeh and one of the few figures capable of navigating the 'morass of intrigue' that had come to typify Iranian politics.[131] For his part, the young shah had many cronies but few friends and cut an isolated figure who was susceptible to influence. In recognition of what Bullard dubbed 'the special nature of their relationship', Britain's diplomatic mission in Tehran was upgraded to embassy status in February 1944. The decision seemed to crystallize London's efforts to influence Iran's internal affairs, meddling that increasingly brought them into conflict with the growing forces of Iranian nationalism and the Soviet Union.[132]

The first oil crisis

When the Majlis returned in March 1944, Mohammad Sa'ed became prime minister but oversaw a parliament that remained deeply divided between fluid factions and subfactions formed along ideological, geographical and opportunistic lines. In a sign of unenviable dislocation, every member of Sa'ed's first cabinet was forced to resign their position, such was the Majlis' hostile reception. The Millspaugh mission remained a lightning rod for criticism of the prime minister. American Chargé d'Affaires Richard Ford reported his surprise at 'the violence of the attacks' in the Majlis and 'the complete lack of any adequate defense of the mission'.[133] Like the shah, Sa'ed found an uneasy ally in Zia who both publicly defended Millspaugh and ordered his newspapers to do likewise.[134] Relying on Zia and factional allies for support, Sa'ed appointed a conservative cabinet with an obvious hostility to the Tudeh. Mossadegh, meanwhile, was reported by British officials to have 'easily topped the poll', a feat they acknowledged reflected the genuine esteem in which the Iranian public held him.[135]

The new Majlis term coincided with international discussions regarding the control and distribution of oil, which manifested themselves in fierce

---

[130] Lascelles to Foreign Office, 27 August 1944, FO 371/40187 (TNA).
[131] Lascelles to Baxter, 27 July 1944; Lascelles to Baxter, 14 August 1944, FO 371/40187 (TNA).
[132] Bullard to Foreign Office, 6 February 1944, IOR/L/PS/12/3691 (BL).
[133] Document 405: The Chargé in Iran (Ford) to the Secretary of State, 25 April 1944, *FRUS 1944 Vol. V*.
[134] Bullard to Eden, 12 May 1944, FO 371/40164; Tehran to Foreign Office, 15 August 1944, FO 371/40164 (TNA).
[135] Military Attaché's Intelligence Summary, 13 February 1944, FO 371/40205 (TNA).

debate over Iranian concessionary rights. The Second World War resulted in unprecedented rates of consumption leading to tentative negotiations as to its future control and supply, initially between the State Department and the heads of those American oil companies operating overseas and subsequently with the British. Despite domestic accusations of cartelization, the American government wanted to 'seek the development of Middle Eastern oil for peacetime commercial purposes in order to promote, for our national security, the relative conservation of strategically located Western Hemisphere supplies'.[136] To this end, they sought to safeguard those Middle Eastern concessions held by American firms and encourage expansion and investment across the region.[137] This included the opening of discussions between the AIOC, Royal Dutch Shell and American firms Standard, Standard-Vacuum and Sinclair Oil in spring 1944 concerning the possibility of a new concession in Iran.[138] Although the British had historically opposed any reduction in their Iranian monopoly, they embraced the intertwining of Anglo-American interests and hoped it would protect their assets against rising nationalism, the Soviet Union and international competition.[139] An agreement would formalize their joint hegemony over Iran's oil industry and guarantee its continued management for private profit. Oil, so fundamental to every aspect of the military and civilian economy, would form a basis from which liberal capitalist cooperation could develop in every area from monetary policy to collective security. American assessments of Britain's diminishing capacity in the Middle East illustrate why obtaining cooperation was so important to London. Surveying their allies' capabilities, American envoy Major General Hurley mused that Britain 'no longer possesses within herself the essentials of power needed to maintain her traditional role as the dominant influence in the Middle East area'.[140]

Although the Anglo-American Petroleum Agreement eventually collapsed in Congress under pressure from domestic oil producers, the close discussion between London and Washington illustrate their shared desire to continue wartime cooperation in peace. Somewhat ironically, however, their pursuit of a settlement raised suspicions in the Soviet Union and added to Moscow's

---

[136] 'Anglo-US Oil Pact Called "A Cartel"; J. Howard Pew Tells Petroleum Council Oil Agreement Gives Government "a Blank Check"', *The New York Times*, 26 October 1944; Document 26: Memorandum by the Assistant Secretary of State (Clayton) to President Roosevelt, undated, *FRUS 1944 Vol. V*.
[137] Ibid.
[138] Document 473: The Secretary of State to the Chargé in Iran (Ford), 4 April 1944, *FRUS 1944 Vol. V*.
[139] Herbert Feis, 'The Anglo-American Oil Agreement', *Yale Law Journal* 55, no. 5 (August 1946), 1175–6; Michael B. Stoff, 'The Anglo-American Oil Agreement and the Wartime Search for Foreign Oil Policy', *The Business History Review* 55, no. 1 (1981), 59–74.
[140] Document 389: General Patrick J. Hurley to the President, 13 May 1943, *FRUS 1943 Vol. IV*.

growing sense of detachment from its allies. In response to the discussions, Assistant Commissar for Foreign Affairs Sergey Kavtaradze demanded that Iran surrender excavation rights over a 200,000 square kilometre area stretching from Azerbaijan to Khorasan in the Soviet occupation zone.[141] Already fearful that communism threatened Iran, the shah responded furiously and claimed that 'the granting of any oil rights to the Soviet government would mean the end of Persian authority' in northern Iran.[142] In discussions with Bullard, the shah revealed that a decision to suspend negotiations for all new concessions until the end of the war would make rejecting the Soviet offer more politically palatable. Now British ambassador, Bullard contended that British firms could not fairly be compared with a foreign state but, under instruction from Eden, reluctantly accepted the proposed Iranian approach.[143]

Despite the Iranian government's best efforts to appear even-handed, the decision to reject Moscow's demands saw them traduced in the Tudeh press as agents of imperialism. Having published a slew of violent articles against Zia, party newspaper *Rahbar* now turned its attention to Sa'ed, describing him as a 'usurper of the rights of the Iranian nation' and a 'fascist' who stood in the way of Soviet-Iranian peace and cooperation.[144] Hastily organized rallies were called across the Soviet zone of occupation and in Tehran allowing the Tudeh's supporters to publicly vent their anger. Red Army soldiers flanked protestors, protecting them from both anti-communist thugs and the Iranian police who were disarmed and rendered useless.[145] According to Bullard a 'war of nerves' had broken out as lorry loads of Soviet troops prowled the streets around the Majlis and put pressure on deputies, reportedly telling one that diplomatic ties between the countries had been severed.[146] Shipments of grain, already in short supply, from Azerbaijan were halted as Moscow sought diplomatic leverage.[147]

---

[141] Document 482: The Ambassador in Iran (Morris) to the Secretary of State, 22 September 1944; Document 483: The Ambassador in Iran (Morris) to the Secretary of State, 2 October 1944, *FRUS 1944 Vol. V*; Bullard to Foreign Office, 1 October 1944, IOR/L/PS/12/3543 (BL); An Account of the Kavir-Khourian Oil Concession in North Persia, 20 September 1945, FO 371/45506 (TNA).

[142] Bullard to Foreign Office, 2 October 1944; Bullard to Foreign Office, 10 October 1944, FO 371/40241 (TNA).

[143] Ibid.; Dixon to Cadogan, 11 October 1944; Young to Starling, 17 October 1944; Foreign Office to Tehran, 18 October 1944, FO 371/40241 (TNA).

[144] Military Attaché's Intelligence Summary, 19 March 1944, FO 371/40205; Bullard to Foreign Office, 13 October 1944, FO 371/40241 (TNA); Azimi, *Iran*, 110; Chaqueri, *The Left in Iran*, 29–34.

[145] Ladjevardi, *Labor Unions and Autocracy in Iran*, 52; Bullard to Foreign Office, 27 October 1944, FO 371/40241 (TNA).

[146] Bullard to Foreign Office, 23 October 1944, FO 371/40241 (TNA).

[147] Bullard to Foreign Office, 24 October 1944, FO 371/40241 (TNA).

The episode was important both in demonstrating a growing closeness between the Soviet Union and the Tudeh and for broadening a sense of national consciousness. Under their occupation the Soviets had allowed the Tudeh to organize freely, but there remained degrees of political independence.[148] Increasingly doctrinaire, this sense of autonomy was severely diminished and the party was widely regarded as Moscow's subordinate. British correspondence from Iran increasingly revealed deep public animosity that their country was being used as a political football and its future thrashed out in foreign capitals.[149] Despite Soviet efforts to cajole editors, a slew of newspapers reported growing discontent and published articles in support of the government's policy. Even hardened Marxists may have baulked at allegations that workers in the Soviet zone of occupation were sacked if they refused to join the Tudeh, and Bullard reported that a number of the party's deputies had privately begun to voice their opposition towards the USSR.[150]

In the Majlis, Mohammad Mossadegh took the initiative and warned against any submission to Soviet pressure.[151] Although supportive of Sa'ed on the oil issue, he attacked the sycophancy and corruption he saw as endemic at the top of government. Floundering, Sa'ed resigned from office amid rumours that Mossadegh was primed to replace him. Undoubtedly popular among many deputies, Mossadegh's desire to retain his Majlis seat should he take on the role proved an unacceptable condition and Morteza-Gholi Bayat became prime minister.[152] His influence, however, was untarnished and on 2 December 1944, with Tudeh demonstrators audible inside the Majlis, Mossadegh rose to table a surprise bill to prevent any new oil concessions from being granted and demand that any violation would lead to three to eight years of solitary confinement and permanent dismissal from government service.[153] Having railed against the Soviet Union, Mossadegh took aim at the British and lionized the Iranian people's

---

[148] Cosroe Chaqueri, 'Did the Soviets Play a Role in Founding the Tudeh Party in Iran?', *Cahiers Du Monde Russe* 40, no. 3 (1999), 514–16; Katouzian, *Musaddiq and the Struggle for Power in Iran*, 49–50.
[149] Bullard to Foreign Office, 16 October 1944; Bullard to Foreign Office, 24 October 1944; Bullard to Foreign Office, 27 October 1944, FO 371/40241 (TNA).
[150] Bullard to Foreign Office, 21 October 1944; Bullard to Foreign Office, 24 October 1944; Bullard to Foreign Office, 30 October 1944, FO 371/40241 (TNA); Military Attaché's Intelligence Summary, 17 December 1944, IOR/L/PS/12/3504 (BL).
[151] Ibid.
[152] Bullard to Foreign Office, 13 November 1944, FO 371/40188 (TNA).
[153] Military Attaché's Intelligence Summary, 4 December 1944; Military Attaché's Intelligence Summary, 17 December 1944, IOR/L/PS/12/3504 (BL); Document 517: The Ambassador in Iran (Morris) to the Secretary of State, 3 December 1944, *FRUS 1944 Vol. V*.

desire for all foreign powers to 'refrain from interfering in our affairs'.[154] Scores of deputies rose to their feet in spontaneous applause. Having championed a theory of negative equilibrium, Mossadegh now looked to implement it and advocated for the self-management of Iranian oil. This was a quasi-revolutionary act that would foreground domestic development at the expense of foreign investment and upend Iran's traditional economic settlement.

Mossadegh's speech sparked parliamentary momentum and his bill to suspend negotiations concerning new oil concessions until foreign troops had left Iran became law. This was no minor achievement but the strongest articulation of Iranian independence since Reza Shah's defenestration. In doing so, it crystallized his status as the lodestar for Iranian nationalism. Having returned from the political wilderness barely three years prior, he was now the clearest alternative to the Soviet-backed Tudeh, British-backed Zia and the forces that had dominated Iranian politics for decades. 'Let us negotiate with every state that wishes to buy oil', he cried, arguing that an end to monopolistic foreign ownership would enhance Iran's ability to trade freely and safeguard its independence. The seeds of a movement that would blossom in years to come had been planted.[155]

Despite Mossadegh's fiery performance, the status quo's preservation was welcomed in Whitehall and by the AIOC, which had objected fiercely to *their* oil being drawn into a dispute between nations.[156] The Tudeh, meanwhile, remained on the offensive, attacking not the popular Mossadegh but Sayyid Zia and the hated British for interfering in Iran's internal affairs.[157] Bullard was under no illusions that the Soviet Union would again seek a concession of their own and insisted that Moscow would inevitably use any agreement to leverage their political influence and move towards the creation of an autonomous satellite state in northern Iran.[158] The question was how Britain would respond to this and whether Iran's fragile political culture would be able to cope with the Tudeh insurgency. Less discussed was the effect Mossadegh's return to the political stage may have on British interests and the balance of power in Iran. While the esteem with which he was held was acknowledged, British diplomatic correspondence offers little by way of analysis concerning his proposals or the impact a policy based on negative equilibrium could have.

---

[154] Katouzian, *Musaddiq and the Struggle for Power in Iran*, 52.
[155] De Bellaigue, *Patriot of Persia*, 123; Bullard to Foreign Office, 3 December 1944, FO 371/40243 (TNA).
[156] Sir William Fraser to Lord Beaverbrook, 18 October 1944, 43853 (BPA).
[157] Bullard to Foreign Office, 22 December 1944, FO 371/40243 (TNA).
[158] Bullard to Foreign Office, 29 December 1944, FO 371/40243 (TNA).

As a source of oil and staging post in the transfer of planes, trucks and weapons to the Soviet Union, Iran had played an important, if understated, role in the Allied victory over Nazi Germany. Although shortages of food and consumer goods were widespread, the country had much improved infrastructure and an oil industry that was delivering more raw and refined products than ever before. The transition from Reza Shah's autocratic rule to something-approaching-democracy had at times been challenging but seemed assured. By these metrics, the invasion and aftermath were judged to be successes. However, Britain's position in Iran at the end of the Second World War was uncertain. The Anglo-Iranian Oil Company had become one of the empire's most important – and profitable – assets and a negotiated settlement on the future of the oil industry seemed imminent. Meanwhile, Iranian nationalism, a dormant threat under Reza Shah, was in the ascendancy and in Mohammad Mossadegh had found a quietly charismatic leader. Similarly, the Tudeh and associated labour movement was increasingly militant and while it had not yet made inroads into Iran's oil fields, it remained a threat to Iranian stability and British interests there. Uncertainty was exacerbated by conditions in Britain itself. Victory was cause for jubilation and for consideration of peace and reconstruction. This task would not, however, fall to the Conservative Party under Winston Churchill but rather Clement Attlee's Labour Party.

2

Labour, imperialism and Iran

By the early afternoon on 26 July 1945 it was clear that the Labour Party had won a landslide general election victory. The final ballots revealed that Labour had enjoyed an unprecedented twelve-point swing, claiming a parliamentary majority of 146 seats. The party's manifesto promised a programme to 'win the peace', including wide-ranging nationalization, universal free secondary education, a National Health Service and improved social insurance. Foreign policy was a secondary concern. Labour pledged – in the most general terms – to 'consolidate in peace the great war-time association of the British Commonwealth with the USA and the USSR' and continue to play a leading role in international affairs. Concerning the empire, self-government for India, Pakistan and Ceylon was prioritized along with the 'planned progress' of Britain's other colonies.[1] However, the Attlee government did not oversee imperial dissolution but rather reorientation around strategically and economically important assets.

Under Labour, two factors intrinsically shaped imperial management. First, the party was committed to improving living standards across the empire as well as domestically. Explaining their obligation, Fabian Colonial Bureau (FCB) secretary Rita Hinden proposed that Britain faced 'a debt to history', which they could repay through improvements to colonial societies. Labour should therefore establish the institutions needed to alleviate poverty and enhance socialist consciousness abroad.[2] Second, and most importantly, Labour, and Foreign Secretary Ernest Bevin in particular, saw the empire as fundamental to preserving Britain's international status and standard of living. With British guidance, Bevin hoped that material conditions across the empire would improve and ties between metropole and dominions strengthened. The result was welfare

---
[1] 'Let Us Face the Future: A Declaration of Labour Policy for the Consideration of the Nation' (The Labour Party, 1945).
[2] Rita Hinden, 'Socialism and the Colonial World', in *New Fabian Colonial Essays*, ed. Arthur Creech Jones (London: Hogarth Press, 1959), 13–14.

imperialism, a new approach that linked the safeguarding of the empire's most profitable assets with schemes to improve living standards.

Officially independent, Iran was nevertheless a central part of Britain's informal empire and its resources treated as such. However, despite its importance Labour struggled to come to terms with the realities of Iranian politics and suffered from the orientalist tendencies that seemed inherent to successive British governments. In particular, they failed to recognize the importance of nationalism in surging left-wing populism and developed plans for reform in something of a vacuum. Additionally, and largely unnoticed at the time, they found themselves powerless to prevent the Iranian government from committing to renegotiate foreign oil concessions with profound consequences.

Labour and the empire

Founded as a coalition of trade unionists and socialists, the early Labour Party tended to prioritize domestic affairs. Labour's position on the empire, where it existed, leant towards reflective anti-imperialism expressed in the most general terms. The party's early leaders Keir Hardie and Ramsay MacDonald had both engaged in imperial debates, touring Britain's colonies and publishing titles such as *Labour and the Empire* and *The Awakening of India* on their findings. Notably, the party did not publish its first serious statement on international affairs until 1917. The Statement of War Aims, adopted at a joint conference with the Trades Union Congress, was drafted three and a half years into the bloodiest conflict in human history and committed the Labour to 'so conduct the terrible struggle in which they find themselves engaged as to bring it, as soon as may be possible, to a secure and lasting peace for the world'. Once peace was assured, Labour's ambition should be no less than the abandonment of imperialism in all its guises.[3]

However, there is little to suggest that Labour's anti-imperialist commitment was anything other than rhetorical. Elected in 1924 and 1930, the first Labour governments' foreign policies differed little from their predecessors and reflected Colonial Secretary Jimmy Thomas' promise that there would be 'no mucking

---

[3] 'The Statement of War Aims', *Labour Voice*, 29 December 1917.

about' with the empire.⁴ Under pacifist leader George Lansbury, Labour were committed to changing 'the policy of imperialism into one of cooperation and commonwealth'; however, this did not necessarily mean the dissolution of British assets overseas.⁵ There remained a strong sense that the empire was a civilizing force and had the potential to raise the socialist consciousness of otherwise backwards and underdeveloped peoples.

The clearest manifestation of Labour's civilizing tendencies was research published by the Fabian Society, the party's intellectual vanguard. In 1900 George Bernard Shaw's *Fabianism and the Empire* railed against the 'purely piratical conquests of weaker states', demanding new imperial management built on socialist principles.⁶ The Fabian Colonial Bureau was subsequently established to refine this position. Outlining Labour's duty towards Britain's overseas territories, FCB co-founder and secretary Rita Hinden claimed that poverty predated imperialism and that rushing towards independence could inadvertently exacerbate it. Suggesting that 'evil is not undone simply by withdrawing from the scene of the crime', Hinden argued that Britain had a moral duty to establish a framework through which stable self-government could eventually be achieved.⁷

Votes cast as the party's 1942 and 1943 annual conferences demonstrate the disconnection between Labour's pacific instincts and the realities of imperial governance. In 1942 delegates endorsed a Charter of Freedom for Colonial Peoples, the principles of which were similar to those expressed in the Statement of War Aims and included: full equality of political, economic and social rights, democratic systems of government based on 'indigenous institutions' and the nationalization of all natural resources. However, just twelve months later, the party adopted an alternative statement drafted by Labour's Reconstruction Committee, headed by FCB chair Arthur Creech Jones, which acknowledged that self-government would not be achieved 'for a considerable time'.⁸ While Labour members instinctively nodded to the moral righteousness of decolonization they had little faith that nations under colonial rule could manage their affairs independently.

---

⁴ C.M.M. Cotton, 'Labour, European Integration and the Post-Imperial Mind, 1960–75', in *The British Labour Movement and Imperialism*, ed. Billy Frank, Craig Horner and David Stewart (Newcastle upon Tyne: Cambridge Scholars, 2010), 151.
⁵ George Lansbury, *Labour's Way with the Commonwealth* (London: Methuen & Co, 1935), 7.
⁶ George Bernard Shaw, *Fabianism and the Empire: A Manifesto by the Fabian Society* (London: Grant Richards, 1900), 46.
⁷ Hinden, 'Socialism and the Colonial World', 13–14.
⁸ David K. Fieldhouse, 'The Labour Governments and the Empire-Commonwealth', in *The Foreign Policy of the British Labour Governments, 1945-1951*, ed. Ritchie Ovendale (Leicester: Leicester University Press, 1984), 85.

Within the party, the National Executive Committee's International Relationships Sub-Committee was the leading organ for foreign policy development during the Second World War, actively considering questions concerning the transition from war to peace, including the role Britain's overseas assets could play in reconstruction and how socialism may be promoted across the empire.[9] These questions were also considered by the Advisory Committee on Imperial Questions, a commission of Labour's International Department, which suggested in 1943 that the party's position should be one of 'trusteeship towards the colonial areas'.[10] It is notable that these bodies were concerned largely with relations with the Dominions and Labour's sister parties in countries like Australia, New Zealand and Canada. Policy towards British colonies in Africa and Asia was described in the broadest and most paternalistic terms as 'training for self government'.[11]

Despite the preparation undertaken by the FCB and Labour's myriad internal committees, the driving force behind the Attlee government's policy overseas was Ernest Bevin, a surprising choice as foreign secretary. Having founded and led the Transport and General Workers' Union (TGWU) before serving as wartime minister of labour, Bevin had anticipated he may become post-war chancellor of the exchequer. However, determined to keep Bevin away from Herbert Morrison who was supervising the nationalization of key industries, Attlee elected to send him to the Foreign Office.[12] Bevin had a decidedly Whiggish view of Britain's transition from island nation to global power to 'the greatest empire in the world.'[13] At the TUC's 1935 annual conference, he had faced down left-wing critics and argued that decolonization would merely lead to a scramble for resources and conflict. Instead of dissolving the empire, it was, the then general secretary argued, the duty of British workers to 'carry it a stage further forward'.[14] In 1938 he travelled to Australia and New Zealand via Canada and the United

---

[9] 'Relief Shall Come' International Relationships Sub-Committee Report, April 1943, International Sub-Committee of the National Executive Committee, 1943-1949 – Box 114 (Labour History Archive and Study Centre – LHA).

[10] Memorandum on Malaya and the Decisions of the Recent Pacific Conference No. 254A, Advisory Committee on Imperial Questions, June 1943, International Sub-Committee of the National Executive Committee, 1943-1949 – Box 114 (LHA).

[11] The International Sub-Committee of the National Executive Committee, Minutes, 16 November 1943, International Sub-Committee of the National Executive Committee, 1943-1949 – Box 114 (LHA).

[12] One of the Labour Party's most enduring legends is that when told that Morrison was his own worst energy, Bevin replied, 'not while I'm alive, he ain't!'

[13] *Peace or War? Full Report of the Momentous Debate at the Margate Trades Union Congress on the Present International Crisis* (London: Trades Union Congress, 1937), 12–15.

[14] *Report of Proceedings at the 67th Annual Trades Union Congress* (London: Co-Operative Printing Society, 1935), 355–7.

States to attend the Commonwealth Relations Conference in Sydney. Meetings with English-speaking trade unionists from across the empire followed by a return journey through India, Aden and Egypt convinced Bevin that imperial management needed to be reformed to deliver for working people across the globe rather than capital or the Colonial Office. Reflecting on his time overseas, Bevin told a parliamentary select committee that Britain's imperial 'crime isn't exploitation, it's neglect'.[15] Instead, he argued in favour of constructing a new socio-economic framework to share expertise and resources across the empire.[16]

Welfare imperialism

The Second World War strengthened Bevin's imperialism. Britain's most powerful trade union leader, he was drafted into parliament in 1940 and made minister of labour in the coalition government. To Bevin and his contemporaries, Labour's management of key ministries at a time of existential crisis was evidence that their movement had come of age and become a vital means of upholding Britain's national and international interests. Bevin's time in office sharpened his awareness that Britain's survival in war and prosperity in peace was inherently linked to the empire and its treasure. This was privately acknowledged by Labour's International Sub-Committee, which in late 1943 found that 'this little island cannot hope very much longer to be a Great Power except as part of a Commonwealth'.[17]

In a broadcast to the nation on the eve of the general election, Clement Attlee promised that his party would 'plan the broad lines of our national life so that all may have the duty and opportunity of rendering service to the nation, everyone in his or her sphere, and that all may help to create and share in an increasing material prosperity free from the fear of want'.[18] These were bold aspirations given the unenviable economic conditions Attlee's government inherited. At the end of the Second World War, Britain was financially exhausted and faced multiple interconnected problems. War damage totalled an estimated £3 billion

---

[15] Alan Bullock, *Ernest Bevin, Trade Union Leader, 1881-1940*, The Life and Times of Ernest Bevin (London: Heinemann, 1960), 627–32; Francis Williams, *Ernest Bevin: Portrait of a Great Englishman* (London: Hutchinson, 1952), 208–10.
[16] Ernest Bevin, 'The Future of the Empire: Co-Ordination', *The Spectator*, 3 February 1939.
[17] The International Sub-Committee of the National Executive Committee Minutes, 16 November 1943, International Sub-Committee of the National Executive Committee, 1943-1949 – Box 114 (LHA).
[18] C. R. Attlee, *As It Happened* (London: Heinemann, 1954), 143.

and had created unparalleled economic dislocation. For six years the British war effort had subsumed civilian industry, a pattern replicated across Europe. A quick return to normal patterns of production and trade was a distant hope. As early as June 1944 the Board of Trade had reported that 'we cannot expect any appreciable long-term improvement of the import/export position for at least two-thirds of Britain's manufacturing industry and there may be some worsening to offset the improvement from the remaining third'.[19] The Board's president was Hugh Dalton, who, following his appointment as chancellor of the exchequer, described Britain's economic outlook simply as 'pretty bleak'.[20] Although a pre-war creditor, Britain's total debt had grown to £24.7 billion by 1946, roughly two and a half times its gross domestic product. Humiliatingly, Britain had also become a debtor to nations in both the formal and informal empire and by the war's end the Treasury owed over £3.5 billion to India, Canada and Australia and a further £475 million to Palestine, Egypt and Sudan.[21]

Britain's financial ailments were added to by the American decision to terminate Lend-Lease, which cut off vital supplies of food, fuel and materials and increased pressure on foreign currency reserves. Although provisions were made in 1943 to allow for the extension of American aid until July 1946, in August 1945 President Harry Truman directed that all outstanding orders be cancelled.[22] Despite subsequent State Department warnings that aid was needed to support British troops stationed in Europe, the president vetoed requests for additional assistance.[23] Before the House of Commons, Attlee acknowledged that the abrupt conclusion of Lend-Lease had put Britain 'in a very serious financial position', not least because the economic burden of war continued throughout the demobilization period.[24] In 1947 over 1.2 million men (around

---

[19] Correlli Barnett, *The Lost Victory: British Dreams, British Realities, 1945-1950* (London: Macmillan, 1995), 56.

[20] The Long-Term Prospects of British Industry, 23 June 1944, CAB 87/14.

[21] Barnett, *The Lost Victory*, 29; John Callaghan, 'In Search of Eldorado: Labour's Colonial Economic Policy', in *Labour's High Noon: The Government and the Economy, 1945-51*, ed. Jim Fyrth (London: Lawrence & Wishart, 1993), 119; Rhiannon Vickers, *The Labour Party and the World, Volume 1: Evolution of Labour's Foreign Policy, 1900-51* (Manchester: New York: Manchester University Press ; Palgrave, 2011), 159.

[22] 'The President's News Conference of August 23, 1945', in *Harry S. Truman, Containing the Public Messages, Speeches, and Statements of the President, April 12 to December 31, 1945*, Public Papers of the Presidents of the United States (United States Government Printing Office, 1961), 232; Document 50: The Secretary of State to the Ambassador in the United Kingdom (Winant), 18 August 1945, *Foreign Relations of the United States: Diplomatic Papers, 1945, The British Commonwealth, The Far East Vol. VI* (Washington DC: United States Government Printing Office, 1969).

[23] Joseph Grew, 'Lend-Lease to Europe', 14 May 1945; Truman to Grew, 2 July 1945, White House Central Files: Confidential File - Box 23: Lend-Lease (Harry S. Truman Library – HSTL).

[24] *Hansard*, HC Debate, Vol. 413 Col. 955, 24 August 1945.

12 per cent of the working population) remained under arms and unable to engage in economically productive labour.[25] The slow pace of demobilization was not without controversy and even prompted a series of mutinies involving 50,000 airmen based in India, South East Asia and the Middle East.[26] Rationing continued, with queues for even the most basic food stuffs ubiquitous, and homelessness became increasingly common. Hugely depleted, Britain needed food, workers and materials to support reconstruction and boost its flagging balance of trade.

Rather than viewing Britain as a nation that possessed distant overseas assets, the Attlee government saw the empire as a single entity in which the peripheries serviced the core. They understood that Britain's vast network of overseas assets, investments, dominions and colonies offered a perhaps unparalleled bounty of riches. Manganese ore from Sierra Leone, rubber and tin from Malaya, Rhodesian coal and precious metals from the Gold Coast were prized as export commodities that would finance post-war reconstruction and maintain Britain's status as a great power. Labour identified imperial reorientation as its ambition, and Bevin promised MPs that he would protect British interests 'in whatever part of the world they may be found'.[27]

The Middle East was central in British policy makers' collective imagination and was described in a War Cabinet memorandum as 'an essential link in the Imperial system, a centre in which are gathered essential arteries of communication and an essential source of power'.[28] It had well-integrated communication and economic networkers with Europe, India and South East Asia and vast oil reserves that were controlled largely by British firms and provided a stream of scarce foreign currency.[29] Home to 7 per cent of known oil reserves and the largest refinery east of Suez, Iran was singled out as particularly significant. In a strident comparison the Ministry of Fuel and Power suggested that the Abadan refinery was worth 'not much less than the estimated cost of retooling and modernizing the coal industry in this country'.[30] Bevin went further, linking British concessions and domestic prosperity by suggesting that without them he could see 'no hope of our being able to achieve the standard of

---

[25] Hugh Dalton, *High Tide and After: Memoirs 1945-1960* (London: Muller, 1962), 170–1.
[26] Political Intelligence Centre Paper No. 80 'Middle East Oil', 1945, IOR/R/15/5/263 (BL).
[27] *Hansard*, HC Debate, Vol. 416 Col. 442, 21 November 1945.
[28] Imperial Security in the Middle East, 2 July 1945, CAB 66/67 (TNA).
[29] Political Intelligence Paper No. 80 'Middle East Oil', undated 1945, IOR/R/15/5/263 (BL).
[30] Ministry of Fuel and Power Memorandum, 17 September 1946, FO 371/52343 (TNA).

living at which we are aiming in Great Britain'.[31] Although total oil production had fallen from 9.6 million tons in 1939 to 6.6 million tons in 1941, it had more than doubled during the war years, reaching 13.3 million in 1944 and 16.8 million tons by 1945.[32] Indeed, Iran's oil production was almost four times that of neighbouring Iraq and more than six times larger than Saudi Arabia.[33] In turn the taxes paid by the AIOC to the Exchequer had increased from £3.32 million in 1939 to £15.53 million in 1945 with the potential for further growth.[34] Between 1941 and 1945 AIOC capital expenditure increased from £0.2 million to over £6.8 million taking refinery capacity to some 15,000,000 tons per annum.[35] In 1945 alone over £1.2 million was dedicated to developing new oil fields, indicating the wealth of untapped resources available in Iran and the Persian Gulf more generally.[36] Expansion was also afoot at the company's Grangemouth and Llandarcy refineries, and there were plans for a new site at the Isle of Grain in Kent.

With withdrawal from India planned, the Middle East took on a new strategic importantance. The region was a critical artery for British trade and communication home to significant military and air force installations at Suez, Aden and Habbaniya. In April 1945 Foreign Secretary Anthony Eden suggested that 'the Middle East is the sole really large source of oil outside America which is available to us' and that within a decade 'neither the British Empire nor even the United States will be able to exert their full war effort' without it.[37] Bevin shared this view, recording simply that 'the Middle East's vast oil reserves were was one of our most important strategic interests and would be vital to us in time of war'.[38] As in the 1800s, the Middle East was identified as a centre of Anglo-Russian competition and even before the end of the Second World War Foreign Office mandarins issued warnings that continued cooperation rested on Moscow's respect for defined spheres of influence and Britain's strategic interests there.[39] Ironically, some officials had expressed concern that the socialist Bevin may seek a rapprochement with the Soviets. These included Principal Private Secretary at the Foreign Office Pierson Dixon who warned that the new

---

[31] Alan Bullock, *Ernest Bevin, Foreign Secretary: 1945-1951*, The Life and Times of Ernest Bevin (London: Heinemann, 1983), 359.
[32] Anglo-Iranian Oil Co Ltd Final Accounts 1939, 90513; Anglo-Iranian Oil Co Ltd Final Accounts 1945, 95587 (BPA).
[33] Political Intelligence Centre Paper No. 80 'Middle East Oil', undated 1945, IOR/R/15/5/263 (BL).
[34] Statement showing AIOC's UK Taxation Liabilities on Accounts, for years 1932 to 1950, 9233 (BPA).
[35] Political Intelligence Centre Paper No. 80 'Middle East Oil', undated 1945, IOR/R/15/5/263 (BL).
[36] Anglo-Iranian Oil Co Ltd Final Accounts 1945, 95587 (BPA).
[37] Defence of the Middle East, 13 April 1945, CAB 66/65 (TNA).
[38] Strategic Requirements in the Middle East, 27 May 1946, CAB 131/1 (TNA).
[39] Orme Sargent Memorandum, 2 April 1945, FO 371/47881 (TNA).

Figure 2.1 Abadan from the air. At the end of the Second World War, it was the world's largest oil refinery and one of Britain's most important overseas assets. Courtesy of Getty Images, Bettmann/Contributor.

foreign secretary had 'a perhaps too pronounced slant towards Russia'.[40] Such assumptions were highly inaccurate.

TUC General Secretary Walter Citrine suggested that Bevin 'personalised almost everything', a tendency that is clear in his inability to separate his views towards the Soviet Union from his experience of communism in the labour movement.[41] As head of the TGWU, Bevin had been a fierce opponent of the Communist Party of Great Britain's attempts to gain a foothold in his union and the wider labour movement.[42] Now foreign secretary, he found it difficult to separate his deep hostility to communism, which he saw as inherently totalitarian, from diplomatic relations with the Soviet Union, effectively viewing them as one and the same. From the podium at the 1946 Labour Party Conference, he told delegates that the only thanks he received for supporting the Russian revolution 'was an attempt by the communists to break up the union that I had built'.[43] As in the TGWU, Bevin saw communism as a challenge to be resisted and the Soviet

---

[40] Piers Dixon, *Double Diploma: The Life of Sir Pierson Dixon, Don and Diplomat* (London: Hutchinson, 1968), 173–4.
[41] Walter Citrine, *Men and Work: An Autobiography* (London: Hutchinson, 1964), 238.
[42] Bullock, *Ernest Bevin, Trade Union Leader*, 518–24.
[43] John Saville, 'C. R. Attlee: An Assessment', *The Socialist Register* 20 (1983), 166.

Union as threatening 'the throat of the British Commonwealth', particularly in Iran and the Middle East.[44] Opportunistic aggression was inherent to the communist and therefore Soviet outlook and could not, the foreign secretary argued, be appeased. Instead, Britain should contribute to the creation of an impenetrable defensive arc that incorporated overseas interests from Asia across the Middle East to Europe.

Imperialism and opposition

To Bevin, Britain's great power status was predicated on its international reach. However, like his Fabian Colonial Bureau contemporaries he did not believe that imperialism was sustainable or desirable if predicated solely on exploitation. Instead, he hoped to galvanize relations between the imperial metropole and peripheries by exporting British expertise – in technology, defence and governance – and capital investment for development projects. In doing so, productivity, profitability and living standards would be raised with mutually beneficial results. The foreign secretary's views were crystallized by the appointment of Denis Healey as secretary of the party's International Department. In this role, the party gave Healey carte blanche to shape its overseas policy and while much of his work focused on developing relations with the United States and left-wing parties in Western Europe, Healey also took an interest in the intersections between the British Empire and emerging international tensions. Codifying Bevinism as party policy, he emphasized the malleability of Soviet-inspired Marxism in exploiting political weakness and working-class discontent. It was therefore vital that political and economic institutions, particularly trade unions, were safeguarded from communism.[45] To avoid ceding political territory to the Soviets, British diplomacy needed to be 'made in mines – or forests or fisheries – as much as in chanceries'.[46]

In the Middle East Bevin argued that Britain's foreign policy 'never reached the ordinary people' and relied instead on relationships with political elites who were themselves often detached from their people. As a result, British imperialism

---

[44] *Hansard*, HC Debate, Vol. 415 Col. 1333, 7 November 1945; Foreign Office Minutes, 24 January 1946, FO 800/513 (TNA); Frank K. Roberts, 'Ernest Bevin as Foreign Secretary', in *The Foreign Policy of the British Labour Governments, 1945–1951*, ed. Ovendale, 30–1; Louis, *The British Empire in the Middle East*, 54.
[45] Cominform and the Labour Movement, undated – 1949, Healey Articles – Box 13/03 (LHA).
[46] Labour Britain and the World, undated – 1947, Healey Articles – Box 13/01 (LHA).

was an easy target for nascent independence movements.[47] The foreign secretary believed that far more needed to be done to advertise the benefits of empire overseas and raise awareness of the alleged partnership that existed between Britain and its overseas interests.[48] The Foreign Office became responsible for publicity work abroad, which was previously the Ministry of Information's purview. In a letter to consular officers, Bevin pressed the importance of renewed propaganda campaigns to promote British interests overseas, the dissemination of which should be varied and tailored to the needs of individual nations and regions.[49]

Bevin's vision was simultaneously Colonel Blimpish and sentimental. Using broad brush strokes he argued that Britain was 'last bastion of social democracy' and had an obligation to improve conditions overseas and simultaneously strengthen ties between the imperial metropole and its extremities.[50] In recognition of the need to win working-class support, 'industrial welfare' was listed as a primary element of British propaganda overseas.[51] Bevin hoped that the 'distinguishing characteristics' of the British economy could be exported, shaping emerging economy's labour movements, workplace legislation and social services.[52] In 1930 he had used his platform at the TUC Conference to announce: 'I know there are lots of people who believe that the British race is finished with, down and out, and is done for. I do not believe it. I believe that we have a culture, we have an ability, we have a craftsmanship that can still render great service to the world.'[53] Now foreign secretary, Bevin's commitment to welfare imperialism was unchanged.

Coinciding with growing Cold War tensions in Europe, Bevin's foreign policy immediately drew criticism from across the British left. At Labour Party Conference in 1946, left-wing delegates attacked the government's alleged continuation of Conservative Party policies and urged rapprochement with Moscow.[54] Similar arguments were made at the TUC Congress in Brighton where delegates cast almost two and a half million votes in favour of a motion that suggested British foreign policy was anti-Soviet and deferential to the United States. The motion was defeated by one million votes but drew the wrath of Clement Attlee who told delegates that it was 'filled with the kind of

---

[47] Bevin to Washington, 12 October 1945, FO 800/484 (TNA).
[48] Ibid.
[49] Bevin to His Majesty' Superintending Consular Officers, 15 January 1947, IOR/R/15/6/397 (BL).
[50] Bevin Memorandum, 13 March 1946, CAB 132/2 (TNA).
[51] Information Newsletter No.1, 28 June 1946, IOR/R/15/6/397 (BL).
[52] Ibid.
[53] *TUC Annual Report* (London, 1930), 257–61.
[54] *Labour Party: Report of the 45th Annual Conference* (London, 1946), 151.

misrepresentation to which we have become accustomed from the members of the Communist Party, their dupes and fellow travellers'.[55] In parliament, fifty-seven Labour backbenchers tabled an amendment to the King's Speech debate urging a socialist alternative to the government's foreign policy. Following criticism from the prime minister, the amendment's author, Richard Crossman, unsuccessfully tried to withdraw it. When divisions were eventually called, no Labour MP voted in favour but more than eighty elected to abstain.[56] The clearest articulation of backbench opposition to Bevinism came in *Keep Left*, a pamphlet written by the aforementioned Crossman and fellow left-wingers Ian Mikardo and Michael Foot, which suggested that Labour's imperialist turn was a 'strategic anachronism' and accused the government of launching an 'anti-Bolshevik bloc of reactionary Arab states in order to secure the oil-fields of Persia, Irak [sic] and Saudi-Arabia'.[57]

Although a staunch defender of his foreign secretary, Attlee was a quiet sceptic of Bevin's bullish imperialism on the grounds of practicality. In March 1945 the Suez Canal Committee, chaired by the then deputy prime minister, reported that 'the time has gone when Great Britain could afford to police the seas of the world for the benefit of others'.[58] Attlee subsequently proposed that the newly formed United Nations was the most effective means of protecting Britain's interests and that defence policy should be predicated on maintaining the international order.[59] In a paper circulated to the Defence Committee in spring 1946, Attlee argued that in any future conflict Britain would struggle to hold its position in the Middle East and that, with India moving towards independence, British strategic thinking must reorientate. 'We must not for sentimental reasons based on the past give hostages to fortune', the prime minister wrote, suggesting 'it may be that we shall have to consider the British Isles as an eastern extension of a strategic area the centre of which is the American continent rather than as a power looking eastwards through the Mediterranean to India and the East'.[60] By focusing on the domestic core, British outposts could be defended through multilateral agreements and, when necessary, long-distance aircraft.[61]

Suggesting that the prime minister's proposal 'would involve leading from weakness', Bevin urged Attlee to reconsider and advocated forcefully that

---

[55] Vickers, *The Labour Party and the World*, 170.
[56] Ibid.
[57] Michael Foot, Richard Crossman and Ian Mikardo, *Keep Left* (London: The New Statesman, 1947), 42–3.
[58] Future Defence Policy in the Suez Canal Area, 20 March 1945, CAB 66/63 (TNA).
[59] Future of the Italian Colonies, 1 September 1945, CAB 129/1 (TNA).
[60] Future of the Italian Colonies, 2 March 1946, CAB 131/2 (TNA).
[61] Attlee to Bevin, 1 December 1946, FO 800/475; Future of the Italian Colonies, 1 September 1945, CAB 129/1 (TNA).

Labour should 'develop the Middle East as a producing area to help our own economy and take the place of India'. Far from exploitative, this redeployment of British capital would, he argued, be mutually beneficial by raising living standards, enhancing stability and creating more integrated markets.[62] Despite Attlee's initial scepticism, the foreign secretary's arguments won out and the Middle East remained firmly at the forefront of British strategic considerations. Though sometimes portrayed as a passive observer, Attlee was not bullied by Bevin but actively delegated responsibility to an ally he trusted above all others. When discussing their relationship some years later, the former prime minister suggested plainly that 'foreign affairs are the province of the foreign secretary . . . if you've got a good dog, you don't bark yourself'.[63] Bevin's authority over British foreign policy was assured but would quickly find itself tested as Iran entered a new period of political turbulence.

The first challenge: Azerbaijan

The Foreign Office's hardening position towards Moscow was given credence by the formation of the secessionist Azerbaijan People's Government in Iranian Azerbaijan in November 1945. Headed by Ja'far Pishihvari, leader of the Democratic Party of Azerbaijan (DPA), the new breakaway government was in receipt of financial and organizational support from the Soviet Union and seen by the Foreign Office as essentially analogous with the Tudeh.[64] Despite protests from Tehran, the Iranian army was powerless to prevent Pishihvari's rise to power as Red Army soldiers blocked roads into the region and supplied arms to hastily assembled DPA militias. Humiliated, the few Iranian troops remaining in Azerbaijan withdrew to Tehran.[65]

The Soviet press depicted the DPA's success as a blow against Western imperialism and hailed its leaders for their part in the fight against despotism. According to an article in Soviet newspaper *Trud* (Labour), the creation of a new state was part of a longer quest for national liberation that successive Iranian

---

[62] Bevin to Attlee, 9 January 1947, FO 800/476 (TNA).
[63] Francis Williams, *A Prime Minister Remembers: The War and Post-War Memoirs of the Rt. Hon. Earl Attlee* (London: Heinemann, 1961), 149.
[64] The Tudeh Party and Iranian Trade Unions, 2 January 1947, FO 371/61993 (TNA).
[65] Bullard to Foreign Office, 26 November 1945, IOR/L/PS/12/3417 (BL); Military Attaché's Intelligence Summary 4 December 1945, FO 371/45459; Wall to Bullard, 12 January 1946, FO 371/52663; Farquhar to Foreign Office, 18 April 1946, FO 416/174 (TNA).

governments had suppressed. The newspaper also claimed that 'in October 1945 several hundred members of democratic organisations were killed and over a thousand imprisoned on false charges', claims that are not substantiated elsewhere.[66]

The Iranian government, now led by Prime Minister Ebrahim Hakimi, had few good options available. To appeal to the public, Hakimi restricted displays of support for either the USSR or the separatist government, forced through new legislation to ban demonstrations and declared that he would not negotiate with the 'anarchists' leading the DPA. Aware that Britain and the United States would not risk conflict with the USSR, Hakimi reached out to the Kremlin and appointed Ahmad Qavam as an intermediary to Moscow. Humiliatingly, the Soviet government responded by suggesting that they would 'prefer to greet in Moscow a Premier Qavam, rather than a Premier Hakimi' and demanded that all emergency legislation be lifted.[67] Despite persistent grain shortages across the rest of Iran, and in direct abrogation of the 1941 Anglo-Soviet-Iranian Treaty, the export of agricultural goods from Azerbaijan was again halted and Red Army soldiers posted along the northern border.[68]

Under enormous pressure from the Soviet Union, the prime minister looked to London for support. A former consul in Moscow, Ambassador Bullard was a well-established critic of the Soviets and demanded that action of some sort must be taken against them.[69] A military response was immediately ruled out on the grounds of practicality. By Bullard's own admission, Britain's military presence in Iran was 'strategically useless' numbering just 5,000 soldiers (one-sixth of the Soviet forces present in Azerbaijan) in December 1945.[70] The ambassador's dismal assessment of Britain's military capabilities was shared by Vice-Chief of the Imperial General Staff Lieutenant-General Frank Simpson who warned that Britain lacked the troops and bases required to guarantee Iran's security in the event of conflict.[71]

Rather than becoming bogged down in a protracted diplomatic standoff, Bullard proposed that Iran be divided into clearly defined Anglo-Soviet spheres of influence. The ambassador had first advocated this approach in spring 1945,

---

[66] British Embassy, Moscow to Foreign Office, 1 February 1946, IOR/L/PS/12/3417 (BL).
[67] Abrahamian, *Iran Between Two Revolutions*, 218–21; Bullard to Foreign Office, 20 December 1945, FO 371/52661 (TNA).
[68] Bullard to Foreign Office, 27 July 1945, FO 371/45433 (TNA).
[69] Bullard to Foreign Office, 27 November 1945, FO 371/45436 (TNA).
[70] Louis, *The British Empire in the Middle East*, 70.
[71] Strategic Requirements in the Middle East, 25 May 1946, CAB 131/2 (TNA).

suggesting that without clear delineation of influence the Soviet Union would gradually encroach on Britain's interests across the Middle East.[72] Developing his position further, Bullard argued that although Iran was a unitary state in principle, competing Anglo-Soviet interests had effectively divided it in practice. In turn, 'over-centralisation' was beginning to undermine stability, which would most effectively be upheld by dividing the country into two semi-autonomous provincial administrations.[73] Under this arrangement the Soviet Union would have authority over Azerbaijan and other northern territories while Britain would control those in the south. The ambassador believed that this system would provide a bulwark, however temporary, against Soviet aggression and won endorsement from consular officials in Ahwaz, Shiraz and Isfahan. Less certain was how the Iranian government may respond. Although Bullard mused on Hakimi and his cabinet acquiescing to the proposals, he indicated that the election of a new, more cooperative prime minister was in London's interests.[74]

Summoned to meet with Bevin, the ambassador warned that taking Azerbaijan was far from the limit of Soviet ambitions and if allowed to secure a foothold in the Persian Gulf they would expand their reach throughout the Middle East. In an early formulation of domino theory, Bullard argued that economic and social unrest would create conditions rife for communism with ruinous results for Western interests. 'If Iraq goes', he suggested, 'Kuwait will be in danger and the oil resources of Kuwait. . . . And from Kuwait to the American oil interests in Saudi Arabia and Bahrain is only a step.'[75] Following this advice, Bevin used the December 1945 Moscow Council of Foreign Ministers meeting to call for the appointment of an Anglo-Soviet-American commission to investigate the Azerbaijan problem and potentially pave the way for Iran's division.[76] The foreign secretary recognized Britain's limited military power and was similarly aware that the ambassador's proposals could be a cost-effective means of maintaining power in the region. While a permanent Soviet satellite in the Persian Gulf was a risk, by drawing clear lines of demarcation the British would in theory secure the partnership of the continuous state in southern Iran and ensure a steady supply of profitable oil.[77]

---

[72] Bullard Memorandum, 25 May 1945, FO 371/45464 (TNA).
[73] Bullard to Foreign Office, 27 November 1945, FO 371/45436 (TNA).
[74] Bullard to Foreign Office, 2 January 1946, FO 371/52661 (TNA).
[75] Bullard Memorandum, 18 December 1945, FO 371/52664 (TNA).
[76] Document 503: The Ambassador in the Soviet Union (Harriman) to the Secretary of State, 28 December 1945, *Foreign Relations of the United States: Diplomatic Papers, 1945, The Near East and Africa Vol. VIII* (Washington DC: United States Government Printing Office, 1969).
[77] Bullock, *Ernest Bevin, Foreign Secretary*, 159.

Faced with the prospect of his country's division, Hakimi requested that the United States serve as an 'unbiased, friendly assistant' in drafting a petition to the United Nations and endorse Iranian complaints that the Soviet Union had broken international law.[78] Insistent upon stringent neutrality, the American government refused to publicly endorse Iran's complaint; however, in private discussions they sought to leverage their influence in both London and Moscow. Explaining the situation to Bevin, the British Ambassador to the United States Lord Halifax, suggested that the Truman administration eyed Anglo-Soviet rivalry in the Middle East as a throwback to previous generations of imperialism and was likely to take an extremely dim view of Bullard's recommendations. Indeed, to pursue Iran's divisions would 'cast serious doubt' on Britain's commitment to the United Nations and the post-war order envisaged in Washington.[79] Halifax's advice was perhaps too restrained. From Tehran, American Ambassador Wallace Murray suggested that the scheme, far from relieving tensions, was likely exacerbate Anglo-Soviet discord.[80] State Department officials, meanwhile, suggested that Bullard's proposals illustrated Britain's inability to effectively safeguard both Iranian independence and their interests there.[81]

In Britain, the proposed division of Iran was succour to Bevin's left-wing critics who, inside and outside parliament, took it as evidence of his pathological hostility to the Soviet Union.[82] In an indicative piece of correspondence with the foreign secretary, Josephine Smith, a long-serving member of Friends of the Soviet Union who had lived in Tehran, attacked Bullard's 'quite unconsciously anti-working class' recommendations and compared British policy in Iran with support for fascism.[83] Reflecting on growing disquiet, Raymond Blackburn, MP for Birmingham King's Norton, used an article in *Foreign Affairs* magazine to report that 'it is often said by extreme left critics that the British Labor [sic] government is pursuing a Socialist policy at home and a Tory policy abroad'.[84]

Despite widespread criticism Bullard insisted that British interests were best served by Iran's partition. In a note for Bevin, he argued that the Azerbaijan issue going before the United Nations was 'likely to kill our Moscow proposals for

---

[78] Murray to Byrnes, 1 January 1946, RG 59 891.00/1-146 (National Archives and Records Administration – NARA).
[79] Halifax to Foreign Office, 2 February 1946, FO 371/51606; Halifax to Foreign Office, 3 January 1946, FO 371/52661 (TNA).
[80] Document 451: The Ambassador in Iran (Murray) to the Secretary of State, 4 December 1945; *FRUS 1945 Vol VIII*; Document 215: The Ambassador in Iran (Murray) to the Secretary of State, 10 January 1946, *FRUS 1946 Vol VII*.
[81] Washington to Foreign Office, 26 November 1945, FO 371/45480 (TNA).
[82] Raymond Blackburn, 'Bevin and His Critics', *Foreign Affairs* 25, no. 5 (January 1947), 239.
[83] Smith to Bevin, 25 November 1945, FO 371/52661 (TNA).
[84] Blackburn, 'Bevin and His Critics', 239.

the appointment of a tripartite commission for the establishment of Provincial Councils for Persia' and called on the foreign secretary to take any action necessary to dissuade Hakimi from tabling a complaint.[85] Recognizing the prime minister's weak position, Bullard appealed for the shah to intervene directly.[86] Convinced that Iran was essentially ungovernable as a democracy, the ambassador suggested that the monarch should play an enlarged role, perhaps even as the dictator of a new state that would be more amenable to British interests.[87] This was far from a minority position within the diplomatic establishment, which increasingly questioned the feasibility of Iran's continued independence.[88]

Bevin found himself in a compromised position. Although he had initially supported Bullard's proposals for Iran's division, he was wary of damaging relations with the United States and recognized the strength of the State Department's opposition. Despite his instinctive suspicion towards Moscow, the foreign secretary was as yet unwilling to break with Washington and potentially undermine his wider ambitions for the empire, informal or otherwise. Cursing the Iranian government for having 'wrecked any chance of Russian acceptance of the proposal for a tripartite commission' he reluctantly agreed to support Iran's petition to the United Nations.[89] Explaining this U-turn in the House of Commons, Bevin suggested that he had simply feared that the United Nations was not yet ready to resolve such a complex dispute and that far from putting pressure on Iran, British advice concerning their relationship with the Soviet Union had been offered on a friendly basis. Rejecting criticism from anti-imperialist backbenches, he argued that Britain's treatment of Iran was justifiable because 'when a small country happens to possess a vital raw material it is for allies to arrange their business so as not to make the small country the victim of controversy between the big allies'.[90] With his proposed policy shelved and lacking the support of his foreign secretary, Bullard's position was untenable and he retired from the Tehran Embassy.

Although Bullard had misjudged the possibility of partitioning Iran, his analysis of Hakimi's weak Majlis support was accurate and on 21 January 1946 the prime minister offered his resignation amid accusations of treason from opposition deputies. His replacement was Moscow's preferred candidate Ahmad Qavam who rallied the support of fifty-two deputies, a majority of just one. The

---

[85] Foreign Office to Tehran, 2 January 1946, FO 371/52661 (TNA).
[86] Bullard to Foreign Office, 4 January 1946, FO 371/52661 (TNA).
[87] Bullard to Foreign Office, 2 January 1946, FO 371/52661 (TNA).
[88] Policy in Persia, 13 April 1946; Howe Minutes, 16 April 1946, FO 371/52673 (TNA).
[89] Foreign Office to Halifax, 5 January 1946, FO 371/52661 (TNA).
[90] *Hansard*, HC Debate, Vol. 419 Col. 1358-9, 21 February 1946.

British Embassy had previously warned that Qavam would ally himself with the Tudeh, and his decision to detain right-wing leaders like Sayyid Zia, withdraw Iran's case from the United Nations and engage in bilateral negotiations with the USSR exacerbated fears that he was under their influence.[91] To resolve the crisis, Qavam spent three weeks in Moscow but achieved few obvious successes. Still indignant that they had been denied a concession in 1944, Soviet Foreign Minister Vyacheslav Molotov demanded one be granted and that the Iranian government recognize Azerbaijan's autonomy. Qavam refused and returned to the United Nations with American support.[92] Facing growing international criticism, the Soviet Union pledged to withdraw its troops within six weeks. In return, the Iranian government agreed to a slew of political and fiscal reforms in Azerbaijan, renegotiate the terms of all foreign oil concessions and establish a jointly held oil company in northern Iran, subject to Majlis approval.[93]

In theory, this arrangement offered the USSR a permanent base in the Persian Gulf; however, Qavam's insistence that the Majlis had to agree to its terms meant that it was not guaranteed to become law. The prime minister publicly referred to the concession as 'long overdue' and a 'natural development' but was under no obligation to campaign for its ratification or call on his supporters to do likewise.[94] The inclusion of a clause necessitating the renegotiation of all foreign concessions was also a canny move. Having reached a settlement with the Soviet Union, and certain that Washington would refuse to support British imperialism, he felt increasingly confident in his ability to win a more equitable settlement from the Anglo-Iranian Oil Company. In March, Reader Bullard had suggested that the Iranians were not only 'untruthful, backbiters, undisciplined, (and) incapable of unity' but simply 'too selfish and slothful' to resist communist subversion.[95] Qavam's skilful approach to diplomacy illustrated the ambassador's misreading of the situation and British primacy in Iran increasingly appeared to be challenged not only by the Soviet Union but also an assertive Iranian government.

---

[91] Bullard to Foreign Office, 4 January 1946, FO 371/52661 (TNA); Document 241: The Secretary of State to the Chargé in the Soviet Union (Kennan), 22 February 1946, *FRUS 1946 Vol VII*.

[92] Foreign Office to Tehran, 4 June 1946, FO 371/52713 (TNA); Inverchapel to Foreign Office, 24 June 1946, IOR/L/PS/12/563B (BL); Document 337: The Chargé in Iran (Ward) to the Secretary of State, 8 May 1946, *FRUS 1946 Vol VII*.

[93] Memo from a Telegraph Report of Ashurov from Tehran, 5 April 1946, 120539; Qavam to Sadchikov, 4 April 1946, 120469 (Wilson Center Digital Archive – WCDA); Azimi, *Iran*, 152.

[94] Document 274: Murray to the Secretary of State, 22 March 1946, *FRUS 1946 Vol VII*.

[95] Bullard to Foreign Office, 15 March 1946; Bullard to Foreign Office, 29 March 1946, FO 371/52670 (TNA).

The second challenge: labour unrest

If the Azerbaijan crisis served to justify British suspicion towards the Soviet Union, the rise of increasingly militant trade unionism linked to the Tudeh Party illustrated the urgent need to improve conditions for Iran's working class. It is not without irony that the Tudeh reacted positively to Labour's election and sent fraternal greetings that appealed for 'British help in establishing real democracy and freedom'.[96]

Although a largely urban party, with centres of support in Tehran and provinces under Soviet control, by January 1946 British Labour attaché Kenneth Hird reported that the Tudeh was gaining popularity in the oil-rich south. He noted that Tudeh's influence was expressed largely through nascent trade unions, which 'gave coherence to workers' grievances' and were gaining strength among the AIOC's previously unorganized workforce.[97] Other officials could not evaluate the Tudeh's growth without lurching into the kind of orientalized analysis that dogged British officialdom. British consul-general in Ahwaz Alan Trott, for example, sneered that 'the poison of Tudeh propaganda has spread with astonishing speed throughout the province; the sorry spectacle of thousands of human beings, who after all have a religion and a sort of culture of their own, suddenly turning communist like sheep following their leader is shocking and disgusting'.[98]

By November 1945 reports had begun to circulate within the AIOC that Tudeh-affiliated trade unions were organizing among oil workers. This was a relatively new phenomenon: historically the AIOC had clamped down on workplace organization to the point where workers were banned from reading or possessing socialist literature and newspapers.[99] The election of a Labour government at home and opening of Iranian politics during the war years meant the company was no longer able to exert such stringent controls over its workers and began to consider the principle of collective bargaining.

With the densest concentration of industrial workers in Iran, it is perhaps unsurprising that trade unionism attracted interest in and around Abadan or that the Tudeh, the most energetic organizing force, became its fulcrum. The Tudeh benefited from a presence in Abadan's social and sports club and an increasingly

---

[96] Bullard to Foreign Office, 6 August 1945, FO 371/45433 (TNA).
[97] Le Rougetel to Foreign Office, enc. Kenneth J. Hird, 'Labour Conditions: Anglo-Iranian Oil Co. - Tehran', 8 January 1947, FO 371/61984 (TNA).
[98] Appreciation of Local Conditions, Nov 1945 – May 1946, date illegible, IOR/L/PS/12/3534 (BL).
[99] Reports of Parliamentary Delegation to Persia, 3 July 1946, FO 371/52718 (TNA).

sophisticated media operation. Its newspaper *Rahbar* had a nationwide distribution network, selling upwards of 100,000 copies per issue and employing up to fifty stridently anti-capitalist and anti-imperialist journalists. According to consular reports, the Tudeh's reach was so great that 'at least seventy percent of the population who represent the working class have been affected'.[100] The language employed was clear: the rapacious AIOC bosses and their lackeys in Iran's traditional parties were responsible for keeping Iran and its workers poor to the point of destitution. *Rahbar* and the party's cadre of organizers gave voice to long-term grievances concerning not only poor pay but also underinvestment, bullying and housing and situated them in a wider Marxist framework. Recognizing their growing popularity, Qavam invited three Tudeh deputies to join his cabinet and overturned Hakimi's ban on public rallies.[101] Despite the prime minister's argument to the contrary, John Le Rougetel, Britain's newly-appointed ambassador, was convinced that the Tudeh was operating with the support of and instructions from the Soviet Union.[102]

The most visible source of domestic opposition to the Tudeh came from conservative political factions and newspapers like *Ra'ad-i Emruz*, which suggested the party would upend Iranian social and political norms and was 'an enemy of Islam'.[103] As in the Second World War, the Foreign Office and British Embassy hoped that Anglophile propaganda and politicians would provide a counternarrative to anti-imperialist rhetoric and prevent the spread of Soviet-influenced Marxism.[104] More assertive, however, was the AIOC, which, recognizing the threat of militant trade unionism, was resolute in its opposition to Tudeh efforts to recruit oil workers.[105] In July 1946, the British consul at Khorramshahr Vere Willoughby, reported that an Arab Tribal Union had been formed by Qashqai and Bakhtiari tribal chiefs to take up arms against the Tudeh with tacit AIOC endorsement.[106] The company subsequently opened discussions to provide arms to the tribesmen through Colonel Herbert John Underwood, a former Indian Army intelligence officer employed by the company as a political advisor.[107] In conversation with the American consul in Basra, William C.

---

[100] Elkington to Berthoud, 22 May 1946, FO 371/52713; British consul in Kerman, 15 August 1945, FO 371/45455 (TNA).
[101] Abrahamian, *Iran Between Two Revolutions*, 229.
[102] Le Rougetel to Foreign Office, 8 June 1946, FO 371/52677 (TNA).
[103] Ervand Abrahamian, 'Factionalism in Iran: Political Groups in the 14th Parliament (1944-46)', *Middle Eastern Studies* 14, no. 1 (January 1978), 40–4.
[104] Young Minutes, 25 July 1945, FO 371/45433 (TNA).
[105] Le Rougetel to Foreign Office, 8 June 1946, FO 371/52677 (TNA).
[106] Le Rougetel to Foreign Office, 20 June 1946; Willoughby to Bevin, 21 July 1946, IOR/L/PS/12/3490A; Trott to Tehran, 26 June, IOR/L/PS/12/1156 (BL).
[107] Rasmus Christian Elling, 'War of Clubs: Struggle for Space in Abadan and the 1946 Oil Strike', in *Violence and the City in the Modern Middle East*, ed. Nelida Fuccaro (Stanford: Stanford University Press, 2016), 202.

Burdett, Willoughby confirmed Underwood's black operation, admitting that 'a few men in the AIOC' had provided support to anti-Tudeh militias.[108] The depth of this arrangement is difficult to substantiate and there is no evidence to suggest they were supported through official Foreign Office channels. Indeed, Le Rougetel complained that 'more harm than good will be done' by encouraging them and wrote to British consular officials to warn against offering assistance.[109] Nonetheless rumours that British intelligence was attempting to instigate an Arab-led uprising became a popular source of anti-British propaganda.[110] According to *Rahbar*, the British were 'intriguing amongst the tribesmen with a view to creating disturbances and disorder' and '3,000 Arabs armed by the British agents are awaiting orders for an attack on Ahwaz'.[111]

With British troops withdrawn from Iran, the AIOC warned that Tudeh organizing among its workforce was becoming increasingly militant and there was now a distinct possibility of 'large scale demonstrations or strikes in Abadan in the near future'.[112] Within a matter of weeks regular meetings involving up to 5,000 workers were taking place during which speakers implored workers 'to use violence' in opposition to the company and its British employees.[113] By early May limited instances of industrial action were beginning to break out. An initial walkout of fifty members of Provincial United Council of the Tudeh-affiliated Trade Union of Workers and Toilers of Khuzestan at the AIOC's locomotive works in response to complaints of bullying by a British foreman was followed by solidarity action involving a further 350 employees of the distillation and bitumen plants at Abadan. Although generally characterized in the most negative terms by British officials, the striking workers proved to be immensely disciplined and quickly drew support from across the company and its auxiliary operations.[114] In correspondence to the Foreign Office, Ambassador Le Rougetel suggested that Tudeh organizers had rallied workers with calls not just for improved terms

---

[108] Document 36: Disturbances in Khuzistan, United States Consulate, Basra, 17 July 1946, F. David Andrews, ed., *The Lost Peoples of the Middle East: Documents of the Struggle for Survival and Independence of the Kurds, Assyrians, and Other Minority Races in the Middle East* (Salisbury: Documentary Publications, 1982), 36.

[109] Le Rougetel to Bevin, 1 July 1946, FO 371/52717 (TNA); Le Rougetel, Consular Circular No. 26, 23 July 1946, IOR/L/PS/12/3491A (BL).

[110] Military Attaché's Intelligence Summary, 1 July 1946, FO 371/52770 (TNA).

[111] 'Strike in Khuzestan', *Rahbar*, 15 July 1946, 66099 (BPA).
Many thanks to Dr Mattin Biglari for directing me to this and a number of other Iranian media sources. See: Mattin Biglari, *Refining Knowledge: Labour, Expertise and Oil Nationalisation in Iran, 1933-51* (Edinburgh: Edinburgh University Press, 2023).

[112] Jones to Elkington, 13 March 1946, 43762 (BPA).

[113] Tehran Inward Telegram, 3 May 1946; Abadan Inward Telegram, 22 May 1946, 43762 (BPA); Berthoud to Starling, 22 May 1946, FO 371/52713 (TNA).

[114] Elkington to Berthoud, 22 May 1946, FO 371/52713 (TNA).

and conditions but also control of the oil fields themselves.[115] Privately, the AIOC leadership agreed and chairman William Fraser acknowledged that the Tudeh's influence had rapidly spread across all facets of the company's Iranian operation.[116]

Despite, or perhaps because of, growing industrial unrest, Qavam hoped to maintain his alliance with the Tudeh and approved a May Day public holiday. In Tehran, 80,000 trade unionists and their supporters marched to the Central Council's headquarters for an open-air rally with similar processions taking place in towns and cities across Iran. The workers' demands included better working conditions, legal protections, and among the first public calls for the oil industry's nationalization. In Abadan the procession of workers was reportedly three miles long.[117] Such was the protestors' strength that Le Rougetel, on Colonel Underwood's advice, reported to Bevin that the security of British personnel and assets relied on 'the goodwill and pleasure of the Tudeh'.[118] The Tudeh's May Day show of strength was followed by weeks of significant industrial unrest centred on the Agha Jari oilfield, around 100 miles east of Abadan. These reached their high point on 13 July when Tudeh-aligned pickets occupied company property and threatened British employees. Disturbances subsequently spread as far as Ahwaz where AIOC staff were attacked by members of the Tudeh-affiliated Provincial Workers Union.[119] As something approaching a general strike broke out in southern Iran, Le Rougetel reported that the Tudeh were 'in complete control' of the oil fields.[120] Convinced that Soviet agents were behind the disturbances, Khuzestan's Governor General Mesbah Fatemi declared a state of martial law and the Iranian Department of War despatched a battalion of soldiers and twenty-four trucks to quell the violence. Although exact figures vary, at least seventeen fatalities and a further 150 wounded pickets were reported.[121]

The Tudeh press responded by accusing the AIOC 'organized terrorism', a message that found sympathy across the Iranian media. *Darya*, a newspaper referred to by the British Embassy as of the 'moderate left', called the strike a reaction to British efforts to partition Iran and a demonstration of workers'

---

[115] Le Rougetel to Foreign Office, 7 May 1946, IOR/L/PS/12/563B (BL).
[116] Fraser to Jackson, 10 July 1946, 43762 (BPA).
[117] Ervand Abrahamian, 'May Day in the Islamic Republic', in *Khomeinism: Essays on the Islamic Republic* (Berkeley: University of California Press, 1993), 65–8.
[118] Le Rougetel to Bevin, 29 May 1946, IOR/L/PS/12/3490A (BL).
[119] Le Rougetel to Foreign Office, 15 July 1946, FO 371/52719 (TNA).
[120] Le Rougetel to Foreign Office, 13 July 1946, FO 371/52719 (TNA).
[121] Le Rougetel to Foreign Office, 16 July 1946, FO 371/52719 (TNA); Abadan Inward Telegram, 15 July 1946, 43762 (BPA).

patriotism.¹²² *Iran e-Ma* adopted a similar position and situated the striking workers within a wider fightback against British imperialism. 'The oil kings', the paper wrote, 'who have sucked the blood of 15 million people were not even prepared to provide the minimum necessities of life for thousands of Iranian workmen ... (they) never thought that 10,000 workmen in a remote desert might rise up in strike against them.'¹²³ Even moderate newspaper *Qiyam-e-Iran* was scathing in its condemnation of British policy and suggested that London was 'continuing her war against Hitler for the domination of the world'. Tellingly, a report prepared by the British Embassy noted that just a single major publication blamed the Tudeh for the strike.¹²⁴ Despite continued efforts to shape opinion in Iran, the realities of AIOC exploitation – of resources and workers alike – were becoming impossible to ignore.

Following discussions with Prime Minister Qavam, Le Rougetel reported that the Khuzestan strike was seen by the Iranian government as having 'no industrial justification whatsoever' and as a purely political move. Industrial action has been declared without legal agreement or notice, offering the pretext for severe action against the Tudeh.¹²⁵ Consequently, three left-wing activists were executed and a further four imprisoned for life. While the disturbances had been quelled by force, the anger that lay behind them required more sensitive resolution. Following discussions with trade union representatives brokered by the Iranian government, the AIOC management agreed to a new welfare policy including a one-sixth pay rise across all grades to ensure workers could take a day of rest.¹²⁶ The company concluded that workers' earnings were insufficient to maintain a family and that their ability to provide was directly related to their potential for militancy.¹²⁷ In a statement prepared for Attlee by the AIOC and the Ministry of Fuel and Power, special emphasis was given to the 'completion of welfare and housing schemes' and raising living standards as a means of quelling unrest.¹²⁸ These relatively trifling improvements were, however, only grudgingly agreed to by the company, and William Fraser continued to insist that the AIOC was a model employer in Iran.¹²⁹ This was

---

[122] Iranian Press Comments on the AIOC strikes, 24 July 1946, FO 371/52721 (TNA).
[123] Untitled, Iran-e Ma, 27 May 1946, 66098 (BPA).
[124] Iranian Press Comments on the AIOC strikes, 24 July 1946, FO 371/52721 (TNA).
[125] Le Rougetel to Foreign Office, 18 July 1946, FO 371/52720 (TNA).
[126] Azimi, *Iran*, 156; Le Rougetel to Bevin, 13 July 1946, FO 371/52720 (TNA).
[127] Le Rougetel to Bevin, 13 July 1946, FO 371/52720 (TNA).
[128] Draft Statement on Anglo-Iranian Oil Company, 7 August 1946, FO 371/52722 (TNA).
[129] Social and Municipal Development Carried Out by the Anglo-Iranian Oil Company Ltd. in Abadan and the South Persian Oilfields, 11 October 1946, FO 371/52726 (TNA).

to become a familiar refrain and a residual point of contention between the company and its government.

Industrial unrest in Iran coincided with fresh warnings of the Soviet threat to British interests. In March 1946, the Joint Intelligence Committee published 'Russia's Strategic Interests and Intentions', its first evaluation of Soviet strategic interests since late 1944. It warned that Russian expansionism was opportunistic and likely to be directed against those regions with limited or weak direct Anglo-American protection. Particularly vulnerable were areas where the United States had few interests, including the Mediterranean, Turkey and Iran. Rather than relying on armed forces, the report suggested that the Soviets would use domestic communist parties and propaganda to 'stir up trouble among colonial peoples'.[130] British Ambassador to Moscow Frank Roberts agreed and stressed that, as their intervention in Azerbaijan illustrated, Soviet expansionism was inherently opportunistic and insatiable. Consequently, reconciling it with British interests would be a challenging undertaking requiring a flexible response.[131]

British fears that the Iranian oil fields would descend into anarchy were reflected in the despatch of *HMS Norfolk* and *HMS Wild Goose* to the Persian Gulf, a decision that drew strong criticism from the Soviet Union and was deemed 'unfriendly' by the Iranian government.[132] Meanwhile, Force 401, roughly 15,000 Indian soldiers, was sent to Basra, Iraq and authorized to cross the border without notice should a threat to British interest emerge.[133] Having already developed links with anti-Tudeh Arab tribesmen, Underwood now attempted to cultivate a network of informants and officials friendly to the AIOC, infiltrate trade union branches and clubs and refine company messaging to more explicitly link organized labour with the Soviet Union.[134] His antipathy towards the Tudeh was relentless and he warned that there would be no respite from communist infiltration until their leadership was 'removed for good (dead or alive)'.[135] In response, *Rahbar* delighted in informing its readers that the company feared Iranian socialists so much that it had promised militias 'armed assistance and ordered them to attack trade union clubs' and demanded that the AIOC be 'banished' from Iran.[136]

---

[130] Joint Intelligence Sub-Committee Report: Russia's Strategic Interests and Intentions, 1 March 1946, CAB 81/132 (TNA).
[131] Roberts to Foreign Office, 20 March 1946, FO 371/56831 (TNA).
[132] Le Rougetel to Foreign Office, 17 July 1946, FO 371/52719 (TNA).
[133] Chiefs of Staff Committee: South Persia - Outline Plan, 23 July 1946, FO 371/52721 (TNA).
[134] Ladjevardi, *Labor Unions and Autocracy in Iran*, 136–9.
[135] Cooke to Pyman, 29 July 1946, FO 371/52721 (TNA).
[136] Ibid.; Peterson to Foreign Office, 6 August 1946, IOR/L/PS/12/1156 (BL).

Figure 2.2 A drilling crew at work in southern Iran. Workplace conditions were often dangerous and the rewards enjoyed by local workers meagre. Courtesy of Getty Images Pictorial Parade/Staff.

Although the AIOC had reached an agreement with its workers, there was little sense that this was a permanent solution. Lord Inverchapel, appointed ambassador to the United States in May 1946, warned against a policy of vengeance and suggested that Washington saw the AIOC as a '"protector of oriental feudalism" in the interests of British imperialism'. Instead, the government should prioritize policies that would illustrate 'that we stand for progress in Middle East and for the betterment of the lot of the common man'.[137] Inverchapel's warning resonated with Le Rougetel and Bevin in particular. Despite Foreign Office requests that the AIOC undertake a renewed propaganda campaign in Iran, Bevin was increasingly frustrated by the company's management, which he believed had failed to show 'the positive side of new Britain' in Iran.[138] Meetings with Fraser did little to assuage the foreign secretary's concerns that the AIOC was incapable of anything but the most superficial improvements and required greater government oversight if not direct management. In a nuanced paper circulated to the Exchequer and Ministry of Fuel and Power, Bevin mused on

---

[137] Inverchapel to Foreign Office, 6 June 1946, IOR/L/PS/12/563B (BL).
[138] Pyman Minutes, 19 April 1946, FO 371/52713; Bevin minutes, undated, FO 930/488 (TNA).

the differences between Britain's domestic and foreign policy, asking, 'what argument can I advance against anyone claiming the right to nationalize the resources of their country?' Advocating a new, collaborative approach with the Iranian people, the foreign secretary explained that the AIOC needed to reflect the tenets of British socialism and do more to safeguard the national interest in Iran.[139]

A parliamentary delegation was subsequently despatched to 'inspect labour conditions in the Anglo-Iranian Oil Company's area'.[140] Its members were Labour MPs Jack Jones (Bolton) and Frederick Lee (Manchester Hulme) and their Conservative colleague William Cuthbert (Rye). Jones and Lee were both experienced trade unionists having served on the executive committees of the British Iron, Steel and Kindred Trades Association and Amalgamated Engineering Union, respectively. Adopting a thoroughly Bevinite tone, their reporting focused on the material interests of the AIOC workforce, not least the 'cave-like' dwellings many of them endured and the continued use of child labour by AIOC contractors. Cuthbert, a former manager at Imperial Bank of Iran branches in Ahwaz and Kermanshah, agreed, noting that the provision of amenities had fallen far behind the AIOC's pursuit of profit. Perceptively, Cuthbert also referenced the depth of feeling felt towards foreign intervention in Iran more generally, stating that an 'anti-British and anti-company attitude [was] shown by the great majority of the Persian employees'.[141] Noting the strength of nationalist feeling among those he met and the popularity of the slogan 'Persian Oil for the Persians', Cuthbert suggested that poverty and workplace exploitation alone could not explain the strength of hostility towards Britain. Despite this acknowledgement, the delegation's final recommendations paid little attention to the fundamental question of foreign intervention in Iran. Indeed, Cuthbert himself suggested that 'the Persians are not strong enough nor morally sound enough ever to form a really democratic government'.[142]

According to Jones, the Tudeh and its unions should not be dismissed as mere Soviet puppets. They were, he believed, 'an industrial force to be reckoned with' and had recruited up to three-quarters of the AIOC's Iranian workforce by mid-1946.[143] This density of organization was seen by the delegation as both

[139] Bevin to Shinwell, 22 July 1946, FO 800/489 (TNA).
[140] Foreign Office to Tehran, 28 May 1946, FO 371/52714 (TNA).
[141] Fraser to Jones, 31 May 1946, 43762 (BPA); Visit of British MPs to Persia, 3 July 1946, FO 371/52718 (TNA).
[142] Ibid.
[143] Jack H. Jones, 'My Visit to the Persian Oilfields', *Journal of the Royal Central Asian Society*, 34, no. 1 (January 1947), 56–8; Berthoud to Starling, 20 May 1946; Elkington to Berthoud, 22 May 1946, FO 371/52713 (TNA).

a threat and an opportunity and they suggested that steps be taken to 'win over the Tudeh trade union officials to British ideas and to constitutional methods'. At the same time, to prevent any future revolutionary foment, Iran's central government should assert its authority in provincial areas more forcefully.[144] Bevin responded warmly to the report and its recommendations. In particular, he hoped that the AIOC's historic anti-trade unionism could be overcome and endorsed the development of workplace councils to improve representation.[145] Despite persistent concerns that the Iranian left was in hock to Moscow, Bevin hopefully told the cabinet that 'it may prove possible to wean the Tudeh Party, or at least some parts of its adherents, from extremist or communist courses'. He believed that 'the sympathetic treatment of labour' would not only foster improved links between the AIOC and its workers but also improve Britain's image in Iran and ultimately safeguard their interests there.[146]

The Anglo-Iranian Oil Company remained an impediment to this policy's implementation and success. Although the British government had representatives on the AIOC board of directors, Bevin suggested that 'none of them has ever taken any interest in labour at all' and had done little to improve the company's relationship with its workers. While acknowledging the underhand and sometimes illegal tactics adopted by Tudeh organizers, he praised their ability to develop a collective consciousness among Iran's industrial workers and suggested they had 'been psychologically much wiser' than the company's leadership in understanding the unifying effect of exploitation.[147] In parliament, Bevin hinted at the AIOC's failures. Having been asked whether he was 'aware that the Anglo-Iranian Oil Company have the reputation of being the best employers in Persia' the foreign secretary cryptically replied that although he was 'not prepared to say what is the best' he believed that 'in all companies in Persia there is room for improvement'.[148] Bevin's view was reinforced by a letter sent to him, and circulated through the Foreign Office, from the MP for Stoke, Ellis Smith, who, having discussed the matter with a former Abadan employee, suggested that the AIOC's approach to labour relations was 'absolutely at sea'.[149]

Despite the foreign secretary's enthusiasm to forge a new path in Iran, Le Rougetel gently pushed back against his analysis. By the ambassador's own admission, he had failed to find conclusive evidence concerning relations between

---

[144] Visit of British MPs to Persia, 3 July 1946, FO 371/52718 (TNA).
[145] Bevin Minutes, 23 June 1946, FO 371/52715 (TNA).
[146] Situation in South Persia, 11 July 1946, CAB 129/11 (TNA).
[147] Bevin Minutes, 23 June 1946, FO 371/52715 (TNA).
[148] Foreign Office to Tehran, 17 July 1946, FO 371/52720 (TNA).
[149] Smith to Bevin, 18 July 1946, FO 371/52722 (TNA).

the Soviet Union and the Tudeh. Nonetheless, he remained convinced that they were part of a 'deliberately planned political offensive, inspired and directed from abroad'.[150] While Le Rougetel did not entirely discount the role trade unions could play in Iran's political and industrial development, he felt that the Tudeh exploited, rather than reflected, workers' grievances and had subsumed the Iranian labour movement into a wider 'communist machine'.[151] If not directing activity, the Soviet Union was at least a revolutionary lodestar that had helped to propagate an ideology malleable enough to encompass both international brotherhood and nationalism.[152] To incorporate even the Tudeh's most moderate elements into a British-style model of industrial relations would, the ambassador feared, risk offering them a permanent outlet for communist unrest. Less considered, but no less important, was the influence of nationalism on the Tudeh's ability to recruit among the AIOC's workforce. An undated Tudeh Party declaration sent to the Foreign Office in December 1946 employed stridently patriotic language, addressing readers not only as 'comrades' but also as 'countrymen'. This document paints a stark portrait of Iranian leaders as collaborators with foreign enemies who were intent on dividing the country. In comparison, the Tudeh was framed as 'the best guarantee of national unity' and a force driven by love of country, as much as class. The declaration signed off with a simple, patriotic call to arms: 'long live the liberty, integrity and independence of Persia!'[153] Such rhetoric grew increasingly common during 1946 and helped to foster support for the Tudeh beyond the Iranian left's usual confines.

Instead of reform, Le Rougetel urged Bevin to 'foster the natural antipathy to communism of religious bodies' and support Islamist movements as a bulwark to communism. Concurrently, he recommended that the British encourage the development of alternative political parties, ideally, though not necessarily, along democratic lines.[154] This strategy would necessitate significant investment in publicity and propaganda and, given the strength of opposition they faced, the ambassador wondered whether the development of alternative oil sources may be a more prudent course.[155] Despite the bullishness of his predecessor and the foreign secretary, Le Rougetel was sceptical as to Britain's ability to reshape

[150] Le Rougetel to Foreign Office, 27 December 1946, FO 371/52710; Le Rougetel to Bevin, 1 July 1946, FO 371/52717 (TNA).
[151] Pyman Minutes, 8 July 1946, FO 371/52717 (TNA).
[152] Le Rougetel to Foreign Office, 26 May 1946, FO 371/52713 (TNA).
[153] Declaration of the Tudeh Party Central Committee, undated, FO 248/1471 (TNA).
[154] Pyman Minutes, 8 July 1946; Le Rougetel to Bevin, 1 July 1946, FO 371/52717 (TNA).
[155] Ibid.

Iranian politics. His concerns were shared by Permanent Under-Secretary of State Orme Sargent who was unconvinced that the Tudeh could be co-opted into the kind of social democratic framework Bevin envisaged.[156] Instead, Sargent suggested that Iranian workers could be replaced with Commonwealth labour and plans developed, as a last resort, to establish an autonomous state friendly to British interests in southern Iran.[157] Emboldened by the opportunity to implement his new approach to imperialism, Bevin nevertheless persisted. In a neat summary of his position, the foreign secretary stressed that 'the way to tackle this problem is vigorous application by the company of their social programme and greater consultation with their work people, and the building up within the undertaking itself of human relationships with the actual men, not on a feudal basis but with the appreciation that all over the world the sense of equality is rapidly developing'.[158] Deferring to his foreign secretary's instructions, Le Rougetel accepted that the 'regular machinery for consultation between the management of the AIOC and their staff and labour' should be established as quickly as possible.[159] In Whitehall, the Foreign Office's Information Policy Department identified Iran as a testbed for welfare imperialism and demanded that a complementary propaganda campaign to promote Britain as the world's 'leading exponent of social democracy in government' be launched.[160]

As Bevin and his staff considered how to improve the AIOC's relationship with its workers, Qavam was reshaping Iran's political landscape. In July the prime minister launched the Democrat Party of Iran, an ideologically amorphous nationalist party built largely on his personal popularity.[161] The Democrats attempted to appeal to Iran's middle and professional classes, to urban youths and to women with proposals to broaden Iran's electoral franchise and liberalize the country. He introduced the first comprehensive labour legislation in Iranian history, Article 21 of which recognized Iranian workers' rights to form workplace unions for the first time.[162] Although framed by his conservative opponents as kowtowing to Russian influence, Qavam's modernizing policies helped to draw less ideological rigid support away from the Tudeh. The labour law contained purposefully unclear promises to pass further legislation pertaining to the governance, registration and regulation of industrial relations in future. This

---

[156] Sargent Minutes, 20 June 1946, FO 371/52715 (TNA).
[157] Sargent to Bevin, 26 June 1946, FO 371/52715 (TNA).
[158] Bevin Minutes, 23 June 1946, FO 371/52715 (TNA).
[159] Le Rougetel to Bevin, 1 July 1946, FO 371/52717 (TNA).
[160] Information Newsletter No. 4, 17 October 1946, IOR/R/15/6/397 (BL).
[161] Document 378: Allen to the Secretary of State, 1 July 1946, *FRUS 1946 Vol VII*.
[162] Le Rougetel to Foreign Office, 8 January 1947, FO 371/61984 (TNA).

vagueness offered Iranian legislators flexibility in dealing with trade union-instigated foment should it arise in future.[163] The labour law also contained Article 32, which required that disputes be considered by a myriad of bodies including factory councils, arbitration boards and, ultimately, the Board for Settlement of Disputes before a strike could take place.[164] Under these terms the Tudeh's preferred strategy of flying pickets supported by propaganda and protests became illegal.

Increasingly confident, Qavam set his sights on fully reincorporating Azerbaijan into Iran, telling American Ambassador George Allen that the 'USSR would remain neutral' if his army invaded. The prime minister correctly believed that having opened the door to its own concession in Iran the Soviet Union would do nothing to defend the Azerbaijani separatists. Instead, he believed that the biggest challenge was being 'castigated as a turncoat and Fascist reactionary' by the Tudeh. He even suggested that Tehran could be imperilled by civil disturbances launched by his alleged allies.[165] Qavam took steps to dull the Tudeh's influence by giving Iranian police and army new powers of 'expulsion' against perceived 'agitators'.[166] Security forces used these powers without prejudice to force the Tudeh's leaders into hiding. Where they continued to organize they also faced armed opposition from supporters of the Democrats.[167] In October, Le Rougetel reported that Qavam's reforms were working and the Tudeh were in retreat. In Khuzestan, a previous hotbed of militancy, the ambassador noted that 'most of the party's agitators have for the time being been banished or shut up and martial law has imposed severe restrictions on party activities of all kinds'. The ambassador reported a similar situation in Shiraz, Isfahan and Kerman and noted the Tudeh press had been reduced to impotently attacking Qavam's oppressive measures.[168] The party continued to produce newspapers and remained well resourced and organized. For the moment, however, its advance had been halted. The prime minister also began to take steps to develop Iran's international relations beyond the traditional Anglo-Russian duopoly and identified the United States as a potential partner in the 'far-reaching economic reforms which Iran needed so urgently'.[169] Previous Iranian leaders had made similar overtures, but Qavam proved successful in procuring $10 million worth

---

[163] Ladjevardi, *Labor Unions and Autocracy in Iran*, 61–3.
[164] Le Rougetel to Foreign Office, 8 January 1947, FO 371/61984 (TNA).
[165] Document 384: Allen to the Secretary of State, 13 August 1946; Document 391: Allen to the Secretary of State, 30 September 1946, *FRUS 1946 Vol VII*.
[166] Le Rougetel to Foreign Office, 15 July 1946, FO 371/52719 (TNA).
[167] Le Rougetel to Foreign Office, 13 November 1946, FO 248/1471 (TNA).
[168] Le Rougetel to Bevin, 8 October 1946, FO 248/1471 (TNA).
[169] Document 391: Allen to the Secretary of State, 30 September 1946, *FRUS 1946 Vol VII*.

of arms having intimated that he may reengage in discussions concerning financial support with the USSR.[170] With this deal secured, Qavam was perhaps at the peak of his power. He announced parliament's dissolution calling for elections to begin in early December and brushed off questions concerning the status of the Soviet oil concession. Hinting at the poor likelihood of ratification, the prime minister contended that this was merely 'something for the future'.[171] He did not, however, express any desire to recant on his pledge to review all other foreign concessions.

On 10 December 1946, 5,000 Iranian troops entered Azerbaijan and recaptured Tabriz within two days. Although there were reports of limited disorder, the American consul in Tabriz Lester Sutton noted that many civilians had taken up arms and were 'hunting out' former separatists.[172] A reported 2,000 people were killed during the conflict. In Washington, where strategy towards the Soviet Union was increasingly crystallizing around what diplomat George Kennan termed the 'firm and vigilant containment of Russian expansive tendencies', the collapse of Pishihvari's government was hailed as a triumph, and Ambassador to Moscow Walter Bedell Smith informed Secretary of State James Byrnes that the 'collapse of Azerbaijan house of cards was a major victory for UN – and for a firm policy toward USSR'.[173] Crucially, Smith also warned that the Soviet Union would continue to manoeuvre for both oil concessions and 'political (and strategic) ascendency in Iran'.[174] Historically detached from Iran as in much of the Middle East, American interest in the region's security was growing.

The twin crises Britain had faced in Iran had gone some way in justifying both the Labour government's suspicion towards the Soviet Union and commitment to implementing a new kind of imperialism. However, while the Soviet withdrawal from Azerbaijan and opportunity to develop a new partnership model between AIOC workers and management could be depicted as victories for Bevin's approach they masked British deficiencies. Moscow had withdrawn its forces not because of British pressure but rather thanks to Iranian diplomacy. Little commented upon in Whitehall, Qavam's commitment to renegotiate Iran's oil concessions was a previously unforeseen and underdiscussed threat to the AIOC. Meanwhile, labour unrest revealed both cracks in the relationship between the

---

[170] Document 393: The Secretary of State to the Acting Secretary of State, 3 October 1946, *FRUS 1946 Vol VII*.
[171] Document 419: Allen to the Secretary of State, 3 December 1946, *FRUS 1946 Vol VII*.
[172] Document 425: Sutton to the Secretary of State, 12 December 1946, *FRUS 1946 Vol VII*.
[173] Kennan to the Secretary of State, 22 February 1946, RG 59 861.00/2-2246 (NARA); Document 430: Smith to the Secretary of State, 27 December 1946, *FRUS 1946 Vol VII*.
[174] Ibid.

British government and the AIOC and the depth of loathing towards London's continued monopoly over Iran's prized assets. Iranian nationalism was a complex, modern ideology that found expression through multifaceted means including Tudeh-influenced trade unionism. Its textures, however, were seldom explored. For Bevin, Soviet intrigue and labour unrest were challenges that necessitated corrective action. In Iran, the foreign secretary saw an opportunity to turn the theory of welfare imperialism into practice and reshape the relationship between Britain and an overseas interest. Whether this was desired by the Iranian people or viable given the limited resources available were questions left unanswered.

3

Development and division

The Labour government saw the waves of industrial action that rocked Iran in the summer of 1946 as evidence that a more active, interventionist policy was required there. Through British guidance, expertise and investment, they believed it would be possible to enhance Iranian civil society, rebuff Soviet intrigue and protect their vast economic interests. Simultaneously idealistic and cynical, their approach demonstrates the complexity of welfare imperialism.

However, the Attlee government's policy struggled to reconcile the realities of Iranian politics or increasingly perilous finances at home. In turn, they increasingly relied on propaganda to mask significant strategic deficiencies. Running in parallel to these challenges was continued division between Whitehall and the Anglo-Iranian Oil Company leading to deep dysfunctionality. By 1949 Iranian nationalism was in the ascent, clearly exposing welfare imperialism's frailties. Patrician, underfunded and ill-suited to responding to the ideological challenge Britain faced in Iran, the high-minded rhetoric of mutually beneficial investment guided by foreign expertise was replaced by more cost-effective alternatives, particularly increased propaganda.

Trade union reform

In November 1946, the TUC informed the Foreign Office that Reza Rousta, a leading Tudeh and labour activist, had contacted them to request an independent appraisal of the AIOC's treatment of its Iranian staff. Although the Foreign Office rejected Rousta's primary allegation – that the company had sacked 5,000 workers without due process – they agreed that further analysis of workplace conditions was a useful endeavour and that the World Federation of Trade Unions (WFTU), of which Rousta was a representative, should conduct this.[1]

---

[1] Foreign Office to TUC General Secretary, 18 December 1946, FO 248/1471 (TNA).

In the interim, the British government continued to cajole the AIOC to adopt a more conciliatory position towards its workers and to encourage the formation of new trade unions unsullied by communist influence. Still resistant to the kind of labour relations envisaged by Bevin, company management hoped that any new organization would not merely be a forum for workers' voices but also a 'firm authority' against the kind of sedition the Tudeh had fomented.[2] The leadership of any new unions, AIOC chairman William Fraser added, should be 'properly accredited' so as to avoid the potential for militancy.[3] On the British Embassy's advice, A. C. V. Lindon was appointed as an industrial relations advisor and talks opened to establish a 'legitimate' workers' organization.[4] Following discussions with trusted local workers, including Mostafa Fateh, the company's most senior Iranian employee, the Oil Workers' Union (OWU) was launched. Nominally independent, the AIOC publicly distanced itself from the union but had privately facilitated its formation.[5] The OWU's first proclamation declared that 'our organisation has actually come to being just to be an industrial union of the workmen and should not have to be involved in political affairs and should only use its power to organize the workmen and protect their rights'.[6] Such tepid statements revealed the OWU's lack of independence and were a transparent attempt to depoliticize industrial relations.[7] Within a month, British diplomats had begun to cast doubts on the OWU's effectiveness and suggested that 'workers are still very suspicious of the motives underlying the formation of this union'.[8] Unlike their Tudeh opponents, the Oil Workers' Union's propaganda lacked ideological clarity and was distributed through saccharine handbills rather than attractive and engaging newspapers. Unsurprisingly, insipid messages like 'this new union of ours has nothing to do with politics. It is simply for the welfare of the workers' and 'do not abuse the government and the company which are always working for your welfare' largely fell on deaf ears.[9] Following their arrival in Iran, the WFTU delegation immediately noted the crude entanglement between the AIOC and OWU. They suggested that AIOC workers were compelled, if not

[2] Elkington to Ministry of Fuel and Power, 29 October 1946, FO 371/52726 (TNA).
[3] Social and Municipal Development Carried Out by the Anglo-Iranian Oil Company Ltd. in Abadan and the South Persian Oilfields, 11 October 1946, FO 371/52726 (TNA).
[4] Report up to Noon, 25 July 1947, FO 248/1475; Elkington to Berthoud, 29 October 1946, FO 371/52726 (TNA).
[5] Report up to Noon, 26 January 1947, FO 248/1475 (TNA).
[6] Oil Workers Union Pamphlet, undated, 35201 (BPA).
[7] Elkington to MacNeill, 25 June 1947, 35201 (BPA).
[8] Khorramshahr to Tehran, 6 February 1947; Khorramshahr to Tehran, 13 March 1947, FO 248/1475 (TNA).
[9] Press Reports – Translated Extracts, 10 February 1947, FO 248/1475; Northcroft to Fateh, 2 July 1947, 35201 (BPA).

forced, to join the new union and prevented from organizing independently.[10] In spite, or perhaps because, of management's best efforts, the OWU's membership peaked at barely 2,000.[11]

It appeared that Bevin's plans to reform Iran's labour movement were already faltering amid mounting WFTU criticism and poor industrial management. The government was handed some reprieve when Edgar Harries, a Welsh TUC official and WFTU delegate, refused to sign off on the federation's report. Harries claimed that the Soviet Embassy had colluded with other delegates to damage British interests, and the Tudeh and the WFTU were behaving as 'one and the same body'.[12] A veteran of the TUC's Organising Department, Harries had spent much of his career fighting off communist attempts to gain a foothold in the British trade union movement and saw the dispute between WFTU delegates as an extension of this struggle. An arch imperialist, Harries took a dim view of the Iranian people's ability to resist Soviet influence, suggesting that the naivety of such 'excitable eastern people' coupled with material deprivation and corporate exploitation made them 'the perfect Marxist textbook case for a revolution'. On his return to London, Harries met with Hector McNeil, Bevin's deputy at the Foreign Office, and reported that the mission's purpose was to score a propaganda victory for Moscow and consolidate Rousta's position in the Tudeh.[13] He recommended that more significant and proactive intervention be pursued, particularly the establishment of a new Iranian workers' federation, much like the British TUC, that could organize resistance to Soviet-inspired elements in the trade union movement. Federalization would prove to be a consistent but largely unsuccessful theme in Iranian industrial politics throughout the late 1940s as successive individuals, groupings and factions vied for influence.

To rout out the Tudeh's lingering influence, and following consultation with the Tehran Embassy's Labour Attaché Kenneth Hird, Qavam's government had taken steps to bolster alternative trade unions, particularly the Central Syndicate of Iranian Craftsmen, Farmers and Workers (ESKI).[14] Established by the Ministry of Labour and Propaganda, workers in government-owned enterprises were forced to join the new union, which was also backed by a state-sponsored newspaper, *Kargaran i-Iran* (Workers of Iran).[15] Though this boosted

[10] Report up to Noon, 21 February 1947, FO 248/1475; Le Rougetel to Bevin, enc. Report by the President of the WFTU Delegation, 24 April 1947, FO 248/1477 (TNA).
[11] Khorramshahr to Tehran, 13 March 1947, FO 248/1475 (TNA).
[12] Le Rougetel to Bevin, enc. Report by the President of the WFTU Delegation, 24 April 1947, FO 248/1477 (TNA).
[13] McNeil Minutes, 15 May 1947, FO 371/61994 (TNA).
[14] Quarterly Report of Events in Persia, 15 January 1947, FO 371/61988 (TNA).
[15] Abrahamian, *Iran Between Two Revolutions*, 238.

nominal membership numbers, it did nothing to stoke genuine enthusiasm among workers or quash questions concerning ESKI's independence. British officials reported that the union's leaders were merely government 'puppets' who intimidated opponents and quashed union democracy to preserve their power.[16] On Harries' suggestion that the government establish a labour federation, the Ministry of Labour and Propaganda ordered that ESKI merge with the independent Central Union of Workers and Peasants of Iran (EMKA) and a series of other smaller organizations.[17] The centralization of Iranian trade unionism was justified on the basis that it would create a single entity with whom the government could negotiate or, more cynically, manage. According to British officials, the bureaucrats at the top of the reorganized Iranian labour movement had 'little real interest in the workers' conditions' and were chiefly concerned with protecting Qavam and furthering their own political interests.[18] It is notable that even independent, social democratic and anti-Tudeh trade unions were repressed, such were the Iranian government's efforts to coordinate and control labour organizing.[19] However, while enthusiastic workplace mobilization was a powerful political force it was difficult to manufacture. During the spring and summer of 1946, the Tudeh had found a campaigning nexus between shopfloor issues, Bolshevism and nationalism, workers' material concerns and sophisticated propaganda. Simply forcing workers to join a new organization with which they had no affinity was not a realistic alternative.

May Day 1947 was a suitably staid affair: public processions and demonstrations were banned, leaving trade unionists confined to their social clubs.[20] Twelve months prior, Iran's labour movement had demonstrated genuine popular appeal and deep industrial organization. Although undoubtedly influenced by the Soviet Union, the movement's power lay in the strength of its membership rather than formal links to Moscow. In contrast, the new unions – whether linked to the AIOC's management or the Ministry of Labour and Propaganda – were shell organizations that lacked active members or much by way of an attractive message. ESKI General Secretary Khosrow Hedayat came in for particular criticism. Previously the director of Iran's railways, Hedayat was urbane, well connected and ambitious. His interest in labour organization seems to have

[16] Review of Conditions in the Isfahan Consular District, 1 July–31 December 1947, 28 February 1948, FO 371/62008 (TNA).
[17] Labour Attaché's Report, 17 June 1947, FO 371/62052 (TNA).
[18] Review of Conditions in the Isfahan Consular District, 1 July–31 December 1947, 28 February 1948, FO 371/62008 (TNA).
[19] Review of Conditions in Isfahan Consular District, 1 July–31 December 1946, 28 February 1947, FO 371/62008 (TNA).
[20] Isfahan Diary for 1947: May, 6 June 1947, FO 371/62008 (TNA).

been wholly self-serving.[21] As 1947 progressed, the British reported growing aloofness among workers who, far from rejecting the Tudeh for a nominally social democratic alternative, were disengaging from labour activism entirely.[22]

In some regards the Iranian labour movement's reorganization enjoyed rapid success. Not only had reform diminished the Tudeh's power base, but it also had reportedly calmed a workforce that had previously appeared to be a major threat to British interests and Iranian stability. Despite the Tudeh's meteoric rise, by mid-1947 the party's influence had been marginalized across Iran. On Qavam's instruction, the party's organizing core was shattered as its leaders were imprisoned or sent into hiding. Lay members found themselves forcibly conscripted or subjected to violence, including from the Iranian army which was given free reign to 'smash the Tudeh' in Isfahan.[23] Within months, British intelligence reported that the party was 'in the eclipse': it played a minimal role in the Majlis elections and was forced to close its popular newspaper, *Rahbar*.[24] Ambassador Le Rougetel went as far as reporting that the party's remaining executive members had agreed to pursue non-revolutionary politics and formally reverse its slide towards Bolshevism.[25] However, on the terms previously set out by Bevin, trade union reform, whether launched from Whitehall or Tehran, had failed. The Tudeh's working-class support had not seamlessly transitioned to more palatable alternatives but detached itself from workplace organization altogether. In mid-1947, the British Embassy launched an organized publicity drive to raise awareness of trade unionism's benefits; however, this had minimal impact and failed to deal with the fundamental contradictions inherent to trade unionism delivered from above.[26]

Within the Labour Party, the conflict between communism and social democracy was seen as nothing less than a moral crusade and trade unions a key battleground. The Foreign Office shared the starkness of this sentiment, if not its romance. Although the Tudeh were for the moment cowed, trade unions that represented either social democratic ideals or a viable bulwark to communism remained elusive. The foreign secretary and his mandarins may have repeatedly outlined their commitment to a new industrial settlement but plans to achieve

---

[21] Persia: Military Attaché's Intelligence Summary No. 50, 22 December 1947, FO 371/61982 (TNA).
[22] Willoughby to Le Rougetel, 23 October 1947, FO 371/62044 (TNA).
[23] Review of Conditions in Isfahan Consular District, 1 July–31 December 1946, 28 February 1947, FO 371/62008 (TNA).
[24] Persia: Military Attaché's Intelligence Summary No. 2, 12 January 1947; Persia: Military Attaché's Intelligence Summary No. 10, 27 March 1947, FO 371/61982; Le Rougetel to Foreign Office, 7 January 1947, FO 371/61988 (TNA).
[25] Ibid.
[26] Isfahan Diary for 1947: July, 31 July 1945, FO 371/62008 (TNA).

such ambitions were minimal and it is difficult to envisage how a reformed labour movement may have been delivered from above. Throughout this period there was no acknowledgement of Iranian workers' autonomy or capacity to manage their own industrial affairs. Indeed, Hird later went on to dismiss their ability to do so and suggest that 'there is little real understanding here of what unionism or democratic government mean or how they work'.[27] Far from siphoning off the Tudeh's more palatable elements, British policy had invertedly helped to crush the Iranian labour movement.

Wages, development and disunity

Alongside attempts to reshape industrial relations, the British government urged the AIOC to improve the living standards enjoyed by Iranian workers. Under pressure from Whitehall a 40 rial a day minimum wage was implemented and salaries increased by up to 100 per cent.[28] Satisfied that salary increases and new trade unions were sufficient to quell dissent, one AIOC official claimed that the company had 'settled all the trouble and calmed all the agitation'.[29] The Foreign Office was less convinced and identified wages as one of several areas that needed to be improved. With just 14,300 lodgings available for over 65,000 workers, housing was a particularly persistent problem.[30] By the mid-1940s, overcrowded, unsanitary conditions were very much the norm, particularly among seasonal workers in the company's oversubscribed 'bachelor quarters'.[31] The AIOC appointed Scottish architect James Mollison Wilson to prepare plans for the modernization of the company's housing stock. Under his proposals segregation would continue with the 'green oasis' of Braim remaining the preserve of European employees. However, significant improvements would be made to labourers' accommodation, including the replacement of mud and temporary structures with new brick homes.[32] Undoubtedly ambitious, details for implementation were

---

[27] Hird to Heron, 30 April 1948, FO 371/68746 (TNA).
[28] Joint Notes: Foreign Office and Ministry of Fuel and Power, 7 November 1946, PREM 8/613; Anglo-Iranian Oil Company Minutes, 28 January 1947, T 236/1337; Willoughby to Le Rougetel, 14 April 1947, FO 371/62044 (TNA).
[29] Anglo-Iranian Oil Company Minutes, 28 January 1947, T 236/1337 (TNA).
[30] Bamberg, *The History of the British Petroleum Company Vol. II*, 347–9.
[31] Social and Municipal Development Carried Out by the Anglo-Iranian Oil Company Ltd. in Abadan and the South Persian Oilfields, 11 October 1946, FO 371/52726 (TNA).
[32] Mark Crinson, 'Abadan: Planning and Architecture Under the Anglo-Iranian Oil Company', *Planning Perspectives* 12, no. 3 (January 1997), 343-57.

limited and no timetable for completion or inventory was provided.[33] Nonetheless, AIOC officials hoped that the building programme could be completed within six years.[34] This proved to be a gross overestimate and almost a decade later over 20,000 Iranian employees still resided in supposedly temporary squatter camps.[35] The company also promised investment in workers' recreation, sports and health facilities, which were in dire need of modernization. In 1944 the company had found that malnutrition was widespread among its lowest earners alongside a host of easily preventable diseases.[36] However, between then and 1947 no appreciable improvements had been made. In January, William Fraser approved upgrades to general medical and health service at Abadan in principle; however, by October, despite ongoing Whitehall cajoling, progress was minimal and the AIOC's building scheme remained largely rhetorical.[37] It would take a further two years for the company to formally approve an extension to Abadan's hospital.[38] To their American allies, the slow pace of British development was at best curious, if not a sign of negligence. In correspondence with Washington, American Ambassador George Allen reported that the British government was 'not deeply concerned whether Iranian political and economic interests are safeguarded' and indicated that intervention from the United Nations may be required to prevent future instability.[39]

British officials in Iran complained that the AIOC actively ignored diplomatic instruction. According to the British consul at Khorramshahr Vere Willoughby, AIOC officials at Abadan behaved as 'a law unto themselves' and should be reminded that the British government was its majority shareholder.[40] Le Rougetel concurred, warning the Foreign Office that the AIOC was resistant to change and becoming 'too big for their boots'.[41] Matters were made worse by corporate dysfunctionality and managers who, unwilling to commit to government objectives, spoke 'with

---

[33] Willoughby to Le Rougetel, 14 April 1947, FO 371/62044 (TNA).
[34] Report on Visit of EHO Elkington to Iran, 17 January to 7 March 1947, 9967 (BPA).
[35] I. Seccombe and R. Lawless, 'Work Camps and Company Towns: Settlement Patterns and the Gulf Oil Industry', *University of Durham, Centre for Middle Eastern and Islamic Studies Working Paper* (1987), 65.
[36] Abadan: The State of Nutritional Health of Men Employed as Labour and Artisans by the Company, undated, 41097 (BPA).
[37] Report on Visit of EHO Elkington to Iran, 17 January to 7 March 1947, 9967 (BPA); Report for the Quarter July–September 1947 on the Affairs of the Anglo-Iranian Oil Company, 23 October 1947, FO 371/62044 (TNA).
[38] Ibid.
[39] Ambassador George V. Allen to Secretary of State James F. Byrnes, 11 January 1947, RG 59 891.6363 (NARA).
[40] Report of the Quarter April–June 1947 on the Affairs of the Anglo-Iranian Oil Company, 10 July 1947, FO 371/62044 (TNA).
[41] Le Rougetel to Butler, 31 May 1947, FO 371/62044 (TNA).

as many tongues as the Tower of Babel'.[42] Discord in Iran was matched by poor relations between the AIOC's chairman and Whitehall officialdom. A vinegar-tongued Scot, William Fraser was famed for his contempt for civil servants, an attitude that was not entirely absent in his dealings with ministers.[43] The archetypal corporate capitalist, Fraser had little by way of a relationship with Bevin, a docker with whom he had previously negotiated at the Llandarcy refinery in 1930. As if foreshadowing future events, Fraser resisted the Transport and General Workers' Union's efforts to reach a new settlement for its members, suggesting instead that 'it would be far better to make a clean sweep and reduce the number of men'.[44] More than a decade later, meetings between the two men were curt encounters that did little to create a shared sense of purpose. The company continued to eye Bevin's trade union with suspicion, suggesting that it should be 'treated with great circumspection' as if it were a proxy for the foreign secretary himself.[45] From the Foreign Office, the AIOC appeared inflexible and maladroit to the realities of what was needed in Iran. For decades the company had operated with almost complete independence from the government and acted as the primary source of British representation in Iran. This arrangement was now clearly at risk.

A new nadir in the AIOC and British government's strained relationship came following the company's decision to seek new lines of credit in the United States, 'hawking' themselves to JP Morgan and other firms on Wall Street in response to perceived underinvestment.[46] Christopher Gandy of the Foreign Office's Economic Relations Department warned that any such commercial arrangements would undermine British credibility in the Middle East and indicate their relative decline vis-à-vis the United States. A commercial loan would also, Gandy warned, lead to the opening of the AIOC's accounts revealing the scale of their profits in Iran and inevitably 'increase the pressure on us to provide even more gold and dollars for Persia'.[47] Orme Sargent was swift to chasten the company, reaffirming that the British government was their primary shareholder and that they required permission from both the Foreign Office and the Exchequer should they wish to proceed with discussions.[48] The

---

[42] Report of the Quarter April–June 1947 on the Affairs of the Anglo-Iranian Oil Company, 10 July 1947, FO 371/62044; Trott to Le Rougetel, 17 May 1947, FO 248/1475 (TNA).
[43] Ronald Hyam, *Understanding the British Empire* (Cambridge: Cambridge University Press, 2010), 136.
[44] Memorandum on Labour at Llandarcy, 10 October 1930, 68639 (BPA).
[45] Elkington to Fraser, 1 December 1948, 93501 (BPA).
[46] Fraser to Sir Donald Fergusson, Ministry of Fuel and Power, 26 November 1947, 8651 (BPA); Inverchapel to Foreign Office, 17 October 1947, FO 371/62059; Gandy to Sargent, 8 October 1947, FO 371/62059 (TNA).
[47] Gandy to Sargent, 8 October 1947, FO 371/62059 (TNA).
[48] Sargent to Gandy, 9 October 1947; Sargent to Bevin, 9 October 1947, FO 371/62059 (TNA).

Figure 3.1 Ernest Bevin, British foreign secretary and the architect of welfare imperialism. Courtesy of Getty Images Frederic Lewis/Staff.

affair coincided with new estimates of the AIOC's value and the suggestion that the Iranian oil industry would 'exceed the value of Malaya rubber' within three years with potential for further growth in future.[49] However, despite the acknowledged difficulties of executing foreign policy through the AIOC, the British government did little to translate a rhetorical commitment to welfare imperialism into concrete action.

Ongoing staffing challenges in Iran did little to help matters. Ann Lambton, one of the most erudite and able British officials in Tehran, returned to London to start a teaching post at the School of Oriental and African Studies and was able only to provide a distant analysis of Persian affairs. At the same time, a slew of controversies forced a number of British officials from service. Intelligence officer Ronald Oakshot was reported to have 'gone native' and succumbed to madness following a struggle with alcoholism. Meanwhile, his commander, Chief of Political Intelligence Basil Bunting was forced to leave Iran having married a fourteen-year-old girl to widespread consternation.[50] Other staffing challenges were more mundane and concerned poor pay, unsatisfactory pensions and low morale.[51] From the Labour Party's International Department, Denis Healey warned that 'farsighted schemes' to raise living standards were being undermined by a lack of investment.[52] For British mandarins, Iran was something of a liminal space that was of interest to not only the Foreign Office

[49] Makins Minutes, 21 October 1947, FO 371/62059 (TNA).
[50] Julian Stannard, *Basil Bunting* (Tavistock: Liverpool University Press, 2018), 17.
[51] Wheeler to Foreign Office, 13 October 1947, IOR/L/PS/12/3491B (BL).
[52] Priming the Pump, July 1947, Denis Healey Papers – Box 13/01 (LHA).

Figure 3.2 British and Iranian AIOC officials, February 1946. William Fraser is fourth from the right in the front row. Ernest Northcroft is third from the left with E. H. O. Elkington on his immediate right. Despite their long experience in Iran, the AIOC's management failed to adequately respond to new challenges in Iran. Courtesy of the BP Archive © BP plc.

but also the Ministry of Fuel and Power, the Treasury, the India Office and the Colonial Office. With responsibilities contested, resources were generally allocated elsewhere. It is notable, for example, that Iran was not included in the 1945 Colonial Development and Welfare Act, which made £120 million available for colonial development.[53] Similarly, although the 1947 launch of the Colonial Development Corporation provided some £100 million worth of credit for overseas infrastructure, no additional funding was made available for nominally independent Iran despite the importance of British interests there.[54] Ruminating on the strategy pursued by his party in government, Healey suggested that crucial assets remained 'strategically exceptionally vulnerable' to

---

[53] Frank Heinlein, *British Government Policy and Decolonisation, 1945-63: Scrutinising the Official Mind* (London: Routledge, 2002), 27-9.

[54] *Hansard*, HC Debate, 25 June 1947, vol. 439 cc 439-44; Priming the Pump, July 1947, Denis Healey Papers – Box 13/01 (LHA).

Soviet intrigue.[55] This was particularly the case in the Middle East where faltering development schemes were creating vacuum that 'must be filled'.[56]

By the end of 1947, the window for revitalized strategic planning was closing as the realities of office set in. Later described by Chancellor Hugh Dalton as an *'annus horrendus'*, the Attlee government experienced a dizzying set of political and economic challenges.[57] In February, Minister of Education Ellen Wilkinson died from a drug overdose to the shock of her colleagues and throughout the year a series of senior ministers, including Bevin, suffered from persistent illnesses. Internecine squabbles fuelled conflict in the Cabinet as socialist MPs from the Keep Left tendency clustered around Aneurin Bevan and *Tribune* magazine to demand military spending cuts and more expansive economic reform. Meanwhile, on the right, young modernizers like Hugh Gaitskell, Evan Durbin and Douglas Jay privately questioned Prime Minister Attlee's capabilities.[58] With ambitious ministers circling, Bevin's Principal Private Secretary Pierson Dixon ruminated as to whether the foreign secretary may be the man to take Attlee's place.[59] Although the prime minister saw off any prospective challenges, Labour's electoral fortunes were poor. The party lost control of councils in Glasgow, Manchester and Birmingham and suffered a series of byelection scares with 8.5 and 10.2 per cent swings against them registered in Islington West and Edge Hill, respectively.[60]

Despite Britain's military withdrawal from Greece and lowering of the union flag in India and Palestine, disarmament remained ponderous leaving the economy starved of labour. A bitter winter gave way to fuel shortages and falling output, followed by the introduction, and subsequent suspension, of sterling convertibility. The cost of Germany's occupation continued to grow and so too did Britain's deficit. The Attlee government had inherited far from enviable economic conditions but benefited from a surplus of optimism. Even this was now dwindling. In parliament, Dalton warned of a 'very grave national emergency' as he set out the multifaceted challenge of wholesale price rises, stagnating exports and a global 'dollar famine'.[61] Against this dire background, plans for a

---

[55] British Labour and the Modern World, July 1948; The Communists and Labour Britain, 1 November 1948, Denis Healey Papers - Box 13/02 (LHA).
[56] British Foreign Policy, 7 March 1949, Denis Healey Papers – Box 13/03 (LHA).
[57] Dalton, *High Tide and After: Memoirs 1945-1960*, 187.
[58] Hugh Gaitskell and Philip Maynard Williams, *The Diary of Hugh Gaitskell, 1945-1956* (London: Cape, 1983), 16.
[59] Kenneth O. Morgan, *Labour in Power, 1945-1951* (Oxford: Oxford University Press, 1985), 333–5.
[60] Andrew Thorpe, *A History of the British Labour Party* (Basingstoke: Palgrave Macmillan, 2015), 136; Chris Cook and John Stevenson, *A History of British Elections Since 1689* (London: Taylor & Francis, 2016), 302.
[61] *Hansard*, HC Debate, Vol. 441 Col. 1654–7, 7 August 1947.

mutually beneficial imperialism based on investment and development seemed increasingly fanciful. Having seen his reputation tarnished, Dalton resigned from office having inadvertently revealed key budget details to a journalist and was replaced by Stafford Cripps. Famed for his asceticism, *Life* magazine described the new chancellor as a left-winger with a taste for 'socialism, sermons and sea-kale salad'.[62] With Cripps at Number 11, austerity became the defining feature of the Attlee government's approach to economic policy. Adopting a strategy dubbed 'export or die', the chancellor prioritized increasing precious foreign currency and reversing the perilous trade balance. As one of the country's primary dollar earners and a key source of fuel and lubrication, officials continued to see the AIOC as critical for Britain's economic recovery.[63]

Propaganda and publicity

Harsh economic realities and the ongoing failure to translate welfare imperialism into policy successes necessitated a change in direction and the Attlee government increasingly favoured using propaganda – euphemistically dubbed publicity – to safeguard British interests in Iran. Colonel Geoffrey Wheeler, formerly of the Indian Political Service and an MI6 operative, was appointed press counsellor at the Tehran Embassy and given a remit to 'reorganize British publicity' there.[64] An enigmatic figure who impressed his seniors in London, Wheeler favoured a broad approach to propaganda in Iran, suggesting that 'I am no more in favour of using half measures in publicity than of pitting Brown Bess against dive bombers'.[65] In the first instance this meant revitalizing Britain's relationship with the Iranian press and redoubling efforts to place stories in local media. Wheeler suggested that '90 per cent' of British propaganda should be positive in tone but encouraged the preparation of anti-Soviet materials.[66] Success was almost immediate, and by mid-1947 an embassy propaganda report boasted that 'we are placing an average of 75,000 words of news and 12,000 words of feature [in the Tehran press] each month'.[67]

---

[62] Noel F. Busch, 'Sir Stafford Cripps', *Life*, 8 March 1948.
[63] Bamberg, *The History of the British Petroleum Company Vol. II*, 325; Foreign Office Views on the Increased Profits of the Anglo-Iranian Oil Company and the Persian Request for Loan of £10 Million Against Royalties, 27 August 1948, FO 371/68731 (TNA).
[64] Pethick-Lawrence to Wavell, 26 June 1946; Wheeler to Donaldson, 27 November 1947, IOR/L/PS/12/3491B (BL).
[65] Wheeler to Pollock, 29 February 1947, FO 953/65 (TNA).
[66] Ibid.
[67] Wheeler Minutes, 14 March 1947, FO 953/64; British Embassy Information Circular, 6 May 1947, FO 953/64 (TNA).

Able to reach a dispersed, often illiterate population, radio was the fulcrum of Britain's information strategy on a day-to-day basis. In July 1946, Lord President of the Council Herbert Morrison published a white paper that called for the BBC's Overseas Service to receive Foreign Office funding while retaining editorial independence. These recommendations formed part of the 1947 Royal Charter and, Morrison argued, would demonstrate that the BBC was not an instrument of the British state. Morrison couched this suggestion in the most equivocal terms and noted that it was 'unthinkable' that the BBC would promote 'at the taxpayer's expense, doctrines hopelessly at variance with the foreign policy of His Majesty's Government'. It was expected that Broadcasting House would 'keep in touch' with the Foreign Office and follow the line set in Whitehall.[68]

In Iran this was clearly the case. As during the war years, the BBC's Persian Service was principally a source of regular news and entertainment programming. However, despite its nominal independence, the British government had agreed that the BBC could be 'brought into action at a few hours' notice' and may be called 'to take direct action in the way of power propaganda'. To this effect, the Persian Service would call upon the British Embassy and Foreign Office to provide 'necessary publicity material' as required.[69] Through correspondence with Le Rougetel, Bevin made clear that the BBC should give 'full publicity' to Britain's reforming agenda.[70] The separate but aligned relationship between the BBC and Foreign Office allowed the former to become a key instrument for the dissemination of British propaganda and, in turn, saw the BBC become a focal point for nationalist opposition. Indeed, Mossadegh's advisor Abolhassan Bani Sadr later referred to the Persian Service as no less than 'the voice of British imperialism'.[71]

Central to British media operations was the Anglo-Persian Institute, a branch of the British Council, which by 1948 had opened centres at Tehran, Isfahan, Shiraz, Tabriz, Resht and Mashhad.[72] The Institute's activities were broad and designed to gently illustrate the benefits of British investment, technical expertise and culture. In this sense, Britain was cast paternalistically as a guide to an inexperienced and developing country.

---

[68] *Hansard*, HC Debate, Vol. 425 Col. 1122–3, 16 July 1946.
[69] F Safiri and H Shahidi, 'The British Broadcasting Corporation', Encyclopaedia Iranica, 2003, https://iranicaonline.org/articles/great-britain-xiii.
[70] Bevin to Le Rougetel, 14 January 1947, FO 371/61993 (TNA).
[71] Sreberny and Torfeh, 'The BBC Persian Service, 1941-1979', 524.
[72] Darius Wainwright, *American and British Soft Power in Iran, 1953-1960: A 'Special Relationship'?* (London: Palgrave Macmillan, 2021), 47–8.

The AIOC was a vital partner in the dissemination of propaganda, providing a public relations team that shared materials with Iranian citizens and workers alike. As well as publishing flyers and pamphlets lauding company investment in housing and health, the company also actively placed articles in friendly newspapers and magazines.[73] An Information Services branch had been opened by the company following industrial unrest in 1946 with a mandate to 'instil pride of service' and 'raise morale' among the company's staff.[74] At Abadan, the company produced nine newspapers and news-sheets for workers in English, Urdu and Persian, including two daily editions. To complement these, the AIOC printed of 5,000 Persian-language pamphlets each week and a further 5,000 weekly newspapers for distribution in Tehran. They also installed loudspeakers across their workplaces to broadcast a diverse programme of lectures, music and radio recordings provided by the BBC. To reach an even larger audience the company purchased broadcasting time on Iranian radio and placed advertisements and articles in the press. To deliver this programme of public relations activity among workers and the Iranian public, the company developed plans to expand its in-country Information Department to more than forty-five permanent employees.[75] The Foreign Office singled out these efforts as a positive example of a British company taking 'active steps to counter hostile propaganda from Russian sources' overseas.[76]

Unlike the British government, AIOC publicity also looked beyond an Iranian audience to an international one. A transcontinental firm with myriad investments, the company's leadership was aware that their image and reputation mattered within and beyond Iran's borders. Glossy company publications published in English and Persian championed the 'extensive character' of new company housing schemes and plans to build over 10,000 new homes at Abadan. These, the AIOC claimed, were not merely functional living quarters but self-contained communities with recreational, educational and health amenities. Readers were assured that 'the social welfare of all those who service the company is a matter of prime concern . . . and a policy of continual advancement is steadily pursued'.[77]

[73] Willoughby to Le Rougetel, 14 April 1947, FO 371/62044 (TNA).
[74] AIOC Information Services in Iran, 3 July 1946, 8662 (BPA).
[75] Report on Visit of EHO Elkington to Iran, 17 January–7 March 1947, 9967 (BPA).
[76] Progress Report: Information Research Department, 13 August 1949, FO 1110/277 (TNA).
[77] *The Anglo-Iranian Oil Company in Iran, A Brief Description of the Anglo-Iranian Oil Company's Social and Welfare Activities for its Employees in Iran* (London/Tehran, 1947), 30827 (BPA).

The message was clear: the AIOC valued not only the pursuit of profit but its workers' health, housing and leisure too. The company made much of the assistance it offered to local municipalities, boasting that it supplied not only 'treated drinking water free of charge and electricity at an exceptionally low cost' but also roads, footpaths, streetlighting, trees and gardens and refuse services.[78] Highly paternalistic in tone, the economic conditions that led to local populaces to rely so heavily on a foreign concern were not touched upon. Instead, company materials depicted senior Iranian staff as apprentices to British managers and intimated that lower-skilled workers required of constant assistance whether through the provision of free accommodation or subsidized food and clothing. Unsurprisingly, the voices of workers themselves was absent from corporate publicity.

British propaganda in Iran embraced both high and low culture to attract audiences. The company championed sport as a means of extolling British values and preventing idleness. Football matches and tournaments were hastily arranged with prizes awarded by senior AIOC officials.[79] Elsewhere, art exhibitions and public lectures were held, sometimes in conjunction with the AIOC, and numerous Persian-language books and periodicals published.[80] Funding was provided for a number of Iranian students to attend British universities and summer schools, and academics with links to Britain, such as Isa Sedigh, a socialist Majlis deputy who had previously taught at Cambridge University, were granted funding for new research.[81] Film was particularly important as the British attempted to mirror the Soviet Union's success in developing striking visual agitprop. In 1943 the British Embassy had helped to finance the *Akhbar* (News) cinema in Tehran and had produced a score of news reels, documentaries and features designed to improve their image.[82] The *Akhbar* proved a hit and a model for propaganda on screen. Recognizing that Iran's predominantly rural population would struggle to reach urban cinemas, embassy and consular staff used mobile film units to project British interests well beyond the capital into regional hubs and even villages that otherwise had little by way of modern media infrastructure. In July 1947, the British sponsored twenty-one screenings throughout Gilan province with audiences that included

---

[78] Ibid.
[79] Donald MacNeill, 'The Lesson of 1946: An Essay on the Personnel Problems of the Oil Industry in South Iran', 12 January 1949, 118823 (BPA); Jack Taylor, 'Oil, Scots and the Great Game in Iran', *Nutmeg: The Scottish Football Periodical*, no. 25 (September 2022), 158–60.
[80] Isfahan Diary for 1947: April, 30 April 1947, FO 371/62008 (TNA).
[81] Report of the British Council, 1947–8, BW 151/9; Report of the British Council, 1948–9, BW 151/10 (TNA).
[82] Paper No. 551A: Plan of Propaganda for Persia, 23 November 1944, IOR/R/15/2/927 (BL).

Figure 3.3 AIOC workers enjoy a performance by the AIOC band at the Labour Cinema, Bahmanshir. Alongside improved housing and working conditions, entertainment was an important means of improving Britain's reputation in Iran. Courtesy of the BP Archive © BP plc.

foreign dignitaries based in the provincial capital, Resht, the Iranian army and AIOC employees.[83]

Entertainment was emphasized as the best means to attract audiences, and the British government reached an agreement with Academy Award-winning director Alexander Korda's Eagle-Lion company to distribute films across the Middle East. The success of this endeavour was, however, mixed. Iranian viewers found some of the films to contain inappropriate themes and content while others arrived without subtitling or dubbing.[84] Such problems were common as officials attempted to cobble together a viable schedule of productions. By 1947 the Anglo-Persian Institute was able to screen film shows on a near-weekly basis with a diverse programme of titles designed to appeal to audiences of all ages. The institute's Ladies' Section held women-only screenings; weekend specials drew in children with Disney cartoons; and 'life in Britain' films were

---

[83] Resht Monthly Diary: July 1947, 1 August 1947, FO 371/62016 (TNA).
[84] James R. Vaughan, '"A Certain Idea of Britain": British Cultural Diplomacy in the Middle East, 1945-57', *Contemporary British History* 19, no. 2 (June 2005), 162; Seager to Wheeler, 11 March 1947, FO 953/64 (TNA).

shown to illustrate the UK's social, scientific and industrial progress.[85] Unlike their Soviet counterparts, British propaganda was not overtly political. Instead, it attempted to offer Iranians a brighter future based around British cultural norms and values and technical and consumer innovation. The AIOC were once again partners, providing facilities for staff to watch blended programmes that included industrial training pictures as well as feature films and newsreels.[86]

Propaganda had a distinctly international character, situating Iran firmly within the wider British world system. Film reels highlighting British investment across the Middle East and Asia were supplemented by pamphlets from the Empire Information Service such as 'Wars Not Yet Won' and 'Progressing Towards Self-Government in the British Colonies', which were widely distributed across Iran.[87] To further promote Britain's interests in what Bevin dubbed the 'spiritual, moral and political sphere', the Information Research Department (IRD) was established in 1948. Although Iran was a nominally independent country, the IRD cultivated networks of journalists, politicians, religious leaders and trade unionists to gather, filter and distribute intelligence materials and promote 'the British ideal of moderation, toleration, social progress and individual freedom'.[88] The British government's Official Committee on Communism (Overseas) noted the importance of stealth in such matters and suggested that 'key men' be identified in the media, trade unions and other institutions to become points of coordination.[89]

Although diverse in form, the effectiveness of British propaganda was questionable. Wheeler had hoped that embassy staff would, like the wartime Public Relations Bureau, forge relationships with key editors and create an effective media network through which propaganda could be disseminated.[90] However, he was sceptical of the emphasis on socio-economic development and sophisticated political messaging that the Iranian public was unlikely to respond to. Surveying the political landscape, he warned that 'the propagation of social

---

[85] Ibid.; British Publicity in Tabriz, 3 July 1947, FO 953/64 (TNA); Hamid Naficy, *A Social History of Iranian Cinema, Volume II: The Industrializing Years, 1941-1978* (Durham: Duke University Press, 2011), 13–16.
[86] Report on Visit of EHO Elkington to Iran, 17 January–7 March 1947, 9967 (BPA).
[87] Rees to Hargrove, 10 March 1947, FO 953/64 (TNA).
[88] Future Foreign Publicity Policy, 4 January 1948, CAB 129/23 (TNA); James R. Vaughan, '"Cloak Without Dagger": How the Information Research Department Fought Britain's Cold War in the Middle East, 1948-56', *Cold War History* 4, no. 3 (August 2006), 56–9; Vaughan, 'British Cultural Diplomacy in the Middle East', 152.
[89] Report on the Work of the Information Research Department of the Foreign Office, 28 March 1950, CAB 143/3 (TNA).
[90] Andrew Defty, *Britain, America, and Anti-Communist Propaganda, 1945-53: The Information Research Department* (London: Routledge, 2004), 43; Seager to Wheeler, 11 March 1947; Wheeler Minutes, 14 March 1947, FO 953/64 (TNA).

democracy in the Middle East is extremely difficult principally because hardly anyone understands what it is and those who do, namely the educated upper classes, think it would be unsuitable for their countries and would in addition undermine their position'.[91]

The AIOC Information Department also proved to be poor partner in improving Britain's image, and it was reported that the majority of Iranians were 'practically untouched' by the publicity material it produced.[92] Similarly, AIOC workers tended to find company propaganda materials to be anodyne and irrelevant. Its news-sheets were largely unread by staff who preferred 'the controversial political issues' that could be found in local publications.[93] As acknowledged by the company's management, the department's head Geoffrey Keatings was 'too imperialistic' resulting in the production of inauthentic and alienating materials.[94] Privately, diplomatic staff was even more critical and described Keatings as a violent, alcoholic gambler who was prone to the 'silliest indiscretions'.[95] They suggested that he was 'quite ignorant of Persian ways of thought and behaviour' and was given to excessive propagandizing that was, ultimately, counterproductive for British interests.[96]

Despite his early successes in galvanizing publicity activity, Wheeler remained underwhelmed by Britain's rhetorical commitment to social democracy and chose to retire after less than eighteen months in post.[97] Following his departure the embassy's propaganda campaigns diminished rapidly. An expose of Soviet-forced labour practices, for example, was covered through a scant 400-word article distributed to trade unions linked to the Iranian government and published in a solitary national newspaper. Although the IRD obtained articles from a wide cast of well-known journalists, academics, and politicians there is limited evidence to suggest these ever made it to Iran.[98] A drive to increase BBC Persian Service listenership was planned but resulted in a piecemeal campaign that delivered as few as 200 advance

---

[91] James R. Vaughan, *The Failure of American and British Propaganda in the Arab Middle East, 1945-57: Unconquerable Minds* (Basingstoke: Palgrave Macmillan, 2005), 43.
[92] Report on the Quarter January–March 1948 on the Affairs of the Anglo-Iranian Oil Company, FO 371/68740 (TNA).
[93] Report on the Quarter April–June 1948 on the Affairs of the Anglo-Iranian Oil Company, FO 371/68740 (TNA).
[94] Comments: Mr Elkington's Report of Visit to Iran, 8 April 1947, 14788 (BPA).
[95] Report on the Quarter October–December 1948 on the Affairs of the Anglo-Iranian Oil Company, FO 371/75501 (TNA).
[96] Pyman Minutes, 22 November 1950, FO 248/1509 (TNA).
[97] Wheeler to Donaldson, 27 November 1947, IOR/L/PS/12/3491B (BL).
[98] Progress Report: Information Research Department, Annex A: Forced Labour Codex, 13 August 1949, FO 1110/277 (TNA).

programme notes across northern Iran.[99] While substantial amounts of anti-communist materials were produced through the IRD hub at Cairo, these were printed in Arabic and useless for circulation in the Iranian press.[100] Even the AIOC's Information Branch employed fewer Farsi than English-speaking staff, a situation the company's deputy staff manager could help but describe as 'absurd'.[101] Despite the stated necessity of improving Britain's image in Iran, a number of basic steps required to achieve this had been ignored.

Domestic politics and reform

While the British government and AIOC struggled to reconcile their faltering publicity strategy, Iranian demands for improved living standards grew louder and found a somewhat unlikely champion in the shah. Recognizing both his country's poverty and the necessity of endearing himself to the public, the monarch used a new year address to attack Iran's 'material and moral' degradation and call for expansive reforms, including the provision of free education and health care, elimination of illiteracy and wholesale improvements in housing.[102] The shah's address was followed by a speech by Qavam announcing a programme for Iran's modernization dubbed the Seven Year Plan. Immensely wide-ranging in scope, Le Rougetel suggested that 'nothing has been forgotten from irrigation to lunatic asylums'. The costs associated with such an ambitious scheme were massive and estimated by the ambassador to be almost 600,000 million rials, approximately £450 million, or 'the equivalent of some fourteen years annual ordinary revenue on the present basis'.[103] Dismissing them as unrealistic to the point of extravagance, the Foreign Office rejected the Iranian proposals out of hand and refused to countenance providing either aid or a line of credit against future AIOC royalties.[104]

The British government accepted that it could not dictate how Tehran should spend its income, but officials were nonetheless concerned that excessive spending could damage their interests and Le Rougetel was instructed to keep a

[99] Hart to Foreign Office, 29 June 1948, FO 953/410 (TNA).
[100] Progress Report: Information Research Department, 13 August 1949, FO 1110/277 (TNA).
[101] Comments: Mr Elkington's Report of Visit to Iran, 8 April 1947, 14788 (BPA).
[102] BBC Monitoring Report, 21 March 1947, FO 371/62001; Le Rougetel to Bevin, 26 March 1947, FO 248/1474 (TNA).
[103] Le Rougetel to Foreign Office, 28 March 1947, FO 371/62001 (TNA).
[104] Bevin to Le Rougetel, 14 April 1947, FO 371/62001 (TNA).

close eye on Qavam's plans.¹⁰⁵ Always couched in sober tones, the implicit threat that AIOC royalties could be suspended should the Iranian government adopt policies unfavourable to London was ever present. Within the embassy, officials sneered at Iran's capacity to undertake significant reform without their direction and dismissed Tehran's plans to seek credit abroad as fanciful. According to one analysis of the Seven Year Plan, the Iranian government 'leads a hand to mouth existence' and struggled financially in large part because 'the Persian is by long tradition a skilful tax dodger'.¹⁰⁶

Undeterred by British scepticism, the shah requested that the Iranian Ambassador to the United States Hossein Ala seek $250 million in economic and military aid from Washington. Recognizing that support on this scale was unlikely to be forthcoming, Ala asked for $100 million in Marshall Aid, a request the Iranian government linked explicitly to deepening Cold War tensions and the necessity of safeguarding their independence from communism.¹⁰⁷ Although this request was unsuccessful, it gained support from Ambassador George Allen, Director of the Office of Near Eastern and African Affairs Loy Henderson and Under-Secretary of State Dean Acheson, who lauded its ambition.¹⁰⁸ With aid unforthcoming, the Iranian government appealed to the International Bank for Reconstruction and Development for credit and appointed Overseas Consultants Inc. (OCI), the firm tasked with Germany and Japan's post-war reconstruction, to provide survey and management services. Under this arrangement, OCI vice president Max Thornburg took residency in Iran and became a close advisor of successive Iranian prime ministers.¹⁰⁹ Although he was a private citizen, Thornburg was well connected on Capitol Hill and his presence was believed locally to signal the American government's growing interest in Iran.¹¹⁰ The appointment of independent advisors financed with American credit also demonstrated a clear alternative to welfare imperialism and had the potential to diminish Britain's influence in an area they assumed they would dominate even

---

¹⁰⁵ Ibid.
¹⁰⁶ The Financial Aspect of Persia's Development Programme, 24 September 1947, FO 371/62003 (TNA).
¹⁰⁷ Document 640: The Ambassador in Iran (Allen) to the Secretary of State, 16 June 1947; Document 644: The Ambassador in Iran (Allen) to the Secretary of State, 28 June 1947, *Foreign Relations of the United States: Diplomatic Papers, 1947, The Near East and Africa Vol. VI* (Washington DC: United States Government Printing Office, 1971).
¹⁰⁸ Dean Acheson, *Present at the Creation: My Years in the State Department* (New York: Norton, 1987), 501–2.
¹⁰⁹ The Seven Year Plan and Overseas Consultants Incorporated, undated, RG 59 3.47; Max Thornburg - The Seven Year Plan, speech to the Iran-American Relations Society of Tehran, 19 October 1949, RG 59 3.410 (NARA).
¹¹⁰ Linda Qaimmaqami, 'The Catalyst of Nationalization: Max Thornburg and the Failure of Private Sector Developmentalism in Iran, 1947–1951', *Diplomatic History* 19, no. 1 (1995), 8–9.

with spending restrained.[111] In a message to the foreign secretary, Le Rougetel warned that the United States was 'capturing trade' in Iran and suggested that the competition for economic influence was increasing.[112] The emerging sense of American encroachment was exacerbated when Iran's persistent requests for military aid were finally rewarded with the sale of $10 million worth of surplus arms.[113]

As prime minister, Qavam had proven himself able to respond to myriad crises and to begin developing a framework for his country's modernization. However, he remained a polarizing figure and was widely criticized for despotic tendencies. During the fifteenth Majlis elections, Qavam attempted to consolidate his power through electoral engineering and took steps to prop up his friends and shoot down his rivals. One British report suggested that 'anyone arriving with a voting paper made out for any other candidate usually had this substituted unless the electoral committee were prepared to allow a certain number of voting papers to be placed in the (ballot) box in another candidate's name so as to make things appear normal.'[114] Such stark fraud prompted outrage and a wave of demonstrations. Denied a seat by ballot stuffing, Mohammad Mossadegh became a ringleader in the campaign for fair elections and led an occupation of the Royal Palace in opposition to Qavam's manipulations.[115] Concluded by the summer of 1947, the elections produced an unsurprising outcome and the Democrats swept to power winning an overwhelming majority that included taking every seat in Tehran. However, Qavam had overplayed his hand and inadvertently helped to forge alliances between his opponents. Islamists, nationalists and republicans had little in common, but they could find a temporary accord in their opposition to the prime minister and his unscrupulous regime. A similarly significant challenge lay in Qavam's heterogenous and fractious electoral coalition, which British officials described as riddled with 'blatant corruption' and held together only by fealty to the prime minister himself.[116]

The new parliament fell into disarray when faced with the proposed Soviet oil agreement. Having refused to endorse the deal he had negotiated, Qavam

---

[111] Atkinson to Pyman, 13 January 1947, FO 371/62003; British Middle East Office, Cairo to Foreign Office, 27 January 1947; Pyman Minutes, 24 February 1947, FO 371/62001 (TNA).
[112] Le Rougetel to Bevin, 3 March 1947, FO 371/62003 (TNA).
[113] Jernegen to Crawford, 1 July 1948; Justification of Estimate: Fiscal Year 1949, undated, RG 59 - Box 36 Folder: Arms Purchases, July–December 1948 (NARA); Le Rougetel to Bevin, 7 December 1948, FO 371/68741 (TNA).
[114] Report Up to Noon, 21 February 1947, FO 248/1475 (TNA).
[115] Le Rougetel to Foreign Office, 16 January 1947, IOR/L/PS/12/1223 (BL); Persia: Military Attaché's Intelligence Summary No.3, 4 February 1947, FO 371/61982 (TNA).
[116] Memorandum on the Persian Government and Internal Situation, 19 March 1947, FO 248/1474 (TNA).

privately acknowledged that the agreement was unlikely to pass and on 21 October 1947 deputies overwhelming voted for a resolution rejecting it.[117] Crucially, legislators did not shut the door to a future agreement with the Soviet Union but instead agreed that all oil concessions would be re-evaluated to ensure they delivered value for the Iranian government. For the first time in generations, Britain's uncontested control of Iran's vast oil reserves was under threat.[118] Despite widespread ballot-rigging, loyalty to Qavam faded quickly and he faced hostility from pro-British and pro-Soviet deputies alike. To claw back credibility with the parliamentary left, Qavam intervened to support Reza Rousta's release from prison but in doing so angered more conservative tendencies. Aware of their leader's vulnerability, ambitious Democrat legislators jockeyed for key positions further splintering his coalition.[119]

With deputies in what Le Rougetel described as 'open revolt' against the prime minister, Majlis business ground to a halt.[120] The Seven Year Plan, which with American oversight had begun to resemble an increasingly viable template for development, went unratified.[121] Nevertheless, Qavam persevered, defending his record and his plans in front of jeering deputies. These attempts were in vain and a vote of confidence was swiftly lost. Attempting to regain populist credibility, the prime minister went on the offensive, using two speeches to attack the British and demand sovereignty over Iran's vast oil reserves. Concerned that Qavam was actively 'stirring up anti-British feeling quite needlessly', the Foreign Office requested American assistance in quelling political unrest. Although the State Department suggested that the Iranian government would be 'well-advised' to avoid such outbursts in future, the damage had been done.[122] Nationalism and resentment towards Britain's outsized influence in Iran had been bubbling for decades but was given a new lease of life by Iran's wartime occupation and subsequent explosion of political activity. Although the Labour government appreciated the effect that popular discontent may have on their interests, steps taken to either address or suppress it had been ineffective. Meanwhile, among the Iranian public, control over *their* oil was increasingly perceived as

---

[117] Document 683: The Ambassador in Iran (Allen) to the Secretary of State, 11 October 1947; Document 686: The Ambassador in Iran (Allen) to the Secretary of State, 23 October 1947, *FRUS, 1947, Vol. VI, The Near East and Africa*.
[118] Ibid.
[119] Le Rougetel to Bevin, 18 December 1947, FO 371/61992 (TNA).
[120] Le Rougetel to Foreign Office, 2 August 1947; Le Rougetel to Foreign Office, 28 August 1947 FO 248/1474 (TNA).
[121] Le Rougetel to Foreign Office, 3 December 1947, FO 248/1474 (TNA).
[122] Document 702: The Chargé in the United Kingdom (Gallman) to the Secretary of State, 22 December 1947, *FRUS, 1947, Vol. VI, The Near East and Africa*.

fundamentally a question of sovereignty, perhaps even of honour. In attacking the concession, Le Rougetel subsequently suggested that Qavam had weakened Britain's negotiating hand and validated long-standing opposition to their presence in Iran.[123]

The Gass mission

Despite his salvos against the hated British, Qavam was unable to arrest his government's collapse and Ebrahim Hakimi was once again elected as prime minister. His inheritance was unenviable and included a parliament that lacked public credibility and an increasingly political shah. To win support from the royal court he invited a number of monarchists to become ministers, which provoked fresh discontent among more liberal deputies. In response, Hakimi withdrew the emergency police powers Qavam had introduced, ending curfews and lifting the ban on public demonstrations. Although a nominally minor legislative change, and part of a wider political balancing act, this decision empowered nationalists, socialists and Islamists alike, reigniting political organizing with an energy unseen since the summer of 1946. Amid rioting and protests from Islamic fundamentalists and revitalized Marxist tendencies, Hakimi lost his grip on power and was replaced by Abdolhossein Hazhir, an ally of the shah, who would be responsible for opening renegotiation talks with the AIOC.

The company was represented by Neville Gass, an experienced director who had spent fifteen years working in Iran following the First World War. Gass arrived in Tehran in late August spending almost a month in preliminary talks before discussions concerning the Supplemental Agreement finally opened on 28 September 1948. The director of Iran's Petroleum Department, Hossein Pirnia, offered a twenty-five-point memorandum for discussion, including: British dividend limitations; the exchange rate used to calculate royalty payments; the need to 'Iranianize' the oil industry; and funding for the Seven Year Plan.[124] Most important, however, was the unfavourable royalty rate Iran received compared to other countries, particularly Venezuela, where the principle of fifty-fifty profit

---

[123] Le Rougetel to Bevin, 9 June 1948, FO 371/68741 (TNA).
[124] Notes of Meetings at the Ministry of Finance, 30 September–13 October 1948, 102080 (BPA); Gass to Wright, 24 January 1949, FO 371/75395 (TNA).

sharing between the government and foreign oil companies had already been introduced.[125]

The breadth of discussion frustrated the AIOC's delegates who reported an absence of clarity concerning 'formulated definite demands' and a lack of 'properly organized procedure'.[126] A particular sticking point was that the Iranian bargaining position stemmed from inexperience in the oil industry and that they had failed to engage external – European or American – support before beginning negotiations.[127] In the early stages of discussions Gass went as far as dismissing the Iranian government's analysis as 'guesswork' predicated on a general misunderstanding of the AIOC's operations and the international market in general. In response, Iranian negotiators accused the company of suppressing information as to production and financial performance.[128]

These complaints were typical of the increasingly unproductive talks. In a particularly bitter exchange, senior AIOC representative Ernest Northcroft accused Pirnia of attacking the company while Iranian delegates suggested that the AIOC was threatening their government.[129] Despite the Iranian memorandum for discussion, British negotiators repeatedly suggested that Pirnia's understanding of the oil industry was confused or inadequate.[130] When talks closed in mid-October only limited progress had been made.[131] The company's hesitancy was a disappointment for the British government, which had hoped for a quick resolution.[132] During tripartite discussions between Treasury, Foreign Office and AIOC officials, Bevin suggested that the Iranian government had a 'legitimate grievance' given the company's huge profitability and relatively trifling royalty rate, and that financial incentives should be offered to them.[133] Resistant to these proposals, the company found an ally in Cripps who overruled the foreign secretary and argued forcefully that while a line of credit could be opened it should not exceed £5 million. The chancellor also encouraged the AIOC to reject any Iranian demands for a royalty increase above 33.5 per cent and agree to a policy of dividend stabilization to prevent budgetary fluctuations.[134]

---

[125] Ibid.; Clinton-Thomas Minutes, 20 August 1948, FO 371/68731; Le Rougetel to Bevin, 6 September 1948, FO 371/68741 (TNA).
[126] AIOC Tehran to AIOC London, 22 December 1948; Foreign Office to Tehran, 14 January, FO 371/75495 (TNA).
[127] Northcroft to Rice, 16 August 1948, 80908 (BPA).
[128] Note of Meeting at the Ministry of Finance, 30 September 1948, 102080 (BPA).
[129] Note of Meeting at the Ministry of Finance, 6 October 1948, 102080 (BPA).
[130] Note of Meeting at the Ministry of Finance, 7 October 1948, 102080 (BPA).
[131] Le Rougetel to Bevin, 3 November 1948, FO 371/68741 (TNA).
[132] Foreign Office to Le Rougetel, 4 September 1948, FO 371/68731 (TNA).
[133] Bevin to Cripps, 4 September 1948, FO 371/68731 (TNA).
[134] Cripps to Bevin, 14 September 1948, FO 371/68731 (TNA).

Foreign Office officials increasingly complained that the AIOC's 'operations and policy are not in any way controlled by His Majesty's Government' and bemoaned the company's tendency to provide spartan information on negotiations.[135] Recognizing the AIOC's vital diplomatic role, for better and worse, Bevin sought to shape the company's bargaining position for wider strategic ends. In contrast, Cripps suggested that the British government was one of many stakeholders in the AIOC and had no authority to bind the company's hands in negotiations.[136] Cripps' argument won out, illustrating the Attlee administration's emerging policy of thrift and Iran's diminishing relative importance in the Foreign Office. Increasingly consumed by the emerging Cold War, British diplomats, and Bevin in particular, were central in establishing the European Recovery Program and North Atlantic Treaty. Bevin's role as an architect of this new international settlement came at a cost to both his health and his attentiveness in other areas. As officials scrambled to reshape the post-war European order, they relegated Iran to something of a second order issue.

British disagreements were nothing compared to the continuing maelstrom of Iranian politics. Lacking a stable majority, Hazhir's position was always vulnerable and within a month of taking office a motion of interpellation had been laid in the Majlis.[137] Unable to count on support in parliament, Hazhir reached out to the shah by appointing monarchist deputies to his cabinet and supporting investment in Iran's armed forces.[138] These manoeuvres were ineffective, and Hazhir found himself unable to pass a budget. Examining the chaotic situation, Le Rougetel suggested that the deputies' behaviour 'is not merely frivolous; it is criminal'.[139] Rumours had begun to circulate that the shah had lost faith in Hazhir and wanted to replace him with a figure capable of bringing about much-needed political reform. A vote of confidence was subsequently lost on 6 November and, following Le Rougetel's advice, the shah took the unconventional step of inviting senior deputies to the palace to request that they invite Mohammad Sa'ed to form a new cabinet.[140] Enraged that the monarch was intervening so blatantly in parliamentary affairs, scores of deputies refused to take their seats, rendering parliament inquorate and ministers unassigned. The unprecedented interregnum lasted almost a month, preventing the new prime minister from

---

[135] Wright to Le Rougetel, 21 December 1948, FO 371/68732; Foreign Office to Tehran, 14 January, FO 371/75495 (TNA).
[136] Bevin to Le Rougetel, 31 January 1949, FO 248/1489 (TNA).
[137] Le Rougetel to Bevin, 13 August 1948, FO 416/101 (TNA).
[138] Abrahamian, *Iran Between Two Revolutions*, 247.
[139] Le Rougetel to Foreign Office, 27 October 1948, FO 371/68708 (TNA).
[140] Azimi, *Iran*, 201; Le Rougetel to Bevin, 7 December 1948, FO 371/68741 (TNA).

presenting his cabinet. Recognizing the potential for general political upheaval to bleed into discussions between the AIOC and the government, Le Rougetel warned that piecemeal adjustments to Britain's oil concession may not be enough to secure its passage through the Majlis.[141]

The success and failure of negotiation

The ambassador's counsel was given credence by the submission of a Majlis' bill to cancel the concession outright. Panicked, negotiations resumed with an Iranian delegation led by Finance Minister Abbas Quli Gulshayan.[142] Like his predecessor, Gulshayan based negotiations on the twenty-five-point memorandum and urged the company to consider a more equitable division of royalties. Once again, AIOC officials regarded this approach as unsatisfactory. Gass not only questioned Gulshayan's authority but even suggested that an external negotiator should be appointed to act on the Iranian government's behalf.[143] In frank discussions with Foreign Office officials, Gass wondered whether negotiations might be in vain, pointing to the tumultuous political environment as evidence that the Iranian government would be unable to secure the Supplemental Agreement's ratification.[144] Fearing a ruse, Le Rougetel warned that the AIOC was attempting to 'spin out the negotiations under cover of a smoke screen of publicity' before forcing the Iranians into an unfavourable, last-minute settlement.[145] Such tactics were, the ambassador believed, most unwise. 'In the long run', he wrote, 'every successive postponement can only work against us; we have recent evidence – which we have reported to the Foreign Office – of increasing dissatisfaction in the country.'[146] As political conditions deteriorated, British officials in Tehran warned that any signs of the oil company 'hanging back' from an agreement could provoke civil unrest and lead to the Sa'ed government's collapse. Were this to happen there were no assurances as to what might replace it.[147]

To deflect from his government's weaknesses, Sa'ed publicly demanded that any settlement must recognize Iran's widespread poverty and the AIOC's

---

[141] Le Rougetel to Foreign Office, 15 October 1948, FO 371/68731 (TNA).
[142] Gass to Wright, 24 January 1949, FO 371/75495 (TNA).
[143] AIOC Tehran to AIOC London, 22 December 1948; Foreign Office to Tehran, 14 January, FO 371/75495 (TNA).
[144] Ibid.
[145] Le Rougetel to Foreign Office, 16 January 1949, FO 371/75495 (TNA).
[146] Le Rougetel Minutes, 7 January 1949, FO 248/1489 (TNA).
[147] Creswell to Burrows, 18 January 1949, FO 248/1489 (TNA).

contrasting wealth. Such comments were mild compared to deputies like Abbas Eskandari who claimed that Iranian oil was 'bring stolen by the British' and urged deputies to elect a new government to liberate their country.[148] In a piece of arch political theatre, Hossein Makki took to the Majlis' floor and read a letter from Mossadegh that suggested 'high treason' was being committed against the nation. In absentia, Mossadegh argued that Iranian politicians had a duty to refuse to enter into an agreement with the hated AIOC.[149] Le Rougetel again warned the Foreign Office about growing unrest, which increasingly manifested itself both in parliament and through public demonstrations. Mounting opposition was so great that the ambassador advised that Britain's concession was clearly under threat.[150]

On 4 February, as tensions reached fever pitch, the shah was shot and wounded while visiting the University of Tehran. A hasty government investigation blamed the Tudeh and suggested that the would-be assassin, Naser Fakhr Arai, was affiliated with the party. In truth, it is likely that Arai was motivated by religious fundamentalism rather than Marxism.[151] The government responded by introducing martial law, placing Mossadegh and a host of other opposition leaders and journalists under house arrest and rounding up the last remnants of the Tudeh.[152] In subsequent discussions with Le Rougetel and American Chargé d'Affaires James Somerville, the shah made clear that he did not want the crisis to go to waste and promised to take 'drastic action' to overcome political dislocation.[153] In the clearest demonstration of his ambitions, the monarch was granted unprecedented powers to dissolve the Majlis, provided new elections were held within three months. He was also given the authority to convene a constitutional assembly to establish a senate, half of whose members he would appoint, effectively returning Iran to the legislative system set out in the country's draft 1906 constitution. Finally, stringent measures suppressing

---

[148] Northcroft to Gass, 28 January 1949, 80908 (BPA); Katouzian, *Musaddiq and the Struggle for Power in Iran*, 67–8.
[149] Ibid.
[150] Le Rougetel to Foreign Office, 3 February 1949, FO 248/1489 (TNA).
[151] Mohammad Reza Pahlavi, *Answer to History* (New York: Stein and Day, 1980), 59; Le Rougetel to Foreign Office, 4 February 1949, IOR/L/PS/12/1225 (BL); Document 268: The Chargé in Iran (Somerville) to the Secretary of State, 4 February 1949, *Foreign Relations of the United States: Diplomatic Papers, 1949, The Near East, South Asia and Africa Vol. VI* (Washington DC: United States Government Printing Office, 1977).
[152] Le Rougetel to Foreign Office, 6 February 1949, FO 371/75464 (TNA).
[153] Document 269: The Chargé in Iran (Somerville) to the Secretary of State, 14 February 1949, *FRUS, 1949, Vol. VI, The Near East, Asia and Africa*; Le Rougetel to Foreign Office, 12 February 1949, IOR/L/PS/12/1225 (BL); Tabriz to Tehran, 7 February 1949; Ogden to Tehran, 10 February 1949; Willoughby to Tehran, 13 February 1949, FO 248/1486 (TNA); Northcroft to Gass, 28 January 1949, 80908 (BPA).

political communications, media and protest were introduced to the outrage of the opposition.[154]

Reflecting on the chaotic situation, British officials turned to the possibility of dispensing with democracy and installing the shah as an autocrat. In correspondence with the Foreign Office, Le Rougetel encouraged his interventions, suggesting that without decisive action the government was likely to collapse. Against the dangerous forces of Marxism and insurgent nationalism, the ambassador urged his government to protect the shah and to refrain from 'doing or saying anything which will weaken his hand'.[155] Although Le Rougetel later suggested that the monarch was either 'a knave or a fool, or both', he remained one of the leading figures in Iran and a potentially-vital counterweight to both the Majlis and the mob.[156] Although no action was taken at this stage, creating something approaching an absolute monarchy was very much under consideration.

With the shah's resolve hardening, negotiations between the Iranian government and AIOC resumed. Despite a mutual desire to reach an agreement, the two sides remained some distance apart particularly concerning Iranian suggestions that royalties be pegged to international gold prices and the gross profits be split on a fifty-fifty basis. Within the oil company both propositions were seen as unworkable. The former because of currency fluctuations and the latter because of the deep integration between their Iranian and international operations.[157] Some progress was, however, made through private talks between Le Rougetel and the shah. Although critical of the AIOC's hard bargaining, the shah recognized that compromise may be needed on the Iranian side and suggested that Max Thornburg be called upon to provide independent advice.[158] Immediately sceptical of the Iranian demands, Thornburg warned that their analysis was 'completely fallacious' and out of step with other international agreements.[159] This blunt assessment deepened rifts between Iranian delegates who privately feared that the collapse of talks could precipitate political unrest and demands for the industry's nationalization.[160] To overcome the impasse, William Fraser personally travelled to Iran for discussions. However, despite the shah's 'expressed wish' for a resolution and reports that royal bodyguards tried

---

[154] Ibid.
[155] Le Rougetel to Foreign Office, 12 February 1949, IOR/L/PS/12/1225 (BL).
[156] Ali M. Ansari, *Modern Iran Since 1921: The Pahlavis and After* (London: Longman, 2003), 105.
[157] Le Rougetel to Foreign Office, 3 March 1949, FO 248/1489 (TNA).
[158] Le Rougetel to Foreign Office, 18 March 1949, FO 248/1489 (TNA).
[159] Ibid.
[160] Berthoud to Wright, 8 April 1949, FO 248/1489 (TNA); Meeting with Sa'ed, 9 March 1949, 126422 (BPA).

to intimidate resistant deputies, an agreement remained elusive.[161] The shah was head of state and keen to flex his muscles, but, without a compromise from the company, Iranian opposition was resolute and righteous in its anger. Reporting to London, Le Rougetel remarked on the 'lack of confidence' the Iranian people felt in their leader and contrasted the shah's bullish approach to politics with ongoing food shortages and inflationary pressures.[162] A deal, the ambassador believed, needed to be concluded quickly lest public dissatisfaction move beyond protests and articles and into more serious civil unrest.

Under significant pressure from the British government, the AIOC used a note to Le Rougetel to establish areas for compromise, particularly regarding royalties paid per ton. Company officials believed that faced with growing financial hardships increasing the 'aggregate amount' received by the Iranian government was a significant concession, and that a Venezuela-style profit-sharing agreement would damage future investment in oil production.[163] The AIOC's evolving position aligned closely with the shah's belief that his government should 'focus on essentials . . . in particular an adequate increase in royalty payments', which would help to accelerate his long desired modernization plans.[164] Somewhat ironically, the memorandum's presentation coincided with the company's decision to defer or cancel a number of its own welfare and development schemes in Iran.[165]

At the Foreign Office, Bevin remained uneasy at the slow progress in negotiations. 'I feel that a major British interest is at stake', he wrote, noting that the AIOC's failure to reach an agreement would have precipitous effects on Anglo-Iranian relations and wider geopolitical interests.[166] Following correspondence with Le Rougetel, the foreign secretary called on the AIOC to provide a guaranteed minimum royalty worth £4 million per annum, thereby establishing an income baseline. Doing so would, he hoped, relieve some of the mounting public pressure and make up for the Iranian delegates' failure to achieve a fifty-fifty profit-sharing agreement.[167] After months of laboured discussions, negotiators had finally reached a breakthrough and by mid-July they

---

[161] Johnson to British Embassy, 13 February 1949; Ogden to British Embassy, 10 February 1949, FO 248/1486; Le Rougetel to Foreign Office, 11 May 1949, FO 248/1489 (TNA); Le Rougetel to Foreign Office, 26 February 1949, IOR/L/PS/12/1225 (BL).
[162] Le Rougetel to Foreign Office, 15 June 1949, FO 248/1489; Le Rougetel to Foreign Office, 27 June 1949, FO 371/75485 (TNA).
[163] Note handed to the British Ambassador, 20 March 1949, 106821 (BPA).
[164] Le Rougetel to Foreign Office, 29 April 1949, IOR/L/PS/12/1225 (BL).
[165] Minutes of a Meeting Held at Britannic House, 11 May 1949; Minutes of a Meeting Held At Britannic House, 16 June 1949, 44165 (BPA).
[166] Bevin to Le Rougetel, 1 July 1949, FO 248/1489 (TNA).
[167] Ibid.

had settled the Supplemental Agreement in principle. The agreement included an increased royalty rate from four to six shillings per ton, a £4 million royalties baseline per annum, the provision of discounted oil within Iran and, despite the Treasury's misgivings, dividend limitation exemptions.[168] Finally, to assuage the complaints of corporate insularity made by nationalists in the Majlis, the company agreed to a steady process of Iranianization and promised that Iranian employees would gradually take over all aspects of domestic extraction and refinement. Retroactively applied to 1948, the measures would enable the AIOC to make a lump-sum payment of little over £5 million to the Iranian government within thirty days of the legislation's passage through the Majlis. Under pressure from the shah, the Iranian delegation accepted the terms on 20 July and it was anticipated that parliamentary ratification would follow in a matter of days.[169]

The National Front

Despite residual sympathy for the wounded shah and attempts to suppress dissent, the Supplemental Agreement provoked an outpouring of fury when it was presented to the Majlis on 23 July. Nationalist deputies railed against a deal that they saw as a betrayal of the Iranian people and which would maintain the country's subjugation by foreign interests. From the gallery enraged citizens decried efforts to impose time limits on speeches and jeered those deputies willing to take a stand in favour of the agreement.[170] The British government and AIOC had greatly misjudged the public mood and failed to the groundswell of opposition to their very presence in Iran. Having previously considered steps to terminate Iranian democracy, Le Rougetel now warned against dissolving the Majlis and suggested that to have 'any real value' the Supplemental Agreement must be fairly ratified. The ambassador stressed that a route to compromise must be found through the Majlis, which, incapable of unity on almost any issue, had found common cause in opposition to the revised concession. For the moment, he advised against reopening negotiations and instead encouraged efforts to win deputies round.[171]

---

[168] 'The Supplemental Agreement Between the Imperial Iranian Government and the Anglo-Iranian Oil Company Ltd', 17 July 1949, 126412 (BPA).
[169] Le Rougetel to Foreign Office, 21 July 1949, FO 248/1489 (TNA).
[170] Le Rougetel to Foreign Office, 27 July 1949, FO 248/1489 (TNA).
[171] Ibid.

Considering the unrest that had rocked the AIOC's oil fields in 1946, field labour supervisor Donald MacNeill wrote that 'if we are pressed, however, we might admit that our Iranian workers had a pretty low standard of living' with housing and services that had suffered from long-standing underinvestment and, in some cases, undergone rapid deterioration.[172] These problems were a microcosm of wider deprivation endured across a country where poor housing, malnutrition, limited access to education and workplace exploitation were common. The Seven Year Plan promised not only to respond to these challenges but also to promote a national drive towards modernity. However, without autonomy over its most valuable assets there appeared little reason for the Iranian people to believe such plans would come to fruition. In a sign of their dependence, sterling's devaluation meant that the real value of the agreement's £4 million royalties baseline was significantly reduced within a matter of months. Having reached a deal in principle, the AIOC refused to consider any amendments.[173]

In July, the fifteenth Majlis ended amid widespread fears that elections would again fall foul to gerrymandering. Growing political alienation was given succour by early reports that ballot-rigging was pervasive in rural areas and that landowners loyal to the shah had pressured generally illiterate peasants to vote for monarchist candidates.[174] In these febrile circumstances, opposition to the Supplemental Agreement provided a fulcrum for popular discontent, encompassing anger towards poverty, self-serving government and exploitation from abroad. On 10 October, Mohammad Mossadegh, eyeing a return to office, called a private meeting of leading liberal newspaper editors and opposition Majlis deputies to discuss electoral strategy and the defence of Iranian democracy.[175] He publicly re-emerged three days later, calling on protestors to take *bast* in the royal palace in opposition to both domestic corruption and the misappropriation of oil, 'Iran's dearest assets'.[176] Mossadegh's call was answered by a diverse coalition of nationalists, students, Islamists and socialists. To unite the protestors, Mossadegh took to a megaphone and shouted, 'silence is our slogan!', as they peacefully descended on the palace.[177] After negotiations, security forces permitted twenty *bastis* entry to the palace grounds to hand a

---

[172] MacNeill, 'The Lesson of 1946', 118823; Abadan Labour Department: Annual Report, 1948, 15917 (BPA).
[173] Lawford to Foreign Office, 26 September 1949, FO 248/1489 (TNA).
[174] Le Rougetel to Burrows, 27 January 1949, FO 248/1486 (TNA).
[175] The National Front in Iran, 28 October 1949, 119116 (WCDA).
[176] Katouzian, *Musaddiq and the Struggle for Power in Iran*, 73.
[177] De Bellaigue, *Patriot of Persia*, 138.

petition to Abdolhossein Hazhir, the former prime minister who was now Iran's minister of the royal court. Unbeknown to the authorities, Mossadegh and his comrades then began a hunger strike. Although called off after three days, the occupation and hunger strike were arch pieces of political theatre, which drew public attention to the veteran nationalist and his new political alliance, the National Front.

Through rallies, pamphlets and newspaper articles, the National Front's election campaign began in earnest and drew support from across Iranian society. Violence was, however, lurking on the fringes and on 4 November a gunman linked to the Fada'iyan-e Islam terrorist group assassinated Hazhir. Coming just nine months after the attempt on the shah's life, the murder of a loyal minister was a major blow to the crown's authority and a warning to politicians who opposed the nationalist cause. Terrified by brewing unrest, the shah declared that all Majlis ballots cast were void and that a fresh round of voting would be held. The election took on a new meaning, effectively becoming a referendum on the Supplemental Agreement and by proxy the very basis of Anglo-Iranian relations. Barely six months before the National Front unified diverse strands of opposition, Assistant Under-Secretary at the Foreign Office Michael Wright had scribbled and underlined the word 'nonsense' next to the suggestion that Iranian public opinion could shape the course of oil negotiations and potentially even cause them to collapse.[178] However, there now existed an energetic coalition that sought to achieve just that. In Mohammad Mossadegh, political dissenters of all stripes had found a figurehead around whom they could rally and who commanded public support of a level unsurpassed by any other Iranian politician.

Since the Second World War, Foreign Office officials had hoped that welfare imperialism would dull nationalist sensibilities and demonstrate the value of British guidance, investment and institutions. The Supplemental Agreement's very public rejection clearly illustrated that their approach had failed. Hamstrung by economic maladies, investment had been minimal. British propaganda was wide-ranging but could do little to mask diminishing living standards or democratic abnormalities. Despite a quiet, constant murmur that Britain could not simply siphon popular discontent into new trade unions or vaguely social democratic institutions, little had been done to correct this. With elections on the horizon, Britain's outsized position in Iran was at risk of disintegrating.

---

[178] Berthoud to Wright, 8 April 1949, FO 248/1498 (TNA).

4

Welfare imperialism in crisis

The 1949 harvest was a poor one and, even before the end of summer, staple crops were in short supply. Ambassador John Le Rougetel reported that conditions in some regions were so bad that Iranians were using opium to barter for wheat. With the Supplemental Agreement still unratified, economic confidence was limited and in the bazaar merchants complained bitterly about a lack of available credit.[1] Having travelled extensively in Iran throughout 1948 and 1949, former diplomat and now SOAS academic Ann Lambton used a speech to the Royal Institute of International Affairs' Middle East Group to reiterate that Iran's maladies were not the result of British imperialism, wartime occupation or dysfunctional politics but 'spiritual and moral weaknesses' expressed through absolutist political movements.[2]

Her position was not unusual in diplomatic circles, and for the most part the British approached Iranian nationalism with little curiosity. Indeed, they barely acknowledged it was a cogent political philosophy at all. Instead, officials dismissed the complaints expressed by Mohammad Mossadegh and his followers as examples of xenophobia, bitterness and psychological deficiency. Concerning opposition to the Anglo-Iranian Oil Company, the British tended to castigate nationalists as ungrateful for the benefits that Western ingenuity had bestowed them. Faced with an increasingly intractable political force, the Attlee government dispensed with any pretence of welfare imperialism and fell back on blunter means of preserving their hegemony in Iran.

---

[1] Le Rougetel to Foreign Office, 27 June 1949, FO 371/75485; Le Rougetel to Foreign Office, 3 August 1949, FO 248/1489; Le Rougetel to Foreign Office, 29 October 1949, FO 371/75481 (TNA).
[2] Recent Political Trends in Persia, 11 November 1949, Ann Lambton Papers - Box 63/2 (DUA).

Imperial revanchism

In January 1950, just a month before the Majlis election were due to conclude, Sa'ed's government collapsed and the beleaguered prime minister was once again forced to cobble together a makeshift cabinet.³ Fearful of the nationalist tide, he elected to exclude National Front supporters and rely instead on monarchist deputies. Sa'ed's fidelity to the crown won plaudits from the shah who called him the only man 'prepared to shoulder the unwelcome responsibility of accepting even this increase of royalty payments in settlement of all outstanding grievances'.⁴ Such praise did not, however, make parliamentary management any easier. Changes were also afoot in the British Embassy. John Le Rougetel departed to become ambassador of Belgium and Francis Shepherd replaced him. Le Rougetel was a capable administrator but he had failed to either improve relations with the Anglo-Iranian Oil Company or communicate the growing nationalist challenge. Previously stationed in the Dutch East Indies, Shepherd had endured protracted civil war and at least one attempt on his life. Ironically given events to come, the new ambassador was promised that his next posting would be in 'a place where we never have any trouble with the natives'.⁵ He travelled to Tehran via Cairo, Beirut and Baghdad, his unpublished memoir revealing an immediately dim view of 'the oriental character'.⁶ After just a month in Tehran Shepherd recorded that 'Persian cynicism and pessimism, combined with a tendency to confess to their own shortcomings, is apparently less a passing phase than a permanent weakness'.⁷ Such blunt assumptions were a consistent and damaging feature of the ambassador's reporting throughout his tenure.

With Shepherd in transit, negotiations on the Supplementary Agreement continued between Chargé d'Affaires Valentine Lawford, the Sa'ed government and the shah. Desperate to modernize Iran and expand his influence, the shah saw the Supplemental Agreement's successful conclusion as essential. However, he also acknowledged the strength of opposition to the agreement's ratification and argued that further concessions were needed before it could achieve parliamentary approval. He called on the British government to do more in

---

³ Le Rougetel to Foreign Office, 12 January 1950; Le Rougetel to Attlee, 19 January 1950, FO 371/82310 (TNA).
⁴ Le Rougetel to Attlee, 1 February 1950, FO 371/82310 (TNA).
⁵ Ervand Abrahamian, *The Coup: 1953, the CIA, and the Roots of Modern U.S.-Iranian Relations* (New York: New Press, 2015), 61.
⁶ Sir Francis Shepherd, *Never Trouble Trouble* – unpublished manuscript, Middle East Centre, Oxford (MEC).
⁷ Shepherd to Strang, 6 April 1950, FO 371/82511 (TNA).

encouraging AIOC malleability but was unable to identify any specific changes he wished to see. Such vagaries led British officials to wonder whether the shah 'had any clear idea' what was really likely to succeed.[8] Despite the distance between them, negotiators returned to the table against a background of economic deterioration and palpable sense of anger towards Iran's exploitation and prostrate leadership.[9]

The country's political malaise was evident when the sixteenth Majlis opened on 9 February 1950 despite ballots from Tehran remaining uncounted. Appointed by the shah using emergency powers, scores of deputies were immediately tainted by corruption. In advice to the Foreign Office, Lambton suggested that 'discontent with present conditions is widespread and growing daily'. In response, all facets of the 'the ruling class' were becoming targets for anger on the streets and in the press.[10] The outlawed Tudeh had begun to re-emerge, using front groups like the Peace Partisans, the Society Organised to Fight Imperialist Oil Companies, and the Women's Organisation of Iran to avoid detection.[11] Observing the breakdown of political consensus, Lambton warned that Britain should not be indifferent to Iranian affairs and pondered whether the population's 'nostalgia for dictatorship' could be exploited in the pursuit of a strong government amenable to their interests.[12] In an indication of the esteem with which the British were held, Lambton also recorded that a stranger lambasted her as a 'reactionary imperialist' while she dined.[13]

Established following widespread industrial unrest in 1946, the AIOC's labour relations framework was clearly faltering, and membership of the government-backed Central Council of Khuzestan Workers fell from 8,000 to just 1,500 members between 1948 and 1950.[14] Local managers blamed the workforce's 'almost impregnable apathy' and 'ignorance of modern democratic industrial practice' for poor participation in elections for AIOC's joint consultation committees and for the Oil Worker's Union's almost total marginalization.[15] In reality, workers' disinterest reflected their detachment from supposedly

---

[8] Lawford to Bevin, 21 February 1950, FO 371/82310 (TNA).
[9] Shepherd to Bevin, 19 February 1950; Shepherd to Foreign Office, 20 March 1950, FO 371/82332B (TNA).
[10] Le Rougetel to Burrows, 27 January 1949, FO 248/1486 (TNA).
[11] Leavett Note, 31 January 1950, FO 371/82314 (TNA); Document 44: Current Strength of the Tudeh Party in Iran, 13 September 1951, *FRUS, 1952-1954, Iran - 2018*.
[12] Le Rougetel to Burrows, 27 January 1949, FO 248/1486 (TNA); Journal Entry, 9 June 1948, Ann Lambton Papers – Box 16/40 (DUA).
[13] Lambton to Rhodes, 17 April 1949, Ann Lambton Papers - Box 48/1 (DUA).
[14] Trade Unions, undated – 1950, 67011 (BPA).
[15] A Report on the Adjustment Board Election, undated - 1950; Refineries Industrial Relations Report, October 1950, 31661 (BPA).

representative organizations over which they had little influence. Despite this apathy, AIOC director E. H. O. Elkington claimed that the relationship between labour and management was 'vastly improved' and the Tudeh and its associated unions were singled out as a marginalized rump of a few thousand remaining supporters among more than 82,000 workers at Abadan.[16] The company's ailing industrial relations framework was reported to the company's leadership by British staff, but complaints that 'one vote per year alone will not produce a sense of participation among workers' were ignored.[17] Indeed, the company's industrial relations report for 1950 noted that the 'vacuum caused by the banning of the Tudeh Party was filled by the establishment of joint consultative machinery' and ruled out any significant changes to it. Reflecting on the lack of participation from local workers, the report blamed illiteracy and ignorance and suggested that 'as is generally found in other Eastern countries' Iranians required a more paternalistic relationship with their employers.[18]

This tendency towards orientalism led the AIOC's leadership to overlook significant developments among their workers, particularly the return of unsanctioned, organic labour activism. Without company permission, previously unorganized staff in auxiliary services like bakeries, restaurants and construction established new trade unions. Meanwhile, up to 8,000 staff took part in protests against electoral malpractice despite a risk of sanction, illustrating a depth of political feeling generally dismissed by management.[19] Research conducted by the International Labour Office in early 1950 found that while avenues for industrial relations had been organized along Western lines, there was an acute distance between the largely British management and the Iranian workforce. It was simply impossible, the ILO suggested, to wholly separate 'political and national feeling' from the labour question given the AIOC's status as a foreign-owned enterprise in which workers had little stake.[20]

The potential challenge Iranian labour might pose to British interests was raised by Minister of Fuel and Power Philip Noel-Baker who wrote to Bevin to express his concern towards the AIOC's 'very exposed position.'[21] His fears were shared across the British labour movement and, having followed developments since Edgar Harries visited Iran, TUC General Secretary Vincent Tewson

---

[16] Elkington Visit to Iran, 17 January–25 February 1949, 9968 (BPA).
[17] MacNeill, 'The Lesson of 1946', 118823; Fateh to Mylles, 28 July 1947, 35201 (BPA).
[18] Industrial Relations, 1950, 27 March 1951, 67011 (BPA).
[19] Trade Unions, undated; Collective Disputes, undated, 67011 (BPA).
[20] Labour Conditions in the Oil Industry in Iran: Report of a Mission of the International Labour Office, January–February 1950, 90434 (BPA).
[21] Noel-Baker to Bevin, 15 November 1950, FO 371/91628 (TNA).

expressed his 'anxiety' that workers' housing remained in short supply and poor condition.[22] Despite widely-reported overcrowding in Abadan's bachelor's quarter, it is notable, for example, that in 1950 and 1951 no new facilities for unmarried labourers were built in Khuzestan.[23] In stark contrast to Noel-Baker and Tewson's complaints, Basil Jackson typified the AIOC leadership's attitude to self-organized labour. Following a brief visit to Iran in spring 1950, the director launched a tirade against the workforce, bemoaning the 'fantastically and wholly undeserved' wages they received and suggesting that the standard of company housing was, if anything, 'too high'. Describing the Iranian workers as insolent, incapable and ungrateful, Jackson revealed the darker side of AIOC paternalism and attacked 'subversive elements' who were sowing discontent among docile and easily led workers. The Iranian government did not escape criticism and Jackson attacked them for continuing to place unwarranted demands on 'the only successful enterprise in the country'.[24] The AIOC workforce's growing disillusionment created space in which the Tudeh was able to develop clandestine cells. In early 1950, Lawford warned that the banned organization had restructured itself having been driven underground and was surreptitiously distributing propaganda through its front groups. Although rhetorical flourishes alluding to brotherhood and solidarity persisted, the Tudeh's message was increasingly targeted at domestic rather than international issues, not least the meddling shah, cruel police and hated British.[25] Aware that Marxist agitprop could quickly spread, diplomats warned against 'dangerous complacency' and recommended more active opposition.[26]

Welfare imperialism had been the foundation of British policy in Iran since 1945 and had encouraged conciliation through socio-economic development supported by multifaceted propaganda. In the face of growing unrest, however, the British government began to explore opportunities to bolster the Iranian state. On the advice of the Official Committee on Communism (Overseas), Iranian police officers travelled to Britain for training in covert operations and anti-subversion tactics with MI5 and MI6 support.[27] More substantively, the British intelligence services began to forge links with the Iranian armed forces and launched a broad suite of anti-communist measures. Before his departure for

---

[22] MacNeill to Fraser, 7 December 1949, 35201 (BPA).
[23] AIOC Housing: Abadan, Mashur and Fields, 7 December 1954, 41669 (BPA).
[24] Notes on Visit to Middle East – February/March 1950, undated, 16990 (BPA).
[25] Lawford to Foreign Office, 18 February 1950, FO 371/82310 (TNA).
[26] Leavett Minutes, 27 April 1950, FO 371/82311 (TNA).
[27] Minutes: Official Committee on Communism (Overseas), 1 March 1950 and 19 May 1950, CAB 134/3; Shepherd to Wright, 26 June 1950; Redacted to Jackson, 3 August 1950; Foreign Office to Tehran, 21 September 1950, FO 371/82391 (TNA).

Brussels, Le Rougetel reported that General Ali Razmara, a senior commander in the Iranian army, had approached him concerning the 'deterioration of the internal situation' and need for British support.[28] Concerned that covert operations could enflame tensions with the USSR, Bevin had previously opposed using them in Iran. However, as a result of angina, successive operations and debilitating medication, the foreign secretary was increasingly bed-ridden and, according to Minister of State at the Foreign Office Kenneth Younger, only 'a shadow of his real self'.[29] Unable to fully participate in policy development, Bevin reluctantly accepted recommendations for David Haldane Porter, an officer in MI5's Overseas Service, to undertake an exploratory mission to Iran.[30] Haldane Porter met with Razmara on four occasions and reported glowingly on the general's willingness to offer British intelligence facilities and support in building their Iranian operation.[31]

Having received a dossier on the Tudeh's modest resurgence, the agent proposed that a British intelligence operative take up residence in Iran and use diplomatic clearance to liaise discreetly and regularly with Razmara. Initially William Jenkin, formerly deputy director of the Intelligence Bureau in India, was suggested for this position; however, he was deemed at risk of exposure owing to the considerable number of Indian and Pakistani workers in Iran.[32] Although an alternative to Jenkin was named in correspondence between MI5 and the Foreign Office, these exchanges remain heavily redacted.[33] It seems likely, however, that the operative placed in Tehran was John Briance, a former colonial police officer in Palestine who spoke fluent Persian. Identified in the diaries of Deputy Director General of the Security Service Guy Liddell as the lynchpin of British intelligence in Iran, Briance's role was to understand Tudeh subversion and to advise on the best means of countering it.[34] To support anti-communist activity, Haldane Porter proposed that senior representatives of the Iranian police and armed force should travel to the UK for additional training.[35] Haldane Porter's mission to Iran represented an intensification of British attempts to exert influence and protect their interests. Crucially, new espionage

---

[28] Le Rougetel to Foreign Office, 24 January 1950, FO 371/82314 (TNA).
[29] Kenneth Gilmour Younger and Geoffrey Warner, *In the Midst of Events: The Foreign Office Diaries and Papers of Kenneth Younger, February 1950-October 1951* (London: Routledge, 2005), 19.
[30] Hankey to Haldane Porter, 10 February 1950, FO 371/82314 (TNA).
[31] Report on Visit to Tehran, 14 April 1950, FO 371/82314 (TNA).
[32] Ibid.
[33] Shaw to Hankey, 20 April 1950, FO 371/82314 (TNA).
[34] Diary of Guy Liddell, 1952, 16 September 1952, KV 4/474 (TNA).
[35] Report on Visit to Tehran, 14 April 1950, FO 371/82314 (TNA).

measures were approved not only within the Foreign Office but personally by Clement Attlee, illustrating the seriousness with which they were treated.[36]

Mansur, Mossadegh and the United States

Defamed in the nationalist press as a British toady and criticized for the debacle surrounding elections for the sixteenth Majlis, Sa'ed's position proved unsustainable and having lost the shah's confidence he resigned from office. His replacement was Ali Mansur, a political veteran who had previously chaired the Seven Year Plan Organization. Mansur was not the British Embassy's first choice, and Shepherd advocated vigorously for an Anglophile strongman like Zia or Razmara to become prime minister. He was, however, well regarded by the royal court and widely viewed as an able dealmaker who the ambassador hoped would be able to cajole the Majlis into accepting the Supplemental Agreement within as little as two months.[37] Such bullishness reflects a naivety concerning the limited political space in which the prime minister would have to operate and the strength of opposition he faced.

Like his predecessor, Mansur's coalition was unstable, besieged by protest and held together by favours. The start of his tenure coincided with the resubmission of ballots in Tehran and with the votes finally counted, the National Front claimed eight deputies, including Mohammad Mossadegh who won the highest number of any candidate.[38] Subsequently joined by a further three deputies, the newly formed National Caucus was numerically small, a feature not of nationalism's popularity but Iranian democracy's contortions. Outside parliament, they could count on the support of newspapers, citizens' groups and merchants' guilds. Among the most high-profile National Front deputies was Ayatollah Sayyid Abul Qasim Kashani, an ultranationalist cleric who was exiled from Iran during the Second World War for his Nazi sympathies. Linked to Fada'iyan-e Islam, the group responsible for murdering Abdolhossein Hazhir, Kashani offered the largely secular movement a degree of religious legitimacy and unscored the breadth of its support. Extremely ambitious and well organized, he was also perhaps the only figure capable of challenging Mossadegh's authority.

---

[36] Proposals for Assisting the Persian Army in Countering Subversive Activities, 9 May 1950; Younger to Prime Minister, 21 June 1950; Hankey Minutes, 24 June 1950, FO 371/82314 (TNA).
[37] Shepherd to Foreign Office, 23 March 1950; Dudgeon Minutes, 27 March 1950 FO 371/82310; Shepherd to Younger, 14 April 1950, FO 371/82307; Shepherd to Foreign Office, 22 April 1950; Leavett Minutes, 27 April 1950, FO 371/82311 (TNA).
[38] Shepherd to Younger, 22 April 1950, FO 371/82311 (TNA).

Figure 4.1 Returned to the Majlis in 1950 Mossadegh was immediately invited to meet with the shah. Perhaps the only leader capable of galvanizing such a broad coalition of nationalist parties and forces, he represented a critical challenge to British power in Iran. Courtesy of Getty Images Keystone-France/Contributor.

When the Majlis reconvened, they deferred consideration of the Supplemental Agreement to an eighteen-member Majlis Oil Committee that included five National Front deputies. Although well short of a majority, Mossadegh became its chair and was able to exert an outsized influence on preceding. In deference to the National Front's obvious public support, the shah invited the veteran nationalist to meet privately with him and the prime minister, affording Mossadegh opportunity to outline his opposition to Britain's continued influence in Iran.[39]

Growing political unrest had not gone unnoticed in the United States, and the State Department repeatedly expressed doubt that the Supplemental Agreement would be ratified.[40] Surveying the country's perilous finances, the National Front's surging popularity and Britain's maladroit handling of the situation, Assistant Secretary of State George McGhee warned that without 'positive American action' Iran was at risk of falling into the Soviet sphere of influence.[41] The Korean War had hardened American convictions that Moscow

[39] Shepherd to Younger, 28 April 1950, FO 371/82311 (TNA).
[40] Foreign Office to Tehran, 6 May 1950, FO 371/82311 (TNA).
[41] Memorandum by the Assistant Secretary of State for Near Eastern, South Asian and African Affairs to the Secretary of State, 25 April 1950, RG 59 788.00/4–1950 (NARA).

would opportunistically exploit peripheral crises to further its influence. Although Mossadegh was certainly no Marxist, American officials believed that Soviet subversion could spread not only through Bolshevik parties but also more ideologically ambiguous forces, and the National Security Council warned that American vulnerabilities would be tested through 'means of subversion, sabotage and civil disorder'.[42] With tensions already inflamed, Iran increasingly looked vulnerable. On McGhee's recommendation, Anglo-American discussions concerning conditions there were arranged in London. Largely exploratory, these ended without firm commitment beyond an agreement to work together to 'raise morale' in Iran, including through financial assistance. American officials insisted that the Supplemental Agreement should be made 'more palatable' to ensure its ratification.[43]

A frank report prepared by the United States Embassy advocated for unprecedented levels of American intervention in Iran. Britain, it argued, had helped to create a sense of hopelessness among the Iranian public, which would provide fertile soil for communism. The State Department must therefore decide whether to 'write Iran off or take effective action of some kind'.[44] The embassy's analysis was endorsed by McGhee and formed the basis of extensive briefing for Secretary of State Dean Acheson.[45] Acheson was advised both that 'there is considerable justification in the Iranian demands' for a new oil agreement and that the British government needed to do more to ensure AIOC conciliation. Led by McGhee, a new diplomatic consensus was emerging at Foggy Bottom that believed London was incapable of preserving Iranian independence and must accede 'wholeheartedly' to a more collaborative policy to protect it from falling into the Soviet orbit.[46]

The man tasked with revitalizing American policy in Iran was Henry Grady, an acerbic economist who had served variously as dean of University of California, Berkeley's College of Commerce, an advisor to Secretary of Commerce Herbert Hoover, and pre-war assistant secretary of state. In 1947 he became the first American ambassador to India. Grady's personal credo married suspicion of British imperialism with an avowed faith in capitalism as the driving force of prosperity. He believed Iran suffered from 'economic colonialism' executed by the

---

[42] Document 100: Report to the National Security Council by the Executive Secretary, 1 July 1950, *FRUS, 1950, Vol. V, The Near East, Asia and Africa*.
[43] Foreign Office to Tehran, 6 May 1950, FO 371/82311 (TNA).
[44] Estimates of the Iranian Situation, 4 March 1950, RG 59 3.300 (NARA).
[45] McGhee to Acheson, 25 April 1950, RG 59 788.00/4–1950 (NARA); Document 236: Position Paper on Iran, 17 April 1950, *FRUS, 1950, Vol. V, The Near East, Asia and Africa*.
[46] Background Memorandum for Meeting Between the Secretary of State, Ambassador Douglas, and Sir Oliver Franks, 7 March 1950, RG 59 611.41/3-750 (NARA).

AIOC with Whitehall's assistance.[47] As a result, Britain had effectively 'established a dictatorial regime in Iran for the sole purpose of safeguarding its illegitimate interests' to the detriment of the country's development and wider geopolitical security.[48] Instead, Grady hoped to see Iranian market liberalized with greater participation from the American private sector, particularly former pupil Max Thornburg. Appointed ambassador in June 1948, his immediate challenge was reinvigorating the Seven Year Plan, which the American government continued to view as essential to Iranian economic development. Grady's strongly held views, and the frankness with which he delivered them, did little to assuage British concerns that their allies overstepping the mark and wading into an area in which they had limited interests or experience. Chargé d'Affaires George Middleton later recalled that 'Henry Grady was not a professional . . . he said to me on one occasion: "I was the saviour of India; I shall be the saviour of Iran."' Such claims were, Middleton euphemistically suggested, 'a little bit splendid'.[49]

Prime Minister Razmara

Grady arrived in Iran to find mounting food shortages, spiralling inflation, rising unemployment and a prime minister struggling to exert political influence.[50] Dogged by criticism in the Majlis and the press, Mansur begged for the Supplementary Agreement to be amended and hoped that its ratification would return Iran to some kind of economic normalcy. In correspondence with London, Shepherd complained that the prime minister remained non-committal as to the kind of 'political lubrication' required to assuage the Majlis and castigated his failure to manage growing discontent.[51] Mansur's inability to corral parliament had not gone unnoticed by the shah, who told Shepherd that he was 'weak vis-à-vis the National Front'. An increasingly active participant in Iranian politics, the shah questioned whether Iran needed a more forceful prime minister who was capable of bringing deputies to heel.[52] British officials were delighted by this proposition and, in correspondence with Kenneth Younger,

---

[47] Henry Grady, *Adventures in Diplomacy* (unpublished manuscript); British-American Policy in Iran, 18 March 1952, Henry Grady Papers - Box 1 (HSTL).
[48] Grady to Middleton, 30 October 1952, Henry Grady Papers - Box 3 (HSTL).
[49] George Middleton: Interview recorded by Habib Ladjevardi, 16 October 1985 (IOHC).
[50] Shepherd to Foreign Office, 2 June 1950, FO 371/82311 (TNA).
[51] Shepherd to Furlonge, 5 June 1950, FO 371/82311 (TNA).
[52] Shepherd to Younger, 12 June 1950, FO 371/82311 (TNA).

Shepherd suggested that they dispense with caution to secure a prime minister favourable to their interests.[53]

Already well known to British diplomats and the intelligence services, the obvious candidate to arrest Iran's slide into chaos was Ali Razmara. Possessing an impressive resume, military experience and wide network of contacts, they hoped that Razmara would face down criticism whether on the streets or in the Majlis and provide a counterweight to Mossadegh and the National Front.[54] Initially cool towards Razmara, the shah was now convinced that only strongman could break through Iran's parliamentary inertia.[55] Amid murmurings that nationalism could lead to republicanism, and with regicide never far from his mind, he also hoped that Razmara's military links might protect him from any future coup.[56] The AIOC's leadership in Iran was less convinced and questioned how sympathetic to their interests the general really was.[57] Reviewing the Majlis' hostile factions, officials considered whether Majlis' dissolution followed by elections that may produce more favourable political conditions. On the one hand, rather than relying on a wide-ranging alliance, the general's support was narrow with prestige derived from his military background and the shah. On the other, they feared that Razmara would demand further concessions and, like his successors, become trapped in a political and legislative quagmire. In the hope for a quick resolution, the company agreed in principle to provide additional financial support to the new prime minister provided he guaranteed 'that ratification of the Supplemental Agreement is definitely part of the government's programme'. Privately, AIOC officials hoped that the general's military authority might simply overawe 'Persian timidity'.[58]

Having once been unfairly mischaracterized by Reader Bullard as 'in the pockets of the Russians', Razmara's star was on the rise in Iranian political circles.[59] Intelligent, energetic and fiercely ambitious, Razmara was described by John Godley, one of the few Western journalists to interview him, as 'restlessly on the move all the time'.[60] A soldier since the age of fifteen, Razmara had received officer training at Saint Cyr academy in France and become Iran's

---

[53] Shepherd to Younger, 30 June 1950, FO 371/82311(TNA).
[54] Shepherd to Foreign Office, 2 June 1950; Foreign Office to Washington, 7 June 1950; Foreign Office to Washington, 27 June 1950, FO 371/82311 (TNA).
[55] Leading Personalities in Persia, 27 June 1947, IOR/R/15/6/392 (BL); Shepherd to Foreign Office, 10 June 1950; Shepherd to Younger, 12 June 1950, FO 371/82311 (TNA).
[56] Shepherd to Younger, 30 June 1950, FO 371/82311 (TNA).
[57] Northcroft to Rice, 28 June 1950, 126346 (BPA).
[58] Northcroft to Rice, 24 June 1950, 126346 (BPA).
[59] Bullard to Foreign Office, 27 October 1945, IOR/L/PS/12/559 (BL).
[60] John Godley, *Living Like a Lord* (London: Gollancz, 1955), 118.

youngest lieutenant general, then the highest military rank, and chief of staff.[61] Unlike Sayyid Zia and other British contacts, Razmara was not an Anglophile but a diplomatic rationalist who saw the Supplemental Agreement as a means of facilitating his country's economic and social development.

Attacked by his enemies as a revanchist right-winger, Razmara's politics are harder to categorize but hint towards a form of militarist social democracy.[62] Among his earliest decisions were the redistribution of some of the states' land assets and he was keen to revitalize Iran's labour movement, becoming the first Iranian prime minister to address a mass trade union meeting.[63] Recognizing the need for ballast in opposing the Tudeh, the prime minister negotiated the creation of a new confederation, the Iranian Trades Union Congress, to represent and organize anti-communist workers.[64] The new organization claimed to represent 100,000–150,000 workers under a management committee headed by Majid Mohiman and Amir Keivan, a long-time opponent of the Tudeh in Isfahan.[65] Keivan was admired by the British and commended as early as 1947 for his attempts to develop 'a really sound trade union' and coordinate anti-communist labour activists.[66] Later described in diplomatic correspondence as one of Iran's few 'genuine' trade unionists, Keivan was a regular source of information for the British Embassy and the AIOC. He also received financial support and instruction from British officials in Iran and during a visit to London.[67]

Even before Mansur's resignation, the shah had contacted Razmara to ask him to lead a new government. Reflecting on Mansur's tenure, Shepherd reported that he had 'done nothing to improve conditions in Iran' and had inadvertently solidified the opposition.[68] The ambassador hoped that Razmara would be an immediate tonic and offer clear leadership in support of the Supplemental Agreement and British interests more generally. Owing to the respect Razmara carried across Iranian society, and despite opposition from the National Front's representatives, the general's appointment was endorsed with a sizeable Majlis

---

[61] Leading Personalities in Persia, 27 June 1947, IOR/R/15/6/392 (BL).
[62] *The Iranian Nation Violently Rejects the Cossack Government*, Mardom, 10 July 1950, FO 248/1494 (TNA).
[63] Labour Attaché's Report, November 1950, FO 371/91628 (TNA).
[64] Rothnie Minutes, 8 January 1951; Labour Attaché's Report, March 1951, FO 371/91628 (TNA).
[65] *Summary of the Labor Situation in Iran* (Washington DC: United States Government Department of Labor, 1955), 7.
[66] Review of Conditions in the Isfahan Consular District, 1 July–31 December 1947, 28 February 1948, IOR/L/PS/12/3529 (BL); Labour Attaché's Report, September-October; Labour Attaché's Report, December 1950, FO 371/91628 (TNA).
[67] Gee Minutes, 16 February 1951, FO 371/91628; Rothnie Minutes, 5 October 1951, FO 371/91464; Pyman Minutes, 24 September 1951, FO 248/1514 (TNA).
[68] Shepherd to Foreign Office, 26 June 1950, FO 371/82312 (TNA).

majority, including a number of opposition deputies.[69] He promised to abide by the constitution but wasted no time in setting out a wide-ranging reform programme that included political decentralization.[70] Under his programme, swathes of economic and political decision-making powers would be devolved to local councils. This redistribution of power away from the Majlis would empower rural, conservative voices at the expense of Tehran's industrial working and intellectual middle classes.[71] Democratically questionable, Razmara's proposals were likely to be advantageous to British interests.

National Front deputies were at the forefront of opposition and attacked 'imperialists whose aim it is to tear Persia apart' for the prime minister's proposals.[72] To Mossadegh and his comrades, decentralization was redolent of the scheme Reader Bullard advocated at the height of the Azerbaijan crisis to carve Iran up and apportion its most profitable regions to foreign powers. That Iran's own supine leadership facilitated this was nothing if not a demonstration of the depths of British imperialism. In a memorable salvo, Mossadegh told an American observer that 'you do not know how crafty they are. You do not know how evil they are. You do not know how they sully everything they touch.'[73] In the Majlis, the National Front leader went on the offensive, attacking Razmara as London's stooge and telling him to 'get lost! Shut the door and don't come back.'[74] Such outbursts delighted nationalists who lionized Mossadegh for his bravery in defiantly standing up against Iran's age-old foe.

In contrast, British diplomats remained puzzled by his appeal. At best, they treated Mossadegh as a wizened eccentric whose public histrionics hinted at deficiencies of the oriental character. At worst, they saw him as a sly and deceitful 'demagogue' who trailed anarchy in his wake.[75] Shepherd, in particular, was perplexed by Mossadegh. Without basis, the ambassador suggested that he 'diffuses a slight reek of opium' and described him as 'more of an extreme nuisance than a serious and constructive statesman.'[76] Blinkered by imperialism, Shepherd singularly failed to interrogate the National Front's appeal. In a widely shared note prepared in 1951, the ambassador compared Iranian nationalists with other

[69] Shepherd to Foreign Office, 5 July 1950, FO 371/82312 (TNA).
[70] Shepherd to Foreign Office, 26 June 1950, FO 371/82312 (TNA).
[71] Lawford to Bevin, 29 June 1950, FO 371/82312; Barnett Minute, 27 October 1950, FO 371/82313 (TNA).
[72] Ibid.
[73] William Roger Louis, 'Musaddiq, Oil and the Dilemmas of British Imperialism', in *Ends of British Imperialism: The Scramble for Empire, Suez and Decolonization: Collected Essays* (London: I.B. Tauris, 2006), 732.
[74] De Bellaigue, *Patriot of Persia*, 147.
[75] Le Rougetel to Foreign Office, 18 June 1947, FO 371/62035 (TNA).
[76] Shepherd, *Never Trouble Trouble* (MEC); Shepherd to Furlonge, 6 May 1951, FO 248/1514 (TNA).

contemporary independence movements. He argued that while the latter were a legitimate evolution from colonial rule, the former were immature and driven only by emotion. Never subsumed into the British Empire, the ambassador stressed that Iran was now 'paying heavily for her immunity from tutelage'.[77] In retrospect, Shepherd's ignorance towards Mossadegh, his movement and his ideology was nothing if not a dereliction of duty. In terms ranging from the legalistic to coarse, the veteran nationalist drew on his decades of experience to explain the distinction between the National Front's movement *for* Iran and British efforts to extract *from* it. Unlike the Tudeh, Mossadegh did not deal in the language of class or transnational solidarity but rather the righteous injustice of British imperialism and Iranian exploitation. In a land blessed with near-unimaginable quantities of oil but persistent poverty, the petronationalist vision projected by the National Front was an intoxicating prospect and the Supplemental Agreement a ready fulcrum around which its supporters could rally.

Iran had not received AIOC royalty payments since July 1949 and was suffering from inflation, food shortages and a deficit growing by 16 per cent each year. Against these dire economic circumstances, Razmara remained convinced that the Supplemental Agreement needed to become law. However, he also understood this was not possible without fresh concessions to win over unsupportive deputies.[78] With Grady's support, the prime minister requested three specific amendments. First, that the AIOC make a cash advance based on production since July 1949; second, that the company open its books to Iranian auditors; and third, that the company accelerate the pace of Iranianization and the technical training of Iranian staff.[79] Despite such specific demands, the AIOC remained obstinately opposed to fresh negotiations. At the company's Finsbury Circus headquarters, the Supplemental Agreement was viewed solely as a commercial agreement, which, having agreed to its terms, the Iranian government was legally bound to honour. Following discussions with their British counterparts, the State Department expressed concern that the company believed the challenge they faced was 'primarily one of raising morale'.[80] In July,

---

[77] Shepherd to Franks, 2 October 1951, FO 371/91464 (TNA).
[78] Walker to Young, 6 May 1950, FO 371/82341; Shepherd to Foreign Office, 27 July 1950, FO 371/82332B (TNA); Iranian Balance of Payments and Foreign Exchange Position, 8 August 1950, RG 59 3.213; George McGhee Memorandum for the Secretary of State, 25 April 1950, RG 59 788.00/4–1950 (NARA).
[79] The Ambassador in Iran to the Secretary of State, 13 July 1950, 888.2553–AIOC/7–1350 (NARA).
[80] Document 530: The United States Delegation at the London Tripartite Foreign Ministers Meeting to the Acting Secretary of State, 16 May 1950, *Foreign Relations of the United States: Diplomatic Papers, 1950, Western Europe Vol. III* (Washington DC: United States Government Printing Office, 1978); Foreign Office to Tehran, 6 May 1950, FO 371/82311 (TNA).

Second Secretary at the American Embassy Joseph Wagner circulated 'The Peculiar Position of the British in Iran', which accused the AIOC of 'act(ing) as a law unto itself' in Iran and 'disregarding' broader Western security interests there. Rather than restraining the company's activity, the report intimated Whitehall's complicity and suggested that they should exert greater pressure to engineer a change in AIOC policy.[81] Secretary of State Dean Acheson, an ally of Bevin and confidant of Ambassador Oliver Franks, struggled to understand British policy in Iran, which appeared to him to be an uncharacteristic blind spot.[82] Without the British Embassy's participation, Grady facilitated discussions between the AIOC, Iranian government, Max Thornburg and the shah on Iran's internal political stability and the Supplemental Agreement. Inconclusive, these talks indicated the distance between Whitehall, the oil company and its closest ally. Grady reported that 'the British look on this matter purely as an oil question, whereas Iranians have come to regard it as political issue'.[83]

In a highly revealing private letter, AIOC director Basil Jackson was unequivocal in his criticism of successive Iranian governments, which should, he believed, take responsibility for the situation they had created. Bemoaning Britain's imperial decline, the director suggested that gunfire would have once provided an easy solution, but 'we have no Indian Brigade or cruiser as our ace in the hole'.[84] Despite Jackson's reticence, the company could not resist growing pressure from Washington and Whitehall and returned to talks with Razmara's three amendments as the basis for discussion. However, while the prime minister's demands appeared clear, AIOC negotiators reported that they were 'rather puzzled' by additional piecemeal requests made by Razmara, including the construction of new cement plants and discounted oil and natural gas.[85] Dismissed as evidence of the Iranian government's continued lack of clarity, the prime minister's appeals reflect his determination to eke out any kind of concession, no matter how small, to sell the agreement to the Majlis. Razmara's uncertainty that a deal could be achieved was reflected in increasingly scattergun communications. In July he suggested that new elections may be required before an agreement could be passed, but little more than a month later claimed that the agreement would be submitted to the Majlis by 11 September.[86] Just three

---

[81] The Peculiar Position of the British in Iran, 29 July 1950, RG 59 641.88/7-2950 (NARA).
[82] The Secretary of State to American Embassy, London, 14 July 1950, RG 59 888.2553/7-1450 (NARA).
[83] Grady to the Secretary of State, 13 July 1950, RG 59 888.2553–AIOC/7–1350 (NARA).
[84] Jackson to Wylie, 16 August 1950, 87230 (BPA).
[85] Razm Ara's Policy: Supplemental Agreement, undated, 72364 (BPA).
[86] Grady to the Secretary of State, 13 July 1950, RG 59 888.2553–AIOC/7–1350 (NARA); Telegram to Fraser, 17 August 1950, 72364 (BPA).

days short of this self-imposed deadline, the prime minister indicated that a deal was not possible without the AIOC 'conceding substantial alterations'.[87]

With royalties unforthcoming, Shepherd warned the Foreign Office that Razmara was likely to request an advance against future payments.[88] In concurrence with the Treasury, Foreign Office officials identified Iran's weak financial position as point of leverage and Shepherd was explicitly told to 'take the opportunity' to point out that the Supplemental Agreement and associated Anglo-American support were a ready-made solution to their financial difficulties.[89] The challenge, Shepherd conceded, was that the Supplemental Agreement's passage was 'no longer purely commercial or financial' but inherently political and involved the fate of Iran's 'most promising government' in years. Considering the strength of opposition to the agreement, the ambassador warned that nationalists increasingly called not for an amended concession but its outright cancellation.[90]

Although Bevin criticized the Iranian government's tendency for the 'bazaar method of negotiating' he accepted that the terms agreed in 1949 were no longer viable and feared the effect that corporate obstinance would have on relations with the United States.[91] In a message to Franks, the foreign secretary warned that if Anglo-American cooperation broke down the Iranian government would inevitably 'try to play us one against the other'.[92] The British Embassy in Washington prepared a report concerning their divergence, which acknowledged that the State Department believed that 'no real progress [could] be made in the economic rehabilitation until this [ratification] is accomplished'. It was important, therefore, that the British government insist on the kind of conciliatory amendments that would ensure Supplemental Agreement's passage through the Majlis.[93]

Demonstrating a flicker of his dimming creativity, the foreign secretary proposed a tentative package of joint Anglo-American assistance until the Supplemental Agreement was agreed.[94] Following talks between McGhee and Foreign Office and Treasury officials, the British government developed plans

---

[87] Telegram to Pyman, 8 September 1950, 72364 (BPA).
[88] Shepherd to Foreign Office, 6 September 1950; Shepherd to Foreign Office, 7 September 1950, FO 371/82342; Shepherd to Foreign Office, 9 September 1950, FO 371/82334 (TNA).
[89] Foreign Office to Tehran, 29 August 1950; Foreign Office to Tehran, 7 September 1950, FO 371/82342; Treasury Minutes, 28 August 1950, FO 371/82342 (TNA).
[90] Shepherd to Foreign Office, 10 September 1950, FO 371/82342 (TNA).
[91] Furlonge to Young, 18 September 1950 FO 371/82342 (TNA).
[92] Bevin to Franks, 12 August 1950, FO 800/489 (TNA).
[93] Burrows to Barclay, 12 September 1950, FO 371/82343 (TNA).
[94] Douglas to the Secretary of State, 10 August 1950, RG 59 888.2553–AIOC/8–1250 (NARA).

for exceptional measures to support the Iranian economy and relieve security concerns. These included the establishment of a credit facility through the American Point Four programme and temporary sterling convertibility to 'promote the execution of the Seven Year Plan' by enabling Iran to service future dollar debts.[95] Having previously suggested that looser convertibility would undermine investments across the Middle East, these concessions represented significant movement from Whitehall.[96] However, although they might provide some respite for the beleaguered Iranian economy, Bevin's proposals remained temporary, technocratic fixes. As Grady noted, any cash the Iranian government received would merely balance their immediate budget and further lines of credit, including from Britain, were required to stimulate economic growth.[97] The proposed changes also did nothing to counter the fundamental logic of Iranian nationalism or advance the Supplemental Agreement's progress through the Majlis.[98] However well-intentioned, piecemeal adjustments would not reconcile the AIOC's blunt refusal to countenance significant reform of their oil concession.[99] In discussions with the Foreign Office, Basil Jackson quashed the suggestion that the AIOC could offer Razmara advance royalty payments, suggesting that the company was 'not a bank' and therefore 'could not lend money'. A similarly unyielding assessment was made of the Iranian request for greater corporate transparency. The company, Jackson argued, could not 'have their books audited by Persians, since this would give infinite opportunities for troublemaking'. He also rejected further steps towards Iranianization on the grounds that up to 'ninety-seven percent' of the AIOC was 'already Iranianised', ignoring the dearth of opportunities for Iranian workers at senior technical or managerial grades.[100]

In a further round of Anglo-American discussions held at the United Nations, Acheson complained that sterling convertibility needed to go further and was a vital step in opening lines of credit between Iran and the United States.[101] Despite Bevin's hopes that this could be achieved, the Treasury was reluctant to loosen currency controls and guaranteed sterling's convertibility

---

[95] Ashe to Ramsbotham, 7 October 1950; Logan to Ashe, 14 October 1950, FO 371/82341; Foreign Office Minutes, 19 September 1950, FO 371/82342 (TNA); Record of Informal United States-United Kingdom Discussions, 21 September 1950, RG 59 780.00/9–1850 (NARA).
[96] Pyman Minutes, 15 September 1948, FO 371/68731 (TNA).
[97] Document 285: Grady to the Secretary of State, 31 October 1950, *FRUS, 1950, Vol. V, The Near East, Asia and Africa*.
[98] Razm Ara's Policy: Supplemental Agreement, undated, 72364 (BPA).
[99] Furlonge to Young, 18 September 1950, FO 371/82342 (TNA).
[100] Foreign Office Minutes, 14 September 1950, FO 371/82342 (TNA).
[101] Jebb to Foreign Office, 29 September 1950, FO 371/82342; Fry to Foreign Office, 2 October 1950; Franks to Foreign Office, 11 October 1950, FO 371/82343 (TNA).

for just twelve months.[102] To Acheson and his colleagues the stalemate in Iran was unfathomable, a 'nonsense' that ignored the growing risk of 'serious trouble' whether expressed through Iranian nationalism or Soviet expansionism.[103] The AIOC, however, remained unmoved by geopolitical arguments and continued to believe that having reached an agreement in principle it was now incumbent on the Iranian government to honour it. Once again, they suggested that the Iranian government's advocacy for the agreement had been insufficient and that Razmara needed to show 'greater determination' in promoting it to sceptical deputies.[104] If this could not be achieved, the company queried whether the agreement could become law without parliamentary ratification and questions were again asked as to the viability of dispensing with democracy in favour of a dictatorship.[105]

Since coming to office Razmara had found the AIOC to be an unmoving negotiating partner from whom he had won little. Deeply frustrated and desperate to overcome his country's economic travails, the prime minister ignored American suggestions that an unreformed Supplemental Agreement was 'political suicide' and reluctantly agreed to support it before parliament.[106] In an attempt to claw back some kind of credibility, he asked the company to make five minor amendments: that Iranian royalties would never fall below the level received by neighbouring Iraq; that Iran would be able to exercise greater control over export levels; the free supply of gas produced during oil extraction; the receipt of 'oil equal in quantity to that used by the company itself in Persia'; and the company's Iranianization 'except for certain chiefs of departments, and other high posts, and necessary experts and technicians'.[107] Scrabbling for a victory to hold up before parliament, the company accepted the prime minister's proposals but acknowledged that they would 'bring relatively trivial benefits' and were unlikely to stand up parliamentary scrutiny.[108] In lieu of advanced royalty payments, Bevin also offered Iran an emergency £3 million loan. Fearful that

---

[102] Makins to Prime Minister, 25 September 1950, FO 800/489; Fry Minutes, 28 September 1950, FO 371/82342 (TNA); Douglas to the Secretary of State, 24 October 1950, RG 59 888.10/10-2450 (NARA).
[103] Ibid.; Rountree Memorandum, 20 December 1950, RG 59 611.41/12-2050; Security of Middle East and Iran, 18 September 1950, RG 59 611.41/9-1850; Summary of Conclusions, US-UK Politico-Military Conversations, 26 October 1950, RG 59 611.41/10-2650 (NARA).
[104] Telegram to Pyman, 25 October 1950; Telegram to Pyman, 13 November 1950, 72364; Rice to Northcroft, 24 November 1950, 126378 (BPA).
[105] Telegram to Pyman, 5 October 1950, 72364 (BPA); Pyman Minutes, 7 November 1950, FO 248/1509 (TNA).
[106] Document 36: Paper Prepared in the Department of State, September 1950, *FRUS, 1950, Vol. V, The Near East, Asia and Africa*; Shepherd to Foreign Office, 2 October 1950, FO 371/82343 (TNA).
[107] Ibid.
[108] Foreign Office to Tehran, 27 October 1950, FO 371/82343 (TNA).

this would be seen by nationalist opponents as example of British coercion, the Iranian government chose not to make the offer public.[109] Meanwhile, to silence accusations that he was acting on London's behalf, Razmara hastily concluded a trade agreement with the Soviet Union and banned foreign broadcasts, including from the BBC, on Radio Tehran. Rather than a sign of genuine dissent, the prime minister was creating a smokescreen as he prepared to take the Supplemental Agreement before the Majlis.[110]

Negotiations and nationalism

Protracted discussions concerning the Supplemental Agreement coincided with a new round of fiscal tightening in the UK and fresh signs that the Attlee government was flagging. In February's general election, Labour's majority fell to just five, leaving the party in a state former chancellor Hugh Dalton described as 'in office without authority or power'.[111] Physically and mentally exhausted, Cripps retired from politics and was replaced as chancellor by Hugh Gaitskell, a young, ambitious modernizer. Gaitskell's inheritance included worsening inflation, an end to the TUC-agreed two-year wage freeze, managing Britain's entry into the European Payments Union and justifying, to an agitated party, the introduction of limited health service charges even as defence spending rose. At Labour's Annual Conference in Margate, Bevin rose to defend British foreign policy and welfare imperialism. In a speech framed around international security and the Soviet menace, the foreign secretary referred not only Britain's 'great interests' in the Middle East but also its 'great works'. He argued that without the latter the region would remain poor and underdeveloped, and without the former 'you could not maintain your standard of life; you could not maintain your power; you could not maintain your position'. Above all else, Bevin insisted that British policy in the Middle East must safeguard 'the maintenance of the *status quo*'.[112] Although the union block vote, defiantly loyal to Attlee and particularly deferential Bevin, protected the leadership on the conference floor, member-led resistance was growing and almost 900,000 votes were cast in opposition to the

---

[109] Furlonge Minutes, 21 October 1950; Shepherd to Bevin, 24 November 1950, FO 371/82343 (TNA).
[110] Elm, *Oil, Power, and Principle*, 70; Document 287: The Secretary of State to the Embassy in Iran, 20 November 1950, *FRUS, 1950, Vol. V, The Near East, Asia and Africa*.
[111] Henry Pelling, *The Labour Governments, 1945-51* (London: Palgrave Macmillan, 1984), 230.
[112] *Labour Party: Report of the 49th Annual Conference* (London: The Labour Party, 1950), 147.

party's foreign policy.[113] Having clearly failed, this was the last hurrah for Bevin's welfare imperialism.

In the Foreign Office, officials hoped that accepting Razmara's proposed changes would 'clinch matters' and secure the Supplemental Agreement's ratification.[114] This proved, once again, to be wildly optimistic. In the Majlis Oil Committee, Mossadegh and his National Front colleagues spent little time studying the proposed agreement before demanding it be thrown out. The committee's other members also recognized its limitations but suggested that further negotiations take place. On 25 November, the committee reached a unanimous decision and passed a resolution stating that the agreement did not safeguard the nation's interests and should be rejected.[115] In response to such clear opposition, Razmara promised to dissolve the committee and to defend the agreement. However, he also told Shepherd that further modifications may be needed to secure ratification.[116]

If the Majlis Oil Committee's findings diminished the Supplemental Agreement's chances of ratification, wider changes in the Middle Eastern oil industry ended them completely. Like Iran, Saudi Arabia had faced economic uncertainties with falling demand for oil in 1949 matched by growing financial commitments. On the advice of former Venezuelan minister for development, Juan Pablo Pérez Alfonzo, the Saudi government requested the renegotiation of Aramco's oil concession and the introduction of the 'Venezuelan principle': the sharing of net profits on a fifty-fifty basis. In contrast to the long and still inconclusive negotiations that typified the Supplemental Agreement, the Saudi-Aramco deal was concluded within little over a month with a new agreement signed on 30 December and backdated to the beginning of 1950.[117] In November, Acheson contacted Bevin via Oliver Franks concerning the fast-moving agreement and warned him that new arrangements would 'make the position of AIOC in relation to financial terms of the proposed agreement far more difficult'.[118] The Saudi-Aramco deal demonstrated that oil concessions needed not only to provide wealth in exchange for extraction rights but also

---

[113] Ibid., 150.
[114] Foreign Office to Tehran, 5 October 1950, FO 371/82343 (TNA).
[115] Shepherd to Bevin, 10 December 1950, FO 371/82309 (TNA).
[116] Pyman Minutes, 29 November 1950; Pyman Minutes, 2 December 1950, FO 248/1509; Shepherd to Bevin, 4 December 1950, FO 371/82313 (TNA).
[117] Policy Statement Prepared in the Department of State, 5 February 1951, RG 59 611.86A/2-551 (NARA); Albion Ross, 'SAUDI ARABIA GETS HALF U. S. OIL PROFIT; Ibn Saud and Aramco Agree to 50-50 Sharing Plan from Jan. 1, 1950', *The New York Times*, 3 January 1951.
[118] The Secretary of State to the British Secretary of State for Foreign Affairs, 20 November 1950, RG 59 888.00/10-2550 (NARA); Franks to Foreign Office, 30 November 1950, FO 371/82343 (TNA).

a sense of partnership between domestic governments and foreign firms. The AIOC tended towards blunt imperialism, executing its will and exploiting Iran's vast oil wealth with little consideration as to the conditions of the country on which it relied. In the context of 'fifty-fifty' their approach was outmoded and unsustainable. The new arrangement caught AIOC officials off guard and surprised Razmara who bemoaned poor Anglo-American coordination.[119] Recognizing the quandary the Aramco deal created, Shepherd urged the Foreign Office to request that its finalization was delayed. Incapable of influencing either Aramco or the American government, his pleas were rejected.[120]

Despite the Majlis Oil Committee's decision to recommend the Supplemental Agreement's rejection, Finance Minister Gholam Hossein Forouhar made an impassioned plea for ratification before the Majlis but was the only minister to do so. Razmara, meanwhile, collected just forty-five signatures for a bill authorizing continued negotiations with the AIOC, thirty short of the number needed. Humiliated, the prime minister told Shepherd that 'his only reasonable course of action was to advise the shah to dissolve parliament'.[121] Mocked, threatened and accused of treachery by his Majlis colleagues, Forouhar withdrew the bill and, when the Saudi-Aramco deal became public, ignominiously resigned.[122] Having defeated Razmara's deal the nationalists went on the offensive. The question was no longer whether the Supplemental Agreement could be reformed but whether Iran's oil industry could be liberated from foreign interference altogether.[123] Taking to the streets, Mossadegh addressed a crowd of over 12,000, telling his supporters that only nationalization could resolve growing social foment.[124] Religious leaders and campaign groups issued supportive press releases and a wave of anti-British fly sheets, newspapers and pamphlets were distributed through Tehran. In grave tones, Shepherd reported that a 'feeling of tension' had fallen over the country and warned that the British government and AIOC were under constant attack.[125] As the National Front's support grew, the ambassador

---

[119] Untitled Memorandum, 17 January 1951, 129296; Northcroft to AIOC London, 2 December 1950, 72364 (BPA).
[120] Elm, *Oil, Power, and Principle*, 73.
[121] Shepherd to Foreign Office, 26 December 1950; Shepherd to Foreign Office, 27 December 1950 FO 371/82377 (TNA).
[122] Razm Ara's Policy: Supplemental Agreement, 72364; Summary of Speech by Minister of Finance in Majlis, 26 December 1950,126349 (BPA); Katayoun Shafiee, *Machineries of Oil: An Infrastructural History of BP in Iran*. Infrastructures Series (Cambridge, MA: The MIT Press, 2018), 166.
[123] Northcroft to Rice, 16 December 1950; Untitled, 3 January 1951, 126349 (BPA).
[124] Abrahamian, *Iran Between Two Revolutions*, 265.
[125] Shepherd to Foreign Office, 21 December 1950, FO 371/82377 (TNA); *Summary of Information No. 42,* February 1951, 129255 (BPA); A. L. Richards to the Secretary of State, 22 December 1950, RG 59 888.2553/2-2250 (NARA).

accused the nationalists of having 'successfully cowed any opposition by appealing to patriotic sentiment with threats of violence if necessary'.[126] Emboldened by burgeoning public support, nationalist deputies submitted a resolution that demanded the 'assertion of national sovereignty over the oil industry'.[127]

On Capitol Hill the move towards fifty-fifty was accepted as irresistible. In contrast to their allies, the State Department believed that more equitable arrangements would help to keep strategically important countries inside the West's sphere of influence, calm nascent nationalism and contribute to economic development. In advice for McGhee, Treasury officials suggested that the Aramco deal offered a 'new basis for stability' in the Middle East and should be replicated by the AIOC to improve conditions in Iran.[128] In this context, British intractability was a source of continued frustration. Even as the Saudi-Aramco deal was finalized, British diplomatic staff mused over piecemeal sweeteners such as corporate donations to the University of Tehran or additional payments to the Iranian government.[129] Facing mounting public and parliamentary opposition, Razmara gave these overtures a cool reception.[130] Exhausted by a recent trip to the United Nations in New York, the ailing Bevin was able to do little but warn Shepherd against 'appearing to dictate to these tiresome and headstrong people'.[131] With correspondence from other ministers going unanswered, Kenneth Younger recorded that the foreign secretary 'simply hasn't the stamina for taking difficult decisions'.[132] The leadership vacuum was exacerbated by William Fraser and Assistant Under-Secretary of State Michael Wright's decision to take vacations in January 1951, which Grady bemoaned as 'typical of the manner in which this vital question has been handled by the Foreign Office and the top officials of the AIOC'.[133]

Privately Shepherd acknowledged that a new 'imaginative solution' was required and recommended that his government press the AIOC for substantive changes to the Supplemental Agreement.[134] Fraught interdepartmental meetings

---

[126] Monthly Report for February 1951, 25 March 1951, FO 371/91449 (TNA).
[127] Abrahamian, *Iran Between Two Revolutions*, 265.
[128] Paul C. Parke to George McGhee, 27 December 1950, RG 59 888.2553 (NARA).
[129] Foreign Office Minute, 24 October 1950, FO 371/82376; Shepherd to Bevin, 24 November 19503; Aid to Persia, 5 December 1950, FO 371/82343 (TNA).
[130] Shepherd to Bevin, 24 November 1950, FO 371/82343 (TNA).
[131] Bevin to Shepherd, 15 December 1950, FO 371/82343; Bevin Minutes, 19 January 1951, FO 371/91522 (TNA).
[132] Younger and Warner, *In the Midst of Events*, 54; Noel-Baker to Bevin, 15 November 1950; Noel-Baker to Younger, 22 February 1951, FO 371/91628 (TNA).
[133] Grady to the Secretary of State, 3 January 1951, RG 59 888.2553 (NARA).
[134] Shepherd to Foreign Office, 31 December 1950; Shepherd to Foreign Office, 10 January 1951, FO 371/91521 (TNA).

between the Foreign Office, Treasury and Ministry of Fuel and Power took place to identify the means by which a fifty-fifty arrangement might be made palatable to the AIOC. In response to company criticism that profit sharing was 'unsatisfactory in practice' owing to the challenge of disaggregating profits from Iranian operations and all others, Eric Berthoud, a former AIOC executive, suggested that the oil company divide itself into two entities, one to manage Iranian oil and one to manage all other interests. While the latter would maintain its independence, the former would enter into an agreement with the Iranian government along similar lines to those established in Saudi Arabia by Aramco and include representatives of the Iranian government on its board of directors.[135] A potentially elegant solution, the AIOC agreed to analyse Berthoud's suggestion and consider the feasibility of a fifty-fifty arrangement if offered by the Iranians.[136] Razmara, however, was in no position to make such an offer. Riding the wave of opposition, Mossadegh used a Majlis Oil Committee meeting on 19 February to again demand oil industry's nationalization, stating without equivocation that the 'moral aspect of oil nationalisation is more important than its economic aspect'.[137]

To a generation of oil men, civil servants and politicians stewed in the culture of empire, Britain's quandary was unfathomable. For Mossadegh and the movement he led, the issue at stake was Iranian sovereignty and their country's ability to control its own destiny. Although the union flag did not fly above Tehran and no governor general was in post, the depths of London's influence was undeniable. In Britain, the National Front's fundamental argument was either misunderstood or entirely ignored. Before the House of Commons, Foreign Office Minister Ernest Davies insisted that the 'fair and reasonable' Supplemental Agreement remained under review and refused to be drawn on possible amendments.[138] Riddled with disease, Bevin was largely absent from proceedings and described by colleagues as a 'a pretty pathetic old wreck'.[139] Despite his protests, Attlee had no choice but to forcibly retire his closest ally,

---

[135] Record of Interdepartmental Meeting Between the Treasury, Foreign Office and Ministry of Fuel and Power, 13 January 1951, FO 371/91522 (TNA); Untitled Memorandum, 17 January 1951, 129296 (BPA); Grady to Secretary of State, 19 March 1951, RG 59 888/2553/3-1851 (NARA); Mary Ann Heiss, *Empire and Nationhood: The United States, Great Britain, and Iranian Oil, 1950-1954* (New York: Columbia University Press, 1997), 47.
[136] Payments to Iranian Government in 1951: Appendix A, 24 January 1951, 129298 (BPA).
[137] Pyman Minutes, 29 January 1951, FO 248/1514 (TNA); Katouzian, *Musaddiq and the Struggle for Power in Iran*, 92.
[138] *Hansard*, HC Debate, Vol. 848 Col. 1261-2, 21 February 1951.
[139] Younger and Warner, *In the Midst of Events*, 68; Grady to the Secretary of State, 3 January 1951, RG 59 888.2553 (NARA).

appointing him Lord Privy Seal on 9 March. Barely a month later Bevin died of a heart attack.

Despite accusation of collusion with the oil company, Razmara remained implacably opposed to nationalization on the grounds of practicality. Appearing before the Majlis Oil Committee, the prime minister warned that Iran lacked the technical expertise to run the oil industry and did not have access to the tankers needed to export oil even if it could be extracted and refined.[140] Unperturbed by the moral argument advanced by Mossadegh in the Majlis and protestors on the streets, Razmara warned that further delays to a settlement with the AIOC would lead to economic ruin.[141] Mossadegh once again went on the offensive, dismissing Razmara as a stooge and a liar. On 7 March, the prime minister was shot three times while visiting a Tehran mosque. His assassin, Khalil Tahmasebi, was a member of the Fada'iyan-e Islam terrorist group, which reportedly had links not only to Ayatollah Kashani but Mossadegh himself.[142] When informed that Razmara had been murdered the National Front leader merely remarked that 'he shouldn't have made that speech' and returned to his work.[143] Just days after the assassination, a crowd of 15,000 people gathered outside the Majlis not to mourn the prime minister but to demand Iran's liberation from British imperialism.[144]

Uncertain as to who should replace Razmara, the shah canvassed Shepherd for his views. The ambassador and Foreign Office had a shared preference for another strongman and suggested that long-time British favourite Sayyid Zia was the most suitable candidate.[145] He urged the monarch to be proactive and warned that the National Front would try to fill any political vacuum.[146] The State Department was opposed to Zia's appointment and warned that a prime minister too closely associated with London would do little to ease political tensions.[147] The shah initially looked to Khalil Fahimi, a minister in Razmara's cabinet, but he failed to win the Majlis' approval. Subsequently he appointed Hossein Ala, this time refusing to ask for a parliamentary vote of inclination.[148]

---

[140] Gifford to Secretary of State, 3 March 1951, RG 59 888.2553/3-351 (NARA).
[141] Tehran to Foreign Office, 4 March 1951, FO 371/91523 (TNA).
[142] Berry Memorandum for Secretary of State Acheson, 14 March 1951, RG 59 788.00/3-1451 (NARA); Shepherd to Foreign Office, 7 March 1951, FO 248/1514; Shepherd to Morrison, 12 March 1951, FO 371/91453; Pyman Minutes, 19 March 1951, FO 248/1514; Middleton to Furlonge, 1 November 1951, FO 371/91464 (TNA).
[143] De Bellaigue, *Patriot of Persia*, 151.
[144] Shepherd to Foreign Office, 10 March 1951, FO 248/1514 (TNA).
[145] Foreign Office to Tehran, 8 March 1951; Shepherd to Foreign Office, 9 March 1951; Embassy Minutes, 16 March 1951, FO 248/1514 (TNA).
[146] Shepherd to Bowker 12 March 1951, FO 248/1514.
[147] The Secretary of State to the American Embassy, Cairo, 28 March 1951, RG 59 788.00/3-2851 (NARA).
[148] Shepherd to Morrison, 20 March 1951, FO 371/91454 (TNA).

Although educated at Westminster School, Ala was no Anglophile but rather a devout patriot and ardent monarchist. Admired by Shepherd for his intellect, he was nevertheless seen as stopgap prime minister.[149] In discussions with American officials, Ala outlined his intention to remain in post 'only until the situation becomes more stable' and indicated a desire to dampen rising unrest.[150] The new prime minister understood the nationalist movement's strength and militancy and felt that he was in no position to oppose it outright. When, under pressure from the National Front, the Majlis Oil Committee agreed to endorse the nationalization, Ala responded by requesting a study into practicalities of implementation.[151] Described by Shepherd as potentially illegal, the exploration of nationalization's mechanics marked a further step in the decline of British power in Iran.

Fallout

Deeply frustrated by the situation in Iran, the British government grew increasingly belligerence under Bevin's replacement, Herbert Morrison. A model Tammany Hall politician, Morrison was previously secretary of the London Labour Party before becoming mayor of Hackney, minister for transport under Ramsay MacDonald and, in 1934, head of London County Council, at the time Labour's most powerful elected politician. A wartime minister and architect of the party's post-war nationalization programme, he was an impressive bureaucrat but one whose vanity, ambition and tendency towards backroom machinations won him as many enemies as friends. It was rumoured that he eyed the foreign secretary position not because of any great interest in international affairs but because it would otherwise go to Aneurin Bevan, his great rival from the Labour left.[152] Described by Younger as 'a little Englander who suspects everyone who is foreign', Morrison was seen in the United States as lacking any real convictions concerning policy overseas.[153] Indeed, the State Department labelled him a 'second-stringer' who lacked his predecessor's drive

---

[149] Shepherd to Foreign Office, 27 March 1951, FO 248/1514 (TNA).
[150] Berry Memorandum for Secretary of State Acheson, 14 March 1951, RG 59 788.00/3-1451 (NARA).
[151] Discussions Between His Majesty's Ambassador and Mr Ala on Current Affairs and Future Policy, 2 April 1951, FO 371/91455 (TNA).
[152] George Brown, *In My Way: The Political Memoirs of Lord George-Brown* (London: Gollancz, 1971), 246.
[153] Younger and Warner, *In the Midst of Events*, 69.

and creativity.¹⁵⁴ Not naturally disposed to cautious diplomacy, Younger reported that Morrison 'hankered after strong-arm methods', a tendency that did little to address American concerns.¹⁵⁵

Assessing conditions in Iran, the American government identified two immediate risks. First, that nationalization would lead to economic ruin and second, that Britain would respond in a dangerous fashion. Both presented significant potential for Soviet intrigue.¹⁵⁶ Seeking resolution, George McGhee was sent to Tehran and London for negotiations as part of a wider diplomatic tour.¹⁵⁷ His reports were uniformly negative, casting aspersions on an anachronistic company that had been 'too rigid and slow to recognize that a new situation had been created' and a government that was 'derelict' in its duties towards an economically and strategically important nation.¹⁵⁸ McGhee found Morrison to be particularly obstinate. The foreign secretary haughtily suggested that Britain's 'long experience of the Middle East' gave them a deeper insight than the United States and insisted that oil would continue to flow regardless of the Iranian government's decision.¹⁵⁹ Similarly intractable, William Fraser suggested that McGhee's analysis relied on 'wrong information' and failed to understand the AIOC's Iranian operation.¹⁶⁰ Following McGhee's visit, the American government questioned whether a settlement predicated on the Supplemental Agreement was possible and indicated that wholesale renegotiation was likely required.¹⁶¹ Oliver Franks liaised closely with the State Department to develop a common strategy and suggested an operation to undermine and divide the National Front. Believing Mossadegh to be a pragmatist at heart, the ambassador pondered whether he could be detached from the nationalist movement's more extreme and potentially violent elements.

---

[154] Holmes to the Secretary of State, 25 August 1951, RG 59 396.1–NE/8–2551 (NARA).
[155] Younger and Warner, *In the Midst of Events*, 75.
[156] Acheson to American Embassy London, 16 May 1951, RG 59 888.2553/5-1651; An Estimation of Soviet Intentions Toward Iran, 25 May 1951, RG 59 888.2553/5-2551 (NARA); Memorandum of Conversation, 17 April 1951, Dean Acheson Papers - Box 77 (HSTL).
[157] Classified Supplement to Annual Petroleum report, 5 March 1951, RG 59 888/2553/3-1551; Memorandum of Informal United States–United Kingdom Discussions, 2 April 1951, RG 59 788.00/4-1051 (NARA).
[158] George Crews McGhee, *Envoy to the Middle World: Adventures in Diplomacy* (New York: Harper & Row, 1983), 325–6; Crocker to the Department of State, 29 March 1951, RG 59 887.2553/3-2951 (NARA).
[159] Foreign Office to Franks, 3 April 1951, FO 371/91184 (TNA).
[160] McGhee, *Envoy to the Middle World*, 333.
[161] American Embassy, London to Acheson, 13 April 1951, Dean Acheson Papers - Box 77 (HSTL); Relations with the United Kingdom, April 1951, RG 59 888.2553/4-151; McGhee to Secretary of State Acheson, 20 April 1951, RG 59 888.2553/4-1051 (NARA); Document 28: Draft Minutes of Discussions at the State–Joint Chiefs of Staff Meeting, 2 May 1951, *Foreign Relations of the United States: Diplomatic Papers, 1951, The Near East, and Africa* Vol. V (Washington DC: United States Government Printing Office, 1982).

However, having tested this suggestions with Secretary of State Acheson, Franks reported that there was little enthusiasm for a scheme that so nakedly meddled in Iranian democracy.[162] While the British government expressed willingness to consider new amendments, they refused to consider anything that may undermine the AIOC's monopoly.[163]

While transatlantic discussions took place, political conditions in Iran deteriorated further. Public demonstrations in support of the oil industry's nationalization were common throughout March and April and included not only Mossadegh's followers but also more radical elements. Islamist extremists and members of Fada'iyan-e Islam, for example, descended on the Majlis and called on 'all true Muslims' to rise up in opposition to foreign interference in Iran.[164] The Tudeh, meanwhile, rallied their front organizations to demand that Iran's oil be brought under popular control.[165] They subsequently issued a statement proclaiming that 'the oil company requires cheap workmen to fill its tankers with our blood and oil and send them all over the world thus filling the pockets of the British capitalists'. Reconstituted to fight British imperialism, the Tudeh-aligned Central United Council of the Trade Union of Workers and Toilers of Iran released a statement that implored Iran's workers to 'fight in favour of peace and against imperialism'.[166] In Tehran, violence between rival groups was now a regular occurrence.[167]

In the oil fields opposition to British misrule and material deprivation converged as ad hoc strikes broke out. Long concerned by rising production costs, the AIOC's management had recently announced a programme for rationalization, which included cuts to workers' already meagre allowances.[168] Described by Shepherd as 'legitimate but unluckily-timed', the changes were the trigger for a wave of unrest.[169] Despite a declaration of martial law on 27 March, flying pickets took to bicycles to encourage their colleagues to down tools. Using underground newspapers and pamphlets, the Tudeh attacked

---

[162] Memorandum of Conversation between Dean Acheson, Paul Nitze, and Oliver Franks, 27 April 1951, Dean Acheson Papers - Box 68 (HSTL); Discussion of the Iranian Situation with the British Ambassador, 27 April 1951, RG 59 788.00 (NARA).
[163] Ibid.
[164] 'Teheran Police Halt Demonstration: Threat to Persian Premier', *The Times of India*, 21 April 1951.
[165] Monthly Report for February 1951, 25 March 1951, FO 371/91449 (TNA).
[166] List of the Proclamations and Pamphlets Published During the Recent Strike and Disturbances in Abadan, undated, 68908 (BPA).
[167] 'Students Clash in Teheran: 12 INJURED AFTER DEMONSTRATION', *The Times of India*, 23 April 1951; Shepherd to Foreign Office, 28 April 1951, FO 248/1514 (TNA).
[168] Ladjevardi, *Labor Unions and Autocracy in Iran*, 188-9; Berry Memorandum, 3 April 1951, RG 59 788.00/4-351 (NARA); Elkington Visit to Iran, 17 January-25 February 1949, 9968; Elkington's Visit to Iran, 14 October 1949-18 February 1950, 67900 (BPA).
[169] Monthly Report for March 1951, 15 April 1951, FO 416/104 (TNA).

British imperialism and promised that 'the will of the nation' would prevail in the face of oppression.[170] Rhetorically intoxicating, the stridently nationalist tone found an audience among the AIOC's demoralized workers.[171] Misreading the situation, Shepherd complained about attempts to 'turn the strike into a political demonstration in favour of nationalisation'.[172] In fact, workplace and national issues were intertwined and impossible to separate. At the root of both was visceral anger towards foreign exploitation. Although the company blamed 'intimidating tactics and aggressive picketing' for shutting down their operations, the number of workers involved illustrated a depth of support that would be difficult to achieve through coercion alone. According to American estimates, up to 15,000 workers, including both permanent and contracted staff, had downed tools.[173] Meanwhile, the AIOC itself acknowledged that more than 85 per cent of workers in the Agha Jari oilfield had left their posts.[174] The British government's own figures put the number at closer to 95 per cent.[175] As a result of industrial unrest, the Abadan refinery was able to run at less than a quarter of its normal capacity.[176] Amid growing concern that the strikes could threaten British assets, three warships were despatched to the Persian Gulf and plans were hastily drawn up for a limited occupation if required.[177]

Although slow to muster, Iranian security forces were violently effective once mobilized. On 12 April, Iranian soldiers faced down a crowd of protesting apprentices, opening fire killing six Iranians and three British AIOC employees.[178] The bloody scenes were followed by outcry and an uneasy truce as peaceful demonstrations were allowed to take place. Although conservative newspapers blamed poor legislation and troublemakers, the strikes were welcomed elsewhere as an act of resistance to British imperialism and the AIOC widely blamed for provoking them. *Shahed*, a National Front title, suggested that the company was responding by arming militias and rehashing plans to

---

[170] 'The Iranian Nation Violently Rejects the Cossack Government', *Mardom*, 10 July 1950, FO 248/1494 (TNA).
[171] 'Concerning the Liberal Bourgeois Movement', *Razm*, 26 June 1950, FO 248/1494; 'Statement by the Central Committee of the Tudeh Party of Persia', 4 February 1951; 'Dr Mossadegh's Government', *Mardom*, 5 May 1951, FO 248/1516 (TNA).
[172] Shepherd to Morrison, 15 April 1951, FO 371/91452; Furlonge to Burrows, 25 April 1951, FO 371/91456 (TNA).
[173] Transmittal of Report on Strike in AIOC, Iran, 10 April 1951, RG 59 888.2553/4-1051; Berry to Acheson, 3 April 1959, RG 59 788.00/4-351 (NARA).
[174] Strike Report – All Fields Areas, 25 May 1951, 68908 (BPA).
[175] Khorramshahr to Foreign Office, 12 April 1951, FO 371/91628 (TNA).
[176] Document 17: Memorandum by the Chief of the Near East and Africa Division, Directorate of Plans, Central Intelligence Agency (Roosevelt), 23 April 1951, *FRUS, 1952-1954, Iran - 2018*.
[177] Abrahamian, *The Coup*, 67.
[178] Strike Report – All Fields Areas, 25 May 1951, 68908 (BPA); Furlonge to Burrows, 25 April 1951, FO 371/91456 (TNA); Ladjevardi, *Labor Unions and Autocracy in Iran*, 189.

divide Iran into autonomous spheres of influence with the Soviet Union. Long discussed in diplomatic circles, such rumours touched on deeply held Iranian concerns.[179] For American officials in Iran, the debacle was further evidence of the 'ineptitude of British labor relations', which could inadvertently offer the Soviet Union a foothold at Abadan.[180] Despite being home to a small number of communists, American Embassy reports warned that the country was in 'an embryonic revolutionary state' with the number of individuals willing to participate in Tudeh-instigated activity likely to rise in parallel with deteriorating quality of life and unmet socio-economic expectations.[181] Offering less nuanced analysis, Ambassador Shepherd acknowledged his bafflement at the situation and meekly complained that Iranian politics was 'so topsy-turvy'.[182]

On 28 April 1951, the Majlis Oil Committee submitted a nine-point resolution to the Majlis for the AIOC's nationalization and constitutionally powerless to block its ratification or continue negotiations, Ala resigned. Although Shepherd hoped to 'inject some common sense into the atmosphere' and rally support for a pro-British candidate, the momentum was firmly with the National Front.[183] Under pressure from the Majlis and the public, the shah was forced to ask Mohammad Mossadegh to become prime minister, an appointment deputies subsequently ratified by a margin of seventy-nine to twenty-one.[184] As a precondition for his acceptance, Mossadegh demanded that parliament ratify the outstanding resolution on the oil question. Despite a final round of sabre rattling, the British were powerless to intervene, and on 1 May 1951 the Anglo-Iranian Oil Company's Iranian assets were nationalized.

Reflecting on the events that led to this decision, it is clear that 1950 and 1951 were disastrous years for British policy in Iran. Having dispensed with any pretence of welfare imperialism they struggled to find an alternative strategy: intelligence operations, protracted oil negotiations and support for an increasingly unpopular prime minister had all failed. While the American government urged their allies to adopt a new, malleable approach this had not manifested and British hard-headedness prevailed. Even as the National Front gained strength in the Majlis and on the street, the Anglo-Iranian Oil Company

[179] Tehran Press Summaries, April to May 1951, 66105 (BPA).
[180] The Station in Iran to the Central Intelligence Agency, 12 October 1951, Harry S. Truman Papers: President's Secretary's Files - Box 180 (HSTL).
[181] Document 1: Despatch From the Embassy in Iran to the Department of State, 23 February 1951, FRUS, 1952-1954, Iran.
[182] Shepherd to Morrison, 29 April 1951, FO 371/91457 (TNA).
[183] Ibid.; Shepherd to Morrison, 27 April 1951, FO 416/104 (TNA).
[184] Cabinet Conclusions, 30 April 1951, CAB 128/19 (TNA).

and Shepherd and his colleagues remained mulishly resistant to strategic change. By the spring of 1951 there is little to indicate that the British truly understood the challenge they faced or how to respond.

Reflecting on the situation and London's hard-headed policy, Secretary of State Dean Acheson suggested that 'never had so few lost so much so stupidly and so fast'. In the State Department, nationalization was the unwelcome conclusion to Britain's unwillingness to acknowledge its imperial decline.[185] The Attlee government, after almost six arduous years in office, now faced challenging questions concerning Britain's response. Fundamentally they still appeared not to comprehend the opposition they faced or the basic tenets of Iranian nationalism. Far from being an emotional spasm or default of the Iranian character, this was a multifaceted, organized political movement backed from growing public support. On the day Mossadegh came to office, Shepherd 'lost no time' in telling the shah that his government had no confidence in the new prime minister.[186] For the first time since 1941 Britain would be forced to negotiate with a government that was not merely ambivalent to their interests but actively opposed to them.

---

[185] Robert L. Beisner, *Dean Acheson: A Life in the Cold War* (New York: Oxford University Press, 2009), 544.
[186] Shepherd to Foreign Office, 28 April 1951, FO 248/1514 (TNA).

5

British responses and British failures

The Iranian oil industry's nationalization posed a significant challenge to Britain's economic and strategic interests. The Anglo-Iranian Oil Company was a major overseas investment, a revenue-generating asset and a producer of the oil-based products needed to fuel the post-war recovery. Losing such a significant undertaking was highly embarrassing for the Labour government, raising questions as to the realities of Britain's international status. Facing the nationalist challenge, the Attlee government was deeply divided on how to react with ministers advocating variously for military intervention, a negotiated settlement and covert operations to remove Mossadegh from power. Unable to reach a resolution before leaving office, the crisis in Iran was inherited by the Conservative Party under Winston Churchill.

Against this backdrop the limits of British power in Iran became obvious, as too did the United States' ascendance as the primary guarantor of Western influence there. Despite the plots against him, Mohammad Mossadegh remained prime minister and the nationalist movement he led was largely unburnished by harsh economic conditions. However, beneath the surface, his coalition of support was increasingly fractious as rivals tussled for influence and British agents did their best to sow disorder.

Understanding Mossadegh

Britain's diplomatic establishment was shocked by the speed with which their monopoly over Iran's oil had crumbled and eyed the new government with deep suspicion. Reporting to London, Ambassador Shepherd described Mossadegh as 'cunning and slippery and completely unscrupulous', the very manifestation of the oriental character's most dubious elements.[1] The National Front, meanwhile, was described as held together only by 'bitter anti-foreign feeling' and spurious 'accusations of colonialism'. Far from being a legitimate or developed ideology, the ambassador saw Iranian nationalism as a collective emotional spasm.[2] In the House of Commons, the foreign secretary acknowledged that it was 'natural and right that the Persian people should now take a greater share in the operation of their main industry' but refused to countenance the unilateral termination of contractual obligations.[3] His statement was followed by a formal request from the AIOC for arbitration, which the Iranian government ignored. Rejecting the 1933 concession as illegitimate, Mossadegh contended that the mandate to decide the oil industry's fate rested solely in Iranian legislators and by extension the Iranian people. Instead, Iran's Ambassador to London Ali Soheily contacted Morrison to express his government's desire for friendship with the British and suggest that with the AIOC nationalized 'the causes of dissatisfaction' between the two countries 'will disappear'.[4] If the Iranians were to negotiate, it was going to be on their own terms.

Labour immediately came under fire from the Conservatives, who depicted the Attlee government as a threat to Britain's remaining overseas assets and Cold War security. Opposition leader Winston Churchill was particularly disparaging of prime minister 'mussy duck', dismissing him as a cartoonish crank that the British should simply swat away.[5] Shadow minister Harold MacMillan explicitly linked Mossadegh's demands with Labour's interventionist approach to the domestic economy and asked whether 'anyone can be surprised if these methods find their imitators abroad?'[6] Asked to respond to these charges, Denis Healey, secretary of Labour's International Department, proposed that while Iran had the right to 'acquire undertakings in its territory' the terms of the 1933 concession explicitly forbade any changes in the commercial arrangement 'even by government legislation' without the AIOC's permission.[7] Distilled into the pamphlet for the party's Talking Points series, Labour claimed that the Iranian government had acted illegally and strong measures were justified in

---

[1] Shepherd to Furlonge, 7 May 1951, FO 248/1514 (TNA).
[2] Ibid.
[3] *Hansard*, HC Debate, Vol. 487 Col. 1011–12, 1 May 1951.
[4] Document 13: Message from the Persian Prime Minister, 8 May 1951, *Correspondence between His Majesty's Government in the United Kingdom and the Persian Government, and Related Documents Concerning the Oil Industry in Persia, February 1951 to September 1951* (London: HM Stationery Office, 1951), FO 371/91615 (TNA).
[5] Steve Marsh, *Anglo-American Relations and Cold War Oil: Crisis in Iran* (New York: Palgrave Macmillan, 2003), 84.
[6] Labour Party Talking Points – Oil in Persia, 9 June 1951, Pamphlet Collection – Box 80.
[7] Ibid.

response. As a first step, they made an application to open proceedings at the International Court of Justice on the basis that the 1933 concession agreement could not be unilaterally amended or annulled.[8]

Like the Conservatives, the British press was unforgiving in their depictions of Mossadegh. *The Times* reported on the prime minister's tendency for the theatrical, treating his idiosyncratic attire – such as pyjamas worn under a camel hair coat – with something between pursed lipped curiosity and outright derision.[9] The media's focus on Mossadegh as a caricature illustrated a challenge that had long affected British policy makers. They had simply failed, perhaps even refused, to interrogate and understand either Mossadegh or the movement he led. The prime minister fundamentally believed that nationalization was a matter of justice and that a foreign company should not be able to deprive Iran of its wealth, returning a pittance that corrupt client politicians inevitable squandered. In an unintentionally pithy summary of the problem, *The Spectator* magazine suggested: 'it is always easier to laugh than to understand, and Dr. Moussadek's fainting-fits, his tears and his iron bedstead in the Mejlis are as intrinsically laughable as, say, Mr. Gandhi's loin-cloth and goat.'[10]

With characteristic flourish, Healey used briefing notes for Labour MPs and ministers to suggest that the crisis 'like an oil-fire itself, has illuminated in a garish hue all the problems and dangers of this key spot in the Cold War'. Defending welfare imperialism, he suggested that problems in Iran were primarily the result of 'political ignorance' and a population that required further education before they could capably manage their own economic and industrial affairs. In contrast to the nationalization of British industry, which Labour designed to elevate living standards and improve productivity, successfully running Iran's oil industry as a national undertaking was simply impossible. Without the technical skills required to operate the industry effectively, or markets in which to sell their products, the Iranian government's endeavour would inevitably lead to economic ruin and opportunities for communism to prosper.[11]

As Mossadegh pressed ahead, diplomats across the Middle East reported their fears that he could inspire other anti-imperialist movements and threaten the entire British world system. Writing in January 1951, British Ambassador to Iraq Henry Mack reported that the local nationalist movement tended

---

[8] Foreign Office to Shepherd, 26 May 1951, FO 371/91536 (TNA).
[9] 'Danger in Persia', 16 May 1951; 'Dr Moussadek's Warning on Oil Dispute', 25 May 1951; 'Dr Moussadek's Collapse', *The Times*, 13 May 1951.
[10] Edward Hodgkin, 'Moussadekism', *The Spectator*, 12 October 1951.
[11] Persian Oil, undated, Labour International Department – Box 134 (LHA).

towards a feeling of 'resentment because they feel that the West does not take them seriously'.[12] His successor John Troutbeck agreed and identified sympathy to Mossadegh's brand of populism as a growing challenge.[13] Similar concerns were raised by British officials in Afghanistan, where the country's political class was reported to fear an 'extremist like Musaddiq', Syria, Turkey, and Lebanon.[14] Following a fact-finding trip through the region, Deputy Under-Secretary of State Roger Makins reported that 'nationalist feeling is not far below the surface' across the Middle East with 'symptoms of strong nationalist and anti-foreign prejudice' particularly prevalent in Iraq and Saudi Arabia.[15] By late summer, even Egypt, home to the Suez Canal and significant numbers of British troops, appeared vulnerable following volatile demonstrations against 'imperialist firms' and 'outright intimidation' on the streets.[16] National Front deputy Hossein Makki did little to calm Whitehall's fears when he used a visit to Egypt to promise that his government would 'help all Middle East countries to break the bonds of imperialism'.[17]

Before the Iranian people, Mossadegh presented himself as a potential martyr who was willing to sacrifice himself in defence of the national interest. 'My life is in danger!' he cried from the Majlis floor, 'the Anglo-Iranian Oil Company is determined to destroy me. I can no longer take the risk of going to my home or my office.'[18] In conspiratorial tones, nationalist newspapers questioned whether 'an ambassador of one of the great powers' may have threatened the prime minister's life and demanded that the police do more to protect him. From the left, the Tudeh press offered support for nationalization and called it Iran's 'sovereign right'. Meanwhile, the nationalist *Atesh* newspaper castigated the 'base hirelings' allegedly hired by the company to discredit the National Front.[19] Responding to the government's enormous public support and rumours that they were meddling in political affairs, AIOC officials could only bemoan the 'Persian genius' for misinterpretation and conjecture.[20]

---

[12] Mack to Bevin, 24 January 1951, FO 487/5 (TNA).
[13] Troutbeck to Foreign Office, 28 May 1951, FO 371/91459; Iraq Annual Review for 1951, 28 January 1952, FO 481/6 (TNA).
[14] Gardener to Eden, 16 October 1951, FO 402/27; Lebanon Annual Review for 1951, 19 February 1952, FO 484/6; Samuel to Eden, 19 June 1952, FO 501/6; Middleton to Ross, FO 248/1531, 4 August 1952 (TNA).
[15] Makins to Eden, 20 March 1952, FO 464/6 (TNA).
[16] Morrison to Attlee, 10 October 1951, FO 800/636; Stevenson to Morrison, 13 October 1951; Cumberbatch to the Board of Trade, 14 November 1951, FO 407/203 (TNA).
[17] Middleton to Foreign Office, 1 November 1951, FO 371/91464 (TNA).
[18] Norman Kemp, *Abadan: A First-Hand Account of the Persian Oil Crisis* (London: Wingate, 1953), 97.
[19] Tehran Press Summaries, April–May 1951, undated, 66105 (BPA).
[20] Seddon to Rice, 2 July 1951; Seddon to Northcroft, 16 July 1951, 72363 (BPA).

Figure 5.1 Demonstrators hold aloft a sign torn from the AIOC's offices in Tehran, July 1951. Courtesy of Getty Images Bettmann/Contributor.

Figure 5.2 Mossadegh addresses supporters outside the Majlis, October 1951.

Plans to commandeer the oil industry developed at pace. As per the Nationalization Law, a committee, dominated by National Front members, was appointed to oversee nationalization. The Iranian government considered the AIOC's local operation to have been dissolved, and the prime minister's office distributed notice that any reference to the firm should include the prefix 'former'.[21] A successor organization, the National Iranian Oil Company (NIOC),

---

[21] Kemp, *Abadan*, 98; Grady to Secretary of State, 24 July 1951, RG 59 888.2553/7-2451 (NARA).

was established to manage the production, refinement and distribution of oil products. Local workers were told that they were expected to continue as normal, and foreign employees were promised the 'respect and affection' of their Iranian counterparts and the nation as a whole if they remained in post.[22]

British and Commonwealth staff found themselves in an unenviable position and the vast majority refused to cooperate with the new Iranian management. The AIOC's leadership recognized the grave situation their employees faced and warned the Iranian government that operations would cease without them.[23] Following reports of seditious activity by British workers, a bill was introduced that promised penalties up to and including death for anyone found to be 'engaging treacherously or with ill intent in activities in connection with the operation of the Persian national oil industry'.[24] Having refused to cooperate, the Iranian government accused AIOC general manager Eric Drake of sabotage and allegedly threatened his life.[25] In response he was hurriedly removed from Abadan and flown back to Britain via Basra.

Following the Iranian government's insistence that tanker captains sign documents acknowledging NIOC's ownership of the oil they carried, AIOC subsidiary, the British Tanker Company (BTC) suspended exports from Abadan. The decision to withdraw BTC cargo vessels left the Mossadegh government unable to export Iranian oil or its by-products. As the AIOC's maritime arm, BTC had one of the world's largest commercial fleets operating almost a third of the world tankers: over 150 vessels including the *British Adventure*, the world's first 'super tanker', with a capacity of over 18,000 gross registered tonnage. In contrast, the Iranian government had access to no tankers at all.[26] With storage capacity limited, a tanker shortage would see oil production grind to a halt. Additional British economic measures, including the freezing of Iranian assets worth £25 million, withdrawal of Iran's right to exchange sterling and export restrictions, compounded Tehran's misery. The World Bank reported that the policy would 'eliminate the imports of luxuries', but even staples such as tea and sugar became scarce as did essential manufactured goods like steel.[27]

---

[22] Proclamation by the Temporary Board of Directors of the National Oil Company, 25 June 1951, 72363 (BPA).
[23] Notes of an Interview Between HE Varasteh, Minister of Finance and Mr NR Seddon, 23 June 1951, 72363 (BPA).
[24] *Hansard*, HC Debate, Vol. 489 Col. 1185–6, 26 June 1951.
[25] Ibid.
[26] Shafiee, *Machineries of Oil*, 193.
[27] Mary Ann Heiss, 'The International Boycott of Iranian Oil and the Anti-Mosaddeq Coup of 1953', in *Mohammad Mosaddeq and the 1953 Coup in Iran*, ed. Mark J. Gasiorowski and Malcolm Byrne (Syracuse: Syracuse University Press, 2017), 180; Nationalization of the Iranian Oil Industry: An Outline of its Origins and Issues, 19 February 1952, 75976 (World Bank Group Archives – WBGA).

Anglo-American hegemony over the oil industry ensured the tanker boycott's effectiveness. Far from seeing the AIOC's woes as an opportunity for expansion, firms on both sides of the Atlantic condemned nationalization outright. In discussions with the State Department, American oil executives were unequivocal: if Iran were allowed to prosper from unilateral nationalization it would create a dangerous precedent, which had the potential to undermine the entirety of American overseas investment and even 'the concept of the sanctity of contractual relations'.[28] In turn, Western oil companies refused to handle Iranian oil, and the governments of the United States, Germany, Holland and a number of other countries banned their citizens from taking up technical roles with the NIOC. These measures immediately undermined the Mossadegh's government's ability to enjoy the fruits of nationalization and left them with a valuable commodity they were unable to sell.

With British citizens still in Iran, Whitehall officials were conscious that sanctions should not bite too hard. However, until an alternative proactive policy could be developed, economic retaliation was one of the only response available. In Cabinet, Hugh Gaitskell urged restraint and wondered whether sanctions could tip Iran into destitution and, eventually, communism.[29] Labour's International Department warned that without 'the fat revenue from oil sales' the Iranian state and army were liable to fall apart with unpredictable consequences.[30] In reality, British economic measures did nothing to dislodge Mossadegh or significantly dent his support. Starved of foreign currency, the Iranian government undertook drastic measures including public bond issues, import limitations and industrial redeployment. Having failed to dislodge the prime minister with sanctions, the British government considered three sometimes interlinked strategies to safeguard their interests in Iran. First was military action, ostensibly to defend citizens and property. Second, in tandem with the United States, were diplomatic negotiations in the hope of reaching a new agreement between the Iranian government and the AIOC. Finally, and ultimately most importantly, was covert action to remove Mossadegh from power.

---

[28] Memorandum of Conversation with Assistant Secretary of State George C. McGhee and Representatives of United States Oil Companies, 10 October 1951, Dean Acheson Papers, Box 69 (HSTL).
[29] Cabinet Minutes, 10 May 1951, CAB 195/9 (TNA).
[30] Failure of a Mission, undated, Labour International Department – Box 134 (LHA).

A splutter of musketry

In an autobiography published just three years after leaving office, Clement Attlee suggested that the British government faced intransigent opponents led by a 'fanatical nationalist' and as a result preparation for armed intervention – 'in the event of danger to our nationals' – was an unfortunate necessity. The former prime minister added, however, that his government had decided that bringing the Iranians to heel through military force was 'out of the question'.[31] The reality was more complicated and while Attlee himself was implacable in his opposition to any invasion, colleagues like Manny Shinwell and Herbert Morrison were staunch advocates of a military response. On the Foreign Office's request, the limited invasion and occupation of Iran was originally explored by the Chiefs of Staff before the AIOC's nationalization in March 1951.[32] The scenarios they envisaged included a limited naval-led response without forces entering Iranian territory; a ground campaign to safeguard British assets and citizens at Abadan; and the military defence of Abadan *and* Iran's southern oil fields. Of these scenarios, the government agreed that the use of military forces beyond Abadan was too dangerous and posed a threat to wider geostrategic objectives. Not only would it test Anglo-American relations, undermine Britain's image across the region and offer the Soviet Union a pretext to occupy northern Iran, but it was also likely to enrage the AIOC's Iranian workers.

Any military action was fraught with difficulty, particularly given Britain lacked adequately trained forces in the Middle East or the means to transport them.[33] The Chiefs of Staff investigated aquatic, aerial and ground invasions of Iran to protect British interests at Abadan, yet none proved immediately satisfactory. Even if British troops were able to land they would likely be met with organized resistance from the four infantry battalions, two marine battalions and squadron of thirteen American-made Sherman tanks based at Abadan.[34] Sceptical of the Iranian army's discipline and training, the chiefs nevertheless warned that such an arsenal presented a 'serious hazard', which was exacerbated by the presence of 2,500 British workers and their 1,500 family members.[35]

---

[31] Attlee, *As It Happened*, 175.
[32] Ian Speller, 'A Splutter of Musketry? The British Military Response to the Anglo-Iranian Oil Dispute, 1951', *Contemporary British History* 17, no. 1 (March 2003), 47–52.
[33] Chiefs of Staff Committee Minutes, 23 May 1951, DEFE 4/43 (TNA); James Cable, *Intervention at Abadan: Plan Buccaneer* (London: Palgrave Macmillan, 1991), 46.
[34] Speller, 'A Splutter of Musketry?'.
[35] Chiefs of Staff Committee Minutes, 23 May 1951, DEFE 4/43; Note: Possible Military Action in Persia, 31 May 1951, DEFE 5/31 (TNA).

Should the requisite resources become available, an invasion of Abadan would take upwards of seven weeks to launch, far from the rapid intervention Shinwell and Morrison had hoped for. In a memorandum, the Chiefs of Staff stated that Britain would need to commission new amphibious vehicles, recall reservists to ensure a force of at least 10,000 men, assemble seventeen personnel and thirty storage ships between Great Britain and the Middle East and charter an unknown number of civilian aircraft.[36] Middle East Command warned that an invasion should be a last resort, making clear that an airlift into Iran required patient build-up and could not be executed without significant planning.[37] Even organizing pre-invasion propaganda was a challenge thanks to a shortage of printers capable of typesetting Farsi in His Majesty's Stationery Office.[38]

Despite these myriad issues, Defence Minister Manny Shinwell remained adamant that an invasion should go ahead. 'We must', Shinwell argued, 'in no circumstances throw up the sponge', suggesting that to do so would be taken as a sign of weakness in other Middle Eastern countries, particularly Egypt.[39] Shinwell believed that events in Iran could precipitate the kind of domino effect that may see the Suez Canal and other British assets nationalization, further necessitating the importance of decisive action. Morrison was also supportive emphasizing the Abadan refinery's strategic and economic value.[40] In contrast, President of the Board of Trade Hartley Shawcross minced few words in warning the Cabinet that Britain would be left with 'not a leg to stand on' before the International Court if they came to be seen as an aggressor. Despite Morrison's insistence that deference to law and international opinion 'can be overdone', Attlee demurred and urged caution in any policy that may damage Anglo-American cooperation.[41] The prime minister's concerns were well founded. Even before Mossadegh had come to power, the State Department warned that Britain may make the 'extremely dangerous' decision to respond to the AIOC's nationalization with force and singled Morrison out as a likely advocate of aggression.[42] Acheson believed that military action against Mossadegh was 'sheer madness' and American diplomats indicated that heavy-handed British action would offer the Soviet Union an easy

---

[36] Chiefs of Staff Memorandum, 29 June 1951, CAB 129/46 (TNA).
[37] Commanders in Chief, Middle East to Chiefs of Staff, 1 June 1951, FO 371/91459 (TNA).
[38] Rothnie Minutes, 31 May 1951, FO 371/91459 (TNA).
[39] Chiefs of Staff Committee Minutes, 23 May 1951, DEFE 4/43 (TNA).
[40] Morrison Memorandum, 20 July 1951, CAB 129/46 (TNA).
[41] Cabinet Minutes, 10 May 1951, CAB 195/9; Attlee to Morrison, 4 July 1951, FO 800/653 (TNA).
[42] Document 12: Memorandum From the Deputy Assistant Secretary of State for Near Eastern, South Asian, and African Affairs (Berry) to Secretary of State Acheson, 3 April 1951; Document 16: Memorandum From the Assistant Director of the Office of National Estimates (Langer) to Director of Central Intelligence Smith, 20 April 1951 FRUS, 1952–1954, Iran - 2018.

propaganda victory.⁴³ Although willing to support steps that prevented Iran from exporting oil and accept London's claims that a contract had been broken, the American position was clearly communicated as being wholly in favour of a negotiated outcome.⁴⁴

Despite the clarity of American reservations, Morrison insisted that tentative British military planning continue. By July, the British Chiefs of Staff had advised that an invasion to secure the Abadan refinery (codenamed Operation Buccaneer) could be made operationally viable by the transfer of three battalions to Shaiba airbase in Iraq.⁴⁵ Privately, Deputy Director General of the Security Service Guy Liddell recorded his hope that the movement of forces alone may be sufficient to 'bring the Persians to reason'.⁴⁶ In tandem, the Foreign Office completed a wide-ranging survey of the possible implications of action to protect British lives and continue operations at Abadan, including in the circumstances that crude oil needed to be imported from fields in Kuwait. To Morrison and its other advocates, Buccaneer would demonstrate Britain's resolution to resist 'eviction' from Iran and illustrate, in the Middle East and beyond, that their overseas interests 'could not be recklessly molested with impunity'.⁴⁷ These theoretical benefits, however, were matched by obvious risks. An invasion, no matter how limited, had the potential to galvanize Mossadegh's support, strengthen his position and undermine the AIOC's domestic labour force. It might also stoke opposition to British imperialism across the Middle East and enflame a region that may be susceptible to Soviet influence.

With limited resources and mounting opposition, the foreign secretary's investigation was an exercise in diplomatic procrastination rather than serious intent. In discussions with American Ambassador to London Walter Gifford, Morrison expressed 'quite frankly' his disappointment with the lack of support Britain had received in Iran but won little sympathy.⁴⁸ Among the Labour MPs – Cabinet members and backbenchers alike – there was widespread condemnation of pursuing a policy that seemed recklessly at odds with the Charter of the United Nations and liable to fan the flames of war.⁴⁹ Refusing to give any further

---

[43] Document 27: Memorandum for the Record, 16 May 1951; Document 29: Villard to Nitze, 24 May 1951, *FRUS, 1952–1954, Iran - 2018*.
[44] Furlonge Minutes, 3 May 1951, FO 371/91533; Franks to Foreign Office, 26 May 1951; Franks to Foreign Office, 28 May 1951, FO 371/91537 (TNA).
[45] Morrison Memorandum, 20 July 1951, CAB 129/46 (TNA).
[46] Liddell Diary Entry, 5 July 1951, KV 4/473 (TNA).
[47] Morrison Memorandum, 20 July 1951, CAB 129/46 (TNA).
[48] Document 31: The Ambassador in the United Kingdom (Gifford) to the Department of State, 26 June 1951, *FRUS, 1952–1954, Iran - Vol. X*.
[49] *Hansard*, HC Debate, Vol. 489 Col. 746–833, 21 June 1951; Cabinet Conclusions, 23 July 1951, CAB 128/20 (TNA).

consideration to an independent military response, Attlee lost patience with his rumbunctious foreign secretary, privately telling Hugh Dalton, 'I am handling Persia.'[50] Later criticized by Churchill for having 'scuttled and run from Abadan when a splutter of musketry would have ended the matter', Morrison's preferred course was ruled out as dangerous, divisive and likely illegal.[51]

Returning to negotiations

In contrast to Morrison's sabre rattling, the Anglo-Iranian Oil Company was keen to reach a mediated settlement that would ensure that oil kept flowing. Having previously resisted offering more favourable concession terms, AIOC officials privately acknowledged that 'any settlement would involve some form of "nationalisation"', the extent of which would determine the compensation received.[52] To calm nerves at home, a series of press briefings and radio broadcast were developed. Describing itself as 'one of the great romances of our age' the company championed its role in educating and training Iranian staff and wringing value from an otherwise backwards, inhospitable land.[53] Corporate publicity materials referred to Iran as 'very backwards' and a 'land of marked contrasts' between rich and poor. In such conditions it was little surprise that a foreign company had become a convenient 'scapegoat' for myriad of socio-economic ills.[54] In Iran, BBC Persian Service transmissions were 'doubled and tripled' to raise morale among the AIOC's beleaguered British workers and to warn Iranians that should the oil industry shut down the economy would grind to a halt.[55] Meanwhile, the company and Tehran Embassy's public relations networks pumped out a similar message to friendly newspapers.[56]

Having reviewed the situation and its potential impact on international security and American oil interests, Assistant Secretary of State George McGhee used talks with Oliver Franks to express his belief that the British must reach

---

[50] Diary Entry, 16 September 1951, Hugh Dalton Diaries – Box 1/42 (London School of Economics Archives – LSE).
[51] Memorandum of Conversation at Dinner at British Embassy, 6 January 1952, RG 59 611.41/1-1452 (NARA).
[52] Hopwood to Butler, 5 June 1951, 121825 (BPA).
[53] Persian Oil, undated, 9233 (BPA).
[54] The Persian Oil Dispute, undated, 9233 (BPA).
[55] Annabelle Sreberny and Massoumeh Torfeh, 'The BBC World Service – From Wartime Propaganda to Public Diplomacy: The Case of Iran', in *Diasporas and Diplomacy Cosmopolitan Contact Zones at the BBC World Service (1932-2012)*, ed. Marie Gillespie and Alban Webb (London: Routledge, 2013), 129.
[56] Stephen Dorril, *Mi6: Fifty Years of Special Operations* (London: Fourth Estate, 2001), 564.

a solution that acknowledged 'some flavour or facade of nationalisation' while maintaining a controlling interest in the development and distribution of Iranian oil.[57] To do so would, he hoped, quell public unrest while protecting the sanctity of contracts. It would also provide a model that could be used should nationalist unrest threaten American interests elsewhere in the Middle East.[58] Still implacably opposed to the manner with which their assets had been expropriated and despite Shepherd's opposition, the British government saw McGhee's proposal for nationalization in principle as worthy of further investigation.[59] Following discussions with the Ministry of Fuel and Power, the AIOC tentatively accepted the assistant secretary's suggested approach but insisted that compensation be paid for any assets lost through such an arrangement. Furthermore, cognizant of the effect any settlement could have on other oil companies operating overseas, the AIOC demanded that any benefits accrued through discussions 'should be clearly attributed not to the fact that "nationalisation" has taken place but to the other provisions of the settlement'.[60]

The McGhee formulation formed the basis of the AIOC's negotiating position when a delegation led by Basil Jackson arrived in Tehran for discussions on 14 June 1951. Having accepted the principle of nationalization, if not the practice, the company appeared willing to substantively move beyond the Supplemental Agreement's terms for the first time. However, discussions were immediately sidetracked by the Iranian delegation, which demanded that the company should agree to pay them 'the total proceeds, less expenses, from sales of Iranian oil as from 20th March 1951'. From this sum, a quarter would be ringfenced and used to settle any claims successfully made by the AIOC.[61] Shocked by the demand, Jackson warned the prime minister that his obstinacy would render a deal impossible. In response, Mossadegh suggested it was 'tragic' that an issue as tawdry as money was preventing the creation of a new, mutually agreeable policy between Tehran and London.[62]

---

[57] Document 13: Rountree Memorandum, 18 April 1951, *FRUS, 1952-1954, Iran – Vol. X*; Franks to Foreign Office, 18 April 1951, FO 371/91471; Franks to Foreign Office, 12 May 1951, FO 371/91533; Shepherd to Foreign Office, 14 May 1951; Franks to Foreign Office, 25 May 1951, FO 371/91537; Franks to Foreign Office, 26 May 1951, FO 371/91537 (TNA).

[58] Document 138: Memorandum of Conversation, 30 October 1951, *FRUS, 1950, Vol. V, The Near East and Africa*.

[59] Foreign Office to Washington, 14 May 1951, FO 371/91533; Foreign Office to Washington, 26 May 1951, FO 371/91537 (TNA); Ervand Abrahamian, *Oil Crisis in Iran: From Nationalism to Coup D'etat* (Cambridge: Cambridge University Press, 2021), 13–14.

[60] Hopwood to Butler, 5 June 1951, 121825 (BPA).

[61] The Company's Interest in Iran, 2 July 1951, 9233 (BPA).

[62] Notes on interviews between Mossadeq and BR Jackson, 13 June 1951, 72363 (BPA).

Following discussions on purely technical matters, Jackson made a counteroffer to the Iranian government, which included a £10 million advance against future payments and a further monthly payment of £3 million while discussions were proceeding. He also proposed establishing a new Persian National Oil Company (PNOC) with oversight over Iranian oil assets. The AIOC would subsequently create a new subsidiary with an Iranian directorship that would operate the refinery and export of PNOC oil.[63] Although a major advance on previous British offers and a demonstration of their commitment to nationalization in principle, Iranian delegates reviewed the offer for just thirty minutes before rejecting it on the basis of non-compliance with the Nationalization Law. Viewed only in legal and commercial terms, the suggestion that nationalization may be a façade misunderstood the Iran government's commitment to control over *their* assets.

Well aware of growing Cold War tensions, Mossadegh put further pressure on the British by warning that if they could not reach an agreement with his government Iran would be 'unable to reject' an olive branch from the Soviet Union.[64] Iranian negotiators also refused the AIOC's request that the British government offer negotiating support on the basis it would constitute interference by a foreign power in purely domestic affair. In the words of one Iranian official 'the era of capitulation was over'.[65] Alarmed by Mossadegh's hints towards Moscow, the American government scrambled to intervene but was unable to prevent discussions from collapsing. On 21 June, AIOC delegates departed for London. In a message to shareholders issued after their return, the company blamed the Iranian government's 'unrealistic and precipitate procedure' for the failed negotiations but gave little indication of their next move.[66]

Coinciding with the failed talks, the International Court's interim ruling found that all oil operations should provisionally proceed as normal until the court decided whether it had jurisdiction over the case, a decision immediately, and unsuccessfully, appealed by the Iranian government. To break the impasse, President Truman proposed that Averell Harriman travel to Iran and broker a *modus vivendi* between the two parties.[67] Harriman would not act as a negotiator per se but rather seek to identify whether 'some common denominator might not be found' that would enable the British and Iranians to return to the negotiating

---

[63] AIOC Tehran to AIOC London, 19 June 1951; Jackson Aide Memoir, 19 June 1951, 129295 (BPA).
[64] Notes on interviews between Mossadeq and BR Jackson, 13 June 1951, 72363 (BPA).
[65] Minutes of Meeting Held in the Office of Government Supervisory Organisation, 25 June 1951, 72363 (BPA).
[66] The Company's Interest in Iran, 2 July 1951, 9233 (BPA).
[67] Acheson to American Embassy, London, 4 July 1951, RG 59 888.2553/7-451 (NARA); Message to the Prime Minister of Iran Following the Breakdown of Oil Discussions with Great Britain, 8 July 1951, Public Papers of the President of the United States - 1951 (HSTL).

table. Although unwilling to countenance military intervention, Truman was not unsympathetic to British interests and recognized, in correspondence with Mossadegh, the essential contribution their 'skill and operating knowledge' made in the refinement and export of Iranian oil.[68] In discussions with Franks, Acheson even suggested that he hoped 'the British would not have to make concessions beyond those already offered.'[69] Despite Morrison's gloomy prediction that Harriman's mission would end in failure, it was endorsed by the Cabinet and described within the Labour Party as an opportunity to 'replace heated fanaticism with cold reason'.[70] In contrast, understanding the chasm between the Iranian and British governments, the secretary of state later recalled that Harriman 'had all the enthusiasm of a really reluctant bride' for his mission.[71]

Along with William Rountree, Walter Levy and General Robert Landry, Harriman arrived in Iran on 13 July and remained there for little over six weeks. The American mission quickly came to understand the strength of support for Mossadegh's hard-line negotiating stance and warned that he 'appears obsessed with the idea of eliminating completely British oil company operations and influence'.[72] Harriman took steps to dampen Iranian enthusiasm for full-blooded nationalization and set out, in discussions with senior figures including Mossadegh, the challenges they would face selling oil on the international market. In a sign of progress, an agreement was reached for direct negotiations with a British government representative acting on the AIOC's behalf. As a precondition, Mossadegh insisted that the Iranian government had rejected Jackson's proposals and would not accept anything along similar lines.[73] Viewed in Whitehall as, on balance, a welcome development – Oliver Franks claimed that the talks were 'a God send' – the British government accepted Mossadegh's offer for further negotiations.[74] The minister selected for the task was Lord Privy Seal Richard Stokes.

---

[68] Ibid.
[69] Acheson to American Embassy, London, 4 July 1951, RG 59 888.2553/7-451 (NARA).
[70] Cabinet Conclusions, 23 July 1951, CAB 128/20; Morrison Memorandum, 20 July 1951, CAB 129/46 (TNA); Failure of a Mission, undated, Labour International Department – Box 134 (LHA).
[71] Transcript: Princeton Seminar Discussion, 15 May 1954, Dean Acheson Papers – Box 81 (HSTL).
[72] Document 44: Harriman to the Department of State, 19 July 1951, *FRUS, 1952-1954, Iran - Vol. X*; Harriman to Secretary of State, 17 July 1951, RG 59 888.2553/7-1751 (NARA).
[73] Document 60: Harriman to the Embassy in Iran, 28 July 1951; Document 61: Grady to the Embassy in the United Kingdom, 29 July 1951, *FRUS, 1952-1954, Iran - Vol. X*; The Harriman Formula, 22 July 1951, RG 59 888.23/7-2351 (NARA).
[74] Morrison to Franks, 25 July 1951, FO 800/653; Cabinet Conclusions 26 July, 30 July and 1 August 1951, CAB 128/20 (TNA); Memorandum of Conversation between Franks, Acheson and Mr. H. Freeman Matthews, 2 August 1951, RG 59 888.2553/8-251 (NARA).

An idiosyncratic industrialist, anti-communist and ally of Morrison, Stokes had visited Iran in his role as managing director of the Ransomes and Rapier engineering firm but had no formal diplomatic experience. Through his membership of the British League for European Freedom, Stokes was reportedly close to intelligence officials and had been involved in the transfer of anti-Soviet assets from Eastern Europe to post-war Britain.[75] He arrived in Tehran on 4 August and extended an offer to Mossadegh for 'co-partnership' in the extraction, refinement and export of Iranian oil through terms not dissimilar to those previously offered by Jackson.[76] Under this arrangement the NIOC would maintain ownership over former AIOC assets in Iran while the British company would hold a twenty-five-year contract to sell oil on the world market. A joint enterprise, including Iranian directorship, would manage operations and British technicians and managers would remain in post. It would also have a mandate to accelerate the Iranianization of the oil industry and to sell oil locally at discounted prices. In effect, the British wanted to leverage their expertise, research and global distribution network in exchange for access to Iran's vast oil reserves. However, Stokes' offer was again rejected as abrogating the Nationalization Law and therefore wholly unacceptable. Concerning British expertise, the Iranian government acknowledged their willingness to utilize AIOC technicians but warned that managers from neutral companies would be employed, a clear attempt to move away from the oil industry's toxic, imperialist culture.[77] In Mossadegh's words, his country had 'divorced the company' and was determined to make a fresh start.[78] After almost three weeks of discussions, Stokes left Iran on 23 August having failed to achieve a breakthrough of any kind.

In the press, the British government suggested that Stokes had been tasked with leading an endeavour doomed to failure owing to the Iranian government's attitude.[79] They felt that Mossadegh had been brought to the table only in deference to the American government and had rejected Stokes' proposals offhand thanks to the 'nationalist fanaticism that he himself had let loose'.[80] Following a nineteen-day journey back to Britain, Stokes holidayed in Cornwall and took the time to write to Attlee and outline his views on the mission most plainly. He expressed doubt as to the wisdom of Britain's 'mean' policy towards

[75] Dorril, *Mi6*, 433–4.
[76] Failure of a Mission, undated, Labour International Department - Box 134 (LHA); Shepherd to Morrison, 6 August 1951, FO 800/653 (TNA).
[77] Mosaddiq to Stokes, 22 August 1951, FO 416/104 (TNA).
[78] Elm, *Oil, Power, and Principle*, 135.
[79] Mr Stokes' Statement to Press on Departure from Iran, 23 August 1951, RG 59 888.2553/8-2351 (NARA).
[80] Failure of a Mission, undated, Labour International Department – Box 134 (LHA).

Mossadegh, not least the AIOC's sizeable compensation demands, and the advice being offered by the 'ungenerous' Shepherd.[81] Stokes appears to have been humbled by the strength of opposition to British imperialism but remained hopeful that stalling negotiations may have 'an educative effect' on sections of the Iranian public who were increasingly disinclined towards their prime minister and protracted economic difficulties. A similar message was recorded by Shepherd, who was confident that deteriorating conditions would inevitably fuel opposition to Mossadegh.[82]

Against the backdrop of ongoing stalemate, British employees and their families were withdrawn from southern Iran leaving a skeleton staff of 395 British, 287 Indian and 246 Pakistani workers at Abadan for essential maintenance purposes.[83] Defended on the grounds of safety and practicality, the spectacle of British retreat in the Middle East had become a key Conservative attack line, which allowed Churchill to claim that Labour had 'cast away one of the major interests of the nation'.[84] The small band of British and Commonwealth workers found themselves in a liminal existence. They were unable to undertake normal work, unsure when they would be able to leave and faced routine intimidation as company cars, aircraft, communication facilities and offices were seized.[85] Shepherd reported that AIOC chief representative Alan Seddon's home had been raided and a cache of AIOC Information Department documents uncovered and published in the local press.[86] According to Mostafa Elm, a translator who attended Seddon's residence and later became a historian of nationalization, the documents were a 'mine field' for the company. They reportedly proved that newspapers had been paid to spread scurrilous rumours about the National Front's leaders and that the company had bribed leading politicians.[87] With tensions mounting, the workers constituted a bargaining chip whose refusal to work could effectively shut down Iran's oil industry. Their morale, however, was

---

[81] Stokes to Attlee, 14 September 1951, Williams, *A Prime Minister Remembers*, 249–51.
[82] Shepherd to Strang, 11 September 1951, FO 371/91463 (TNA).
[83] Khorramshahr to Foreign Office, 8 June 1951, FO 371/91624; Morrison Memorandum, 11 July 1951, FO 129/46; Cabinet Conclusions, 12 July 1951; Cabinet Conclusions, 23 July 1951, CAB 128/20; Khorramshahr to Foreign Office, 16 September 1951, FO 371/91625 (TNA).
[84] Scheme for Total Evacuation of AIOC Employees, undated; Khorramshahr to Foreign Office, 13 July 1951; Benbow to Logan, 26 July 1951, FO 371/91625 (TNA); *Hansard*, HC Debate, Vol. 491 Col. 995, 30 July 1951.
[85] Failure of a Mission, undated, Labour International Department – Box 134 (LHA); Capper to Middleton, 24 June 1951, FO 371/91461 (TNA).
[86] Shepherd to Foreign Office, 5 July 1951, FO 371/91624; Shepherd to Morrison, 9 July 1951, FO 371/91450 (TNA).
[87] Elm, *Oil, Power, and Principle*, 120.

waning and Shepherd advised that evacuations should begin immediately to exert pressure on the Iranian government.[88]

With talks still ongoing and stung by Conservative accusations of weakness, the Labour government was reluctant to agree to Shepherd's recommendation but acknowledged that British citizens were suffering from the most humiliating treatment.[89] Having failed to take decisive action, Mossadegh called their bluff and, on 25 September, informed the AIOC that their staff had to leave Iran within a week. His order came amid a reported surge in anti-British propaganda, including the establishment of a government unit for this purpose.[90] Before a crowd chanting 'death to Britain!' the prime minister wept with joy and lauded his country's movement for liberation.[91] Not to be outdone, Mossadegh's leading rival within the National Front, Ayatollah Kashani declared a national strike against imperialism.[92] Despite last-ditch protests from Whitehall, at 09.15 on 3 October 1951, the few remaining British AIOC staff at Abadan boarded *HMS Mauritius*, setting sail for Basra little over three hours later. As the ship departed, the Royal Navy band struck up 'Colonel Bogey's March', a military anthem that lent itself to defiantly off-colour lyrics sung by the otherwise dejected workers. After half a century of dominance this was the most visible manifestation of the collapse of British power in Iran.

Having failed to influence their Iranian counterparts, the British government claimed that the prime minister's ultimatum constituted a violation of the International Court's interim ruling and requested that the United Nations Security Council intervene in the dispute. This was a further British misstep. Travelling to New York to defend his government's decision offered Mossadegh the opportunity to pose with President Truman, Dean Acheson and a host of other leading figures from American politics; address opinion makers at the National Press Club; and draw parallels between his country's struggle for independence and the United States' own by visiting sites like the Supreme Court and the Liberty Bell. Given to public-fainting fits and taking meetings in bed at the Ritz Tower Hotel, Mossadegh's eccentricities charmed the American public

---

[88] Notes of an Interview Between H. E. Varasteh, Minister of Finance, and Mr N. R. Seddon, 23 June 1951, 72363 (BPA); Shepherd to Morrison, 9 July 1951, FO 371/91450 (TNA).
[89] Failure of a Mission, undated, Labour International Department – Box 134 (LHA); Shepherd to Morrison, 18 August 1951, FO 371/91451; Shepherd to Morrison, 12 September 1951, FO 371/91463 (TNA).
[90] Foreign Office to Chancery, 29 September 1951, FO 371/91464 (TNA).
[91] Shepherd to Foreign Office, 28 September 1951, FO 371/91464 (TNA).
[92] Shepherd to Foreign Office, 29 September 1951, FO 371/91464 (TNA).

Figure 5.3 Mossadegh inspects the Liberty Bell during his visit to the United States, Harry S. Truman Library & Museum.

who were not unsympathetic to the righteousness of his cause.[93] In discussions with State Department officials, the prime minister was uncompromising on the necessity of the Iranian government preserving total control of the ownership, production and distribution of their country's oil and ruled out McGhee's suggestion that erecting a façade of nationalization would suffice.[94] Mossadegh was similarly undaunted when appearing before the Security Council, arguing that the dispute was solely between Iran and the AIOC, a private enterprise, and therefore constituted a purely domestic affair. Following a period of deliberation, the Security Council adjourned having failed to reach a decision. His public relations triumph was complete when he visited Egypt on his way back to Iran and was greeted by crowds reportedly in the millions. Having signed a treaty of friendship with his opposite number, Mostafa el-Nahas Pasha, Mossadegh promised that the two countries would work together to 'demolish British imperialism'.[95]

Although British officials hoped that the public would turn against Mossadegh as economic conditions worsened there was no sign that this was

---

[93] De Bellaigue, *Patriot of Persia*, 175–85; Elm, *Oil, Power, and Principle*, 183–93; Document 49: THE CURRENT IRANIAN SITUATION, 10 October 1951, *FRUS, 1952-1954, Iran - 2018*; Foreign Office Minutes, 5 October 1951, FO 371/91464; Foreign Office Intel Report: Persia, 25 October 1951, FO 953/1205 (TNA).
[94] Memorandum of Conversation with Prime Minister Mosadeq, 18 October–19 November 1951, RG 59 888.2553/8-1051 (NARA); Memorandum of Conversation with Prime Minister Mosadeq, 24 October 1951, Dean Acheson papers – Box 69 (HSTL).
[95] McGhee, *Envoy to the Middle World*, 404.

happening. Indeed, the prime minister appeared to be in the ascendancy. The British Embassy at Cairo warned that Mossadegh and Pasha had presented themselves as the leaders of 'two small but gallant countries struggling to free themselves from the shackles of blood-sucking imperialism'.[96] Against this intoxicating rhetoric, legal and technical points concerning the mechanics of nationalization carried little weight. Two days after Britain's unceremonious exit from Abadan, with a general election looming, Clement Attlee publicly reaffirmed his continued belief in alignment with the United Nations and again ruled out action that might further inflame the 'red hot nationalist campaign' in Iran.[97] Even after the failure of multiple diplomatic missions, Attlee was adamant that military action could not be warranted. However, the Labour government did not intend to surrender British interests in Iran unilaterally and increasingly placed its faith in covert operations to pave the way for Mossadegh's removal.[98]

Spies, thugs and Oxford dons

Perhaps the first suggestion that Mossadegh should be removed by external forces came in June 1951 during discussions at the International Labour Organization in Geneva. During the conference, Iranian anti-communist trade unionist Amir Keivan met not only with Frederick Lee, a junior minister at the Ministry of Labour and participant in the 1946 parliamentary mission to Iran, and assistant Under-Secretary for the Middle East and North Africa at the Foreign Office James Bowker, but also M. A. C. MacNeill, a senior member of the AIOC staff department. During discussions Keivan proposed 'firm measures even to the extent of lending forces to save Persia and Persian oil from communism' and explicitly called for Mossadegh to be toppled, recommending that 'Generals Zahedi and Arfa would be good for a coup d'état'.[99] He suggested the shah was

---

[96] Elm, *Oil, Power, and Principle*, 193.
[97] Healey Speaking Notes for Attlee, 5 October 1951, Labour International Department – Box 134 (LHA).
[98] A significant number of British files concerning covert operations in Iran remain inaccessible to researchers despite successive Freedom of Information Act requests under FOIA Section 23(1) 'information supplied by, or relating to, bodies dealing with security matters'. It appears that a number of files have also been lost or destroyed at both the National Archives and BP Archives.
Similar problems face researchers in the United States where, for example, documents concerning the Office of Greek, Turkish, and Iranian Affairs of State's Bureau of Near Eastern, South Asian, and African Affairs are reported to have been lost and/or destroyed.
[99] Notes on talks in Geneva during the last 10 days of June with Iranian Trade Union Congress Representative Amir Kaivan, 10 July 1951, 129298 (BPA); Bowker Minutes, 3 July 1951; Bowker to Shepherd, 5 July 1951, FO 371/91461; Mason Minutes, 5 July 1951; Foreign Office to Tehran, 7 July 1951; MAC MacNeill Minutes, 10 July 1951, FO 371/91628 (TNA).

critical to any operation's success and provided MacNeill with a list of Majlis deputies who could help cajole him towards participation. Keivan appears to have been driven by a desire to preserve the Iranian Trades Union Congress' independence and autonomy from government. Having refused to align itself with the National Front, Keivan warned that Mossadegh would now attempt to 'crush the free trade union movement' and told British officials that workers in government-owned factories were threatened with dismissal if they refused to join the Toilers, the National Front's labour wing.[100] A veteran of struggles to protect Iran's nascent labour movement from communism, he also feared that Mossadegh could catalyze the Tudeh. Rather than creating a binary between communism and nationalism, Keivan encouraged the British government to facilitate an international 'Cominform of democracy' and support labour organizations like his own across the Middle East.[101] The discussions between Keivan and British officials are revealing both in demonstrating the AIOC's role in coordinating activity across the political spectrum and foreshadowing events to come.

Keivan's meetings with British officials coincided with Ann Lambton's recommendations on how to deal with Mossadegh. The prime minister, she suggested, was impervious to reason and it was therefore simply 'not possible to do business with him'.[102] Criticizing the British government's tendency for negotiation, Lambton instead suggested that they should instead undertake a public relations campaign to change the 'climate' in Iran and create conditions suitable for a change of government. It would, she argued, be possible 'by covert means (a) to under-mine the position of Mr. Moussadek; and (b) to give encouragement to the substantial body of Persian friends we still have'.[103] Convinced that Iranian society was in a state of flux, Lambton used an anonymous article in *The Times* to suggest that Mossadegh may be succeeded by an even more dangerous force.[104] It was therefore vital that the British government intervene and actively select his successor. Lambton recommended long-time British favourite, Sayyid Zia, but identified Ahmad Qavam, the AIOC's preferred option, as a worthy second choice.[105]

---

[100] Labour Attaché's Report, April to July 1951; Labour Attaché's Notes on Recent Trade Union Developments, 26 September 1951, FO 371/91628 (TNA).
[101] Notes on talks in Geneva during the last 10 days of June with Iranian Trade Union Congress Representative Amir Kaivan, 10 July 1951, 129298 (BPA).
[102] Berthoud Minute, 15 June 1951, FO 371/91548 (TNA).
[103] Ibid.
[104] Special Correspondent, 'The Crisis in Persia', *The Times*, 22 March 1951.
[105] Berthoud Minute, 15 June 1951, FO 371/91548 (TNA); CIA Information Report, 28 March 1951, CIA-RDP82-00457R007300570016-6 (CIA Electronic Reading Room – CIA).

To lay the groundwork for Mossadegh's removal, Lambton recommended that Professor Robin Charles Zaehner take up residence in Iran. The history of British intelligence operations is littered with brilliant eccentrics, but even among these Zaehner cuts a particularly idiosyncratic figure. Popularly known as 'Prof', Zaehner was a gifted linguist – speaking over twenty modern and ancient languages with varying degrees of expertise – and a scholar of Zoroastrianism who spent much of the Second World War at the British Embassy in Tehran ostensibly as a press attaché. In truth, he had been heavily involved in counterintelligence operations to maintain control of Iran's railway network. After returning to Britain, Zaehner provided ongoing linguistic support to MI6 and taught Ancient Persian at All Souls College, Oxford. Short and bespectacled with thick milk bottle glasses, he appeared to exist in a state of distraction. Seldom seen without a cigarette or glass of gin, Zaehner was a lifelong bachelor, Roman Catholic convert with a deep interest in mysticism and a Tommy Steele fanatic. Although cleared of any wrongdoing, in later years he was accused of being a Soviet asset. Supporting Zaehner was a small team of gentlemen agents including Christopher Montague 'Monty' Woodhouse, a prizewinning Oxford scholar and MI6 officer who had headed Britain's military mission to Greece during the Second World War; Sam Falle, a talented linguist and former British consul at Shiraz; and Norman Darbyshire, Zaehner's Persian-speaking assistant who possessed a deep knowledge of Iranian culture and politics. According to the latter, their mission was simple: 'go out, don't inform the ambassador, use the intelligence services to provide you with any money you might need and secure the overthrow of Mossadegh by legal or quasi-legal means.'[106] Interviewed in the late 1980s, Chargé d'Affaires George Middleton brushed off claims of any unique British wrongdoing. Bribery of officials was, he intimated, was a regular occurrence and could be justified provided it helped them to achieve the right decision.[107]

At the heart of Zaehner's intelligence network were the Rashidian brothers, Seyfollah, Qodratollah, and particularly Assadollah. The brothers' father, Habibollah, had made a small fortune in property, trade and banking having previously worked as a British Embassy driver. A follower of Sayyid Zia, the senior Rashidian was imprisoned by Reza Shah before being released by the British in 1941. Like their father, the brothers were avowed Anglophiles and Zia loyalists. On their father's request – and likely with British agreement – they had

---

[106] Transcript: Interview with Norman Darbyshire for End of Empire (NSA).
[107] Transcript: Interview with George Middleton, 'Iran', *End of Empire*.

travelled to Palestine to persuade Zia to return from exile. Thereafter they were crucial in the relaunch of his National Will party and in developing commercial and intelligence ties with the British. After the war, the Rashidians remained in close contact with Tehran Embassy officials and Ann Lambton stoking rumours that they were under their instruction.[108] Given the brothers' closeness with Zia and well-evidenced relationship with British intelligence, this does not seem unlikely.

Owners of multiple businesses including the Theatre-Cinema Rex in Tehran – later used as a meeting place for anti-Mossadegh conspirators – the Rashidians were a crucial link between Iranian high politics, the bazaar and the mob. Described euphemistically by Sam Falle as 'passing a few demands to a likely lad (and) paying a crowd', the brothers recruited thugs from Tehran's *zurkhaneh* gym to act as the anti-nationalist movement's street fighting wing.[109] Ostensibly organized to protect Zia and his supporters from political opponents, the hooligans were employed to disrupt National Front and Tudeh demonstrations and incite political unrest as directed.[110] In an internal agency history, CIA operative Donald Wilber reported that alongside their bands of thugs, the Rashidians had successfully cultivated contacts in 'such fields as the armed forces, the Majlis, religious leaders, the press, street gangs, politicians, and other influential figures'.[111] Indeed, Wilber's colleague Richard Cottam suggested that they had the ability to influence up to 80 per cent of the Iranian media.[112] Zaehner facilitated this 'straightforward bribery' with wads of cash from a biscuit tin he carried with him and, according to Darbyshire, the brothers received around £10,000 per month from the British and over £1.5 million in total.[113]

Alongside the Rashidians, Zaehner built links with senior figures in the royal court. Particularly important was Ernest Perron, the shah's personal secretary,

---

[108] Le Rougetel to Foreign Office, 14 September 1946, IOR/L/PS/12/3490A; Le Rougetel to Foreign Office, 26 September 1946, IOR/L/PS/12/3448 (BL); Diary Entry, undated, Ann Lambton Papers – Box 16/2; Diary Entry, 4 November 1948, Ann Lambton Papers – Box 16/40 (DUA).

[109] Transcript: Interview with Sam Falle, 'Iran', *End of Empire*; Shepherd to Attlee, 11 September 1951; Shepherd to Foreign Office, 14 September 1951; Pyman Minutes, 24 September 1951, FO 248/151 (TNA); Ali Rahnema, *Behind the 1953 Coup in Iran: Thugs, Turncoats, Soldiers, Spooks* (New York: Cambridge University Press, 2015), 62.

[110] Woodhouse, *Something Ventured*, 111.

[111] Clandestine Service History: Overthrow of Premier Mossadeq of Iran, November 1952–August 1953, March 1954 (NSA).
Note: This document was originally leaked to the *New York Times* and partially published by the paper on 16 April 2000. A full version with digital redactions was subsequently published on 18 June 2000. A number of 'unredacted' copies have subsequently been produced using decryption software to reveal the hidden text. Given it is not possible to verify these, this study refers only to the copy hosted by the National Security Archive.

[112] Transcript: Interview with Richard Cottam, 'Iran', *End of Empire*.

[113] Transcript: Interview with Norman Darbyshire for End of Empire (NSA).

who provided a steady stream of palace gossip which indicated that the shah was 'anxious' to remove Mossadegh and increasingly willing to act against him.[114] The information Perron provided was at times questionable and, as Zaehner noted, his boldest claims usually came after several whiskies.[115] However, despite this tendency for exaggeration, he remained a valuable intermediary who offered otherwise unavailable insight into the shah's shifting mindset. Although Middleton later claimed that intelligence operatives influencing heads of states was 'not really the style of British diplomacy', it is clear that by late 1951 an interface had been created between the royal household and British intelligence.[116] The aim at this stage, Falle suggests, was relationship building and 'talk(ing) to as many Iranians as possible'.[117] Through discussions with the Rashidians, Perron 'and dozens of others' the British kept abreast of the machinations of Iranian politics and, according to Norman Darbyshire, provided instruction on 'what needed to be done' to secure Mossadegh's removal.[118]

Although the networks established by Zaehner became crucial to the United States' own covert operations in Iran, the State Department viewed British intelligence activities dimly. The AIOC was seen to have botched negotiations with the Iranian government, but American officials remained hopeful that a mediated solution might be possible. They recognized Mossadegh's extraordinary popular appeal, which they understood created its own political legitimacy. Reports from the American Embassy went as far as suggesting that 'for the first time in many years a prime minister is in power who has the confidence of the majority of Iranians'.[119] As 1951 progressed, this assessment was tempered by embassy reports that extremist factions within the nationalist movement could undermine conciliation to the point any compromise would lead to the prime minister 'suffering the same fate as Razmara'.[120] In terms not dissimilar to Bevinite welfare imperialism, American officials even investigated whether they could offer Mossadegh the kind of 'support, advice and possibly economic

---

[114] Woodhouse, *Something Ventured*, 111; Zaehner Minutes, 27 August 1951; Zaehner Minutes, 21 September 1951; Zaehner Minutes, 1 October 1951; Zaehner Minutes, 10 November 1951; Zaehner Minutes, 13 November 1951, FO 248/1514 (TNA).
[115] Zaehner Minutes, 27 August 1951, FO 248/1514; Zaehner Minutes, 20 March 1952, FO 248/1531 (TNA).
[116] George Middleton: Interview recorded by Habib Ladjevardi, 14 October 1984 (IOHC).
[117] Falle, *My Lucky Life*, 78.
[118] Transcript: Interview with Norman Darbyshire for End of Empire (NSA).
[119] Document 23: Despatch From the Embassy in Iran to the Department of State, Attachment: Estimate of the Political Strength of the Mosadeq Government, 4 May 1951, *FRUS, 1952-1954, Iran - 2018*.
[120] Document 43: Despatch From the Embassy in Iran to the Department of State, 20 August 1951, *FRUS, 1952-1954, Iran - 2018*.

assistance' needed to safeguard his government from more radical elements.[121] Ruled out on the basis that the American government could not be seen to reward unilateral action against foreign investments, the State Department maintained that compromise from London was required, and that Iranian stability should be prioritized over Britain's economic and diplomatic interests with the United States acting as a broker between them.[122]

Although the State Department hoped that Mossadegh could be a force, however imperfect, for stability, the CIA took a different position. In 1948, having helped to set up Overseas Consultants Inc., Allen Dulles travelled to Iran to advocate for and develop the Seven Year Plan under Max Thornburg's direction. Now, three years later, he was the CIA's deputy director for plans and an early – and vocal – advocate for Mossadegh's removal. Dulles' position was informed by not only agency briefings and personal contacts in Iran but also a deep animosity towards communism that verged on paranoia. In his world view the prime minister was a vector for communism whether expressed through new social foment or engagement with the Soviet Union.[123] In a particularly stark briefing, American agents warned that a 'dictatorship of the streets' had been created in which Mossadegh was a mere prisoner of an increasingly violent mob.[124] Indeed, within days of Razmara's assassination the agency reported that 'unless something was done about it' Iran was liable to fall to Tudeh subversion and following the Nationalization Law's passage Dulles argued that the shah should 'throw out Mossadeq, close the Majlis and temporarily rule by decree' rather than risk a communist takeover.[125] The State Department's insistence on a negotiated solution, he believed, ignored communism's inherent opportunism and merely offered the Soviet Union and its lackies time to grow.[126] Many within the British government and Anglo-Iranian Oil Company followed a similar logic. According to Shepherd, even the National Front's legitimacy as a

---

[121] Document 23: Despatch From the Embassy in Iran to the Department of State, Attachment: Estimate of the Political Strength of the Mosadeq Government, 4 May 1951, *FRUS, 1952-1954, Iran - 2018*.
[122] Memorandum of Conversation with Prime Minister Mosadeq, 18 October–19 November 1951, RG 59 888.2553/8-1051 (NARA); Memorandum of Secretary's Conversation with the President, 10 October 1951, Dean Acheson Papers – Box 69 (HSTL).
[123] Koch, *Zendebad, Shah!*, 15.
[124] Document 51: Telegram from the Station in Iran to the CIA, 12 October 1951, *FRUS, 1952-1954, Iran - 2018*.
[125] Hewitt to Cline, 15 March 1951, CIA-RDP79R01012A000200050011-4, (CIA); Document 25: Minutes of Director of Central Intelligence Smith's Meeting, 9 May 1951; Document 26: Memorandum for the Record, 10 May 1951, *FRUS, 1952-1954, Iran - 2018*.
[126] Document 29: Memorandum From Henry Villard of the Policy Planning Staff to the Chairman of the Policy Planning Staff (Nitze), 24 May 1951 *FRUS, 1952-1954, Iran - 2018*.; Situation in Iran, 20 April 1951, CIA-RDP79R00904A000100020092-0 (CIA).

nationalist movement was debateable. It was, he argued, merely 'a preliminary flicker of nationalism', which could create chaos and sow discontent but was incapable of achieving the kind of national liberation the Iranian people hoped for.[127] While the Tudeh were not yet able to challenge Mossadegh's government, his tenure did nothing to mitigate their threat.[128] Despite continued State Department scepticism towards a change of government, tentative collaborative operations and stay-behind activities between British and American intelligence agents in Iran began.[129] The Tudeh remained the United States' primary target with resources dedicated to evaluating their political and military influence and understanding its interaction with the National Front. Revealingly, CIA minutes of a meeting involving unnamed agents suggest that should the situation deteriorate to the point where a Tudeh coup became a viable prospect British and American operations would effectively become cooperative.[130] In his diary, Guy Liddell made note of the thanks offered by anonymous CIA operatives for the 'considerable' assistance being offered by British agents on the ground in Iran, indicating some tentative collaboration in the intelligence sphere.[131]

The speed with which the British intelligence network grew was so great that less than six weeks after AIOC staff were evacuated from Iran, Berthoud reported that 'unofficial efforts to undermine Dr Mussadiq are making good progress' and warned against any compromise.[132] Like Shepherd, he believed that Mossadegh's broad coalition was unlikely to survive significant internal or external pressure. Having retired from the British Embassy in January 1948, Colonel Geoffrey Wheeler temporarily returned to provide propaganda support and was convinced that a coup could be launched 'without difficulty or disturbance' if a common position was agreed between London and Washington.[133] In private conversations with his American counterparts, Middleton suggested that embassy officials believed Mossadegh's time in office was limited and a list of possible successors was under review.[134] Sayyid Zia, with whom British Embassy and intelligence staff

---

[127] Shepherd to Franks, 22 October 1951, FO 371/91464 (TNA).
[128] Middleton to Foreign Office, 5 November 1951, FO 371/91464; Furlonge Minutes, 6 November 1951, FO 371/91465 (TNA).
[129] Document 47: Memorandum From Henry Villard of the Policy Planning Staff, Department of State, to the Chairman of the Policy Planning Staff (Nitze), 26 September 1951; Document 48: Operation in Iran, 9 October 1951; Document 53: Memorandum for the Record, 9 November 1951, *FRUS, 1952-1954, Iran - 2018.*
[130] Ibid.
[131] Liddell Diary Entry, 9 November 1951, KV 4/473 (TNA).
[132] Berthoud Minute, 2 November 1951, FO 371/91609 (TNA).
[133] Wheeler to Bowker, 29 October 1951, FO 371/91464 (TNA).
[134] Document 42: Memorandum From the Counsellor of Embassy (Richards) to the Ambassador to Iran (Henderson), 15 August 1951; Document 46: Telegram From the Embassy in Iran to the Department of State, 21 September 1951, *FRUS, 1952-1954, Iran - 2018.*

were meeting regularly, was once again singled out as the preferred candidate and, in a message forwarded to Attlee, Shepherd made clear that he was 'the one man who would be able, and anxious, to get a reasonable oil settlement for us'.[135]

Britain's transition towards covert operations was not universally celebrated in government. Particularly acerbic in his criticism was Kenneth Younger, who had grown disillusioned by Labour's policy in Iran. In a draft memorandum found among his personal papers, Younger wrote that he could not recall 'when, very belatedly, it was decided that the only thing to do was to try to pull Mossadeq down and get in Sayed Zia' but only that doing so had been left in the hands of 'some gifted amateurs from England' with little Foreign Office oversight. Bemoaning the department's failure to adequately influence Iranian politics before Mossadegh came to power, Younger poured scorn on ignorant diplomatic and AIOC staff. He saw covert operations not as a viable route to Mossadegh's removal but as a demonstration of British shortcomings in Iran. Despite 'preaching' to Washington that they knew how to manage the Middle East, the Foreign Office's analysis was found wanting, and they had been forced to rely on a motley crew of academics turned spies to defend one of the UK's most important overseas interests. While welfare imperialism was a cogent policy position, albeit one that failed, Labour's latest approach was reactive, ill-considered and potentially-toxic to Britain's international reputation.[136] Younger's salvo was timely full stop on Labour's policy in Iran. For six years Anglo-Iranian relations had been a minor but contentious issue for the party. On 26 October 1951, despite winning the popular vote, Clement Attlee left 10 Downing Street for the last time and Winston Churchill became prime minister with a slim majority. Exhausted by six years in office, Labour ministers appeared ready to offload the thorny issues of oil, nationalism, diplomacy and espionage to their Conservative successors. In Attlee's own words the crisis in Iran had 'illustrated the kind of problem that arises when insurgent nationalism comes into conflict with old-established commercial interests'. Out of office, the former prime minister had time to reflect on his government's own shortcomings and suggest that while there had been an opportunity to change the course of Anglo-Iranian relations, they had failed to take it.[137]

---

[135] Bowker to Attlee, 2 September 1951, FO 371/91463 (TNA).
[136] Younger Minute, 6 October 1951, Younger and Warner, *In the Midst of Events*, 97–101.
Marked 'top secret' the subject matter and language used by Younger is of a strength seldom seen in diplomatic correspondence. Littered with typographical errors, the document remains in draft form. Unfortunately, corresponding copies have been lost in the National Archive perhaps misplaced, destroyed or still unavailable to the public.
[137] Attlee, *As It Happened*, 175; Williams, *A Prime Minister Remembers*, 254–5.

Change and continuity

If Attlee was remorseful that his government had failed to resolve the crisis in Iran, Churchill was resolute that it must be overcome. Despite a shared imperialist outlook, the new government would not be advised by Ambassador Shepherd who, increasingly seen in Whitehall as having bungled his portfolio, requested an early end to his posting.[138] An orientalist and fluent Persian speaker, Foreign Secretary Anthony Eden approached the crisis with vigour, establishing an interdepartmental coordinating group to continue negotiations and commissioning new research into the nationalist movement.[139] The National Front was increasingly understood as the embodiment of an uneasy national spirit brokered between Iran's lumpen, xenophobic masses and more aspirant urban classes, represented by technocratic officialdom and the bazaar. The former, the Foreign Office believed, were 'out of touch with the latter, and the intellectuals, failing to understand the masses, despise them'.[140] Lacking a shared set of interests or values and held together largely by its figurehead, the nationalist movement was believed to be a paper tiger that would crumble should its leader lose power. On Ann Lambton's advice that Britain must 'keep steady nerves', the foreign secretary endorsed and expanded efforts to undermine Mossadegh.[141] While Eden's predecessor had organized intelligence operations through the Foreign Office, MI6 officers, led by Head of the Tehran Station Monty Woodhouse, now took charge. Like Zaehner, Woodhouse was of an academic disposition but was an experienced field operative who had spent much of the Second World War behind enemy lines in Greece. Woodhouse built on Zaehner's relationship with the Rashidians and continued to finance their network. He also established links with tribal forces hostile to Iran's central government, furnishing them with smuggled arms.[142] British operations benefited from new additions to his network, not least a senior Iranian civil servant, referred to only as Omar, who attended Mossadegh's Council of Ministers meetings and offered British intelligence a source at the heart of government.[143]

Change was also afoot at the American Embassy where Loy Henderson replaced Henry Grady as ambassador. A career diplomat, Henderson had more

---

[138] Foreign Office Minutes, 31 October 1951, FO 800/812 (TNA).
[139] Eden to Churchill, 31 October 1951, FO 800/812 (TNA).
[140] Sarell Minutes, 13 February 1952, FO 371/98596 (TNA).
[141] Berthoud Minute, 2 November 1951, FO 371/91609 (TNA).
[142] Document 175: Memorandum Prepared in the Central Intelligence Agency, undated, *FRUS, 1952-1954, Iran - 2018*; Woodhouse, *Something Ventured*, 115–16.
[143] Ibid., 112–13.

than two decades of experience studying the Soviet Union and the Comintern. Hawkish in his outlook, he was critical of previous American overtures to Moscow and, like his CIA colleagues, believed that communism presented a fluid, opportunistic threat.[144] Woodhouse welcomed Henderson's appointment, suggesting that he 'changed the atmosphere' among American officials and fostered a new collaborative spirit in Iran.[145] In a joint report prepared with their British counterparts following the new ambassador's arrival, American Embassy staff noted that Soviet propaganda in Iran had increased to the point that 'the USSR is queen of the airwaves in this area' broadcasting nationwide in a variety of local languages. Assessing Iran's economic and political outlook, the report found that Mossadegh's character, anti-British xenophobia and 'almost megalomaniac desire to act as champion of the Iranian people' were contributing to political fissures and economic mismanagement. In a significant change of direction, it also found that latent pro-British factions could be mobilized, should the right circumstances present themselves, to oppose the Tudeh and other extremist forces.[146] Following the failure of Harriman and Stokes' missions to Iran and talks with Mossadegh in the United States, American resolve appeared to be hardening.

In private discussions with the shah, Henderson remarked that Mossadegh's leadership was 'destructive instead of constructive' and raised the prospect of his replacement.[147] Through intermediaries, Zaehner and his colleagues had ascertained that the monarch was ready to discuss the 'ways and means' of removing the prime minister but remained concerned that without an organized opposition preserving the façade of democracy would be an insurmountable challenge.[148] Instead, the shah suggested that a coup followed by a 'temporary dictatorial regime' was perhaps the only means of replacing Mossadegh. Henderson was not yet willing to countenance American participation in any such operation but expressed an interest in succession planning and the steps his government and its British allies could take to fill a power vacuum should one emerge.[149] Alongside the threat of communism, lobbying from the American oil industry raised fears that Iran could become a point of contagion and inspire

---

[144] Interview with Loy Henderson, 14 June 1973, Oral History Interviews (HSTL).
[145] Woodhouse, *Something Ventured*, 110.
[146] Document 55: Despatch From the Embassy in Iran to the Department of State, Attachment: Joint Estimate of the Situation in Iran, 23 November 1951, *FRUS, 1952-1954, Iran - 2018*.
[147] Document 138: The Ambassador in Iran (Henderson) to the Department of State, 26 December 1951, *FRUS, 1952-1954, Iran - Vol. X*.
[148] Zaehner Minutes, 10 November 1951, FO 248/1415 (TNA).
[149] Document 138: The Ambassador in Iran (Henderson) to the Department of State, 26 December 1951, *FRUS, 1952-1954, Iran - Vol. X*.

other countries to nationalize resources under foreign control. To prevent this, American oil executives told the State Department that it needed to do more to 'protect the sanctity of contracts' and, ideally, 'get rid of Mosadeq'.[150] However, opinion remained divided as to the effect his removal might have in Iran and across the Middle East. In particular, fears persisted that premature action would lead to socio-economic unrest and 'give good fishing' to the Tudeh.[151]

The Truman government pressed their British allies to resume negotiations. 'Anxious that we and the Americans should speak with one voice', Eden agreed but did not suspend covert operations in Iran.[152] In January 1952, Churchill made his first official visit to the United States since returning to office, a trip that coincided with Mossadegh firmly imprinting himself into American public consciousness. He appeared on the cover of *Time* twice and the magazine named him its 'man of the year' for 1951. This award and accompanying article were not particularly complementary. Described variously as a 'strange old man' and 'dizzy old wizard', *Time* identified Mossadegh as the living embodiment of Middle Eastern anti-imperialism and the emerging split between east and west.[153] Analysing the emerging crisis, the magazine encouraged the American government to step in and offer the kind of active leadership that their allies were incapable of. To Churchill's frustration, Acheson did not criticize the Labour government's lack of firmness in Iran but instead referred to the structural challenges created by historic British misrule there.[154] The prime minister's suggestion that past mistakes were 'not a reason for weakness in the face of Mossadeq's impossible conduct' received a similar response, suggesting that a genuinely shared position remained some way off.[155]

Notionally committed to a negotiated settlement but divided on where compromises could be made, Anglo-American attention now turned to elections for the seventeenth Majlis, which were taking place amid a fresh wave of political unrest. In December, armed security forces were called in to quell violence between the nationalist Toilers Party, students and right-wing thugs outside the

---

[150] Funkhouser to McGhee, 13 September 1951, RG 59 822.2553/91351 (NARA).
[151] Document 57: Webb to the Embassy in the United Kingdom, 29 November 1951; Document 63: National Intelligence Estimate: Probable Developments in Iran in 1951 in the absence of an Oil Settlement, 4 February 1952, *FRUS, 1952-1954, Iran - 2018*; Memorandum of Conversation Between President Truman and Mr. Churchill, 10 December 1951, RG 59 611.41/12-1051; Memorandum of Conversation on Iran, 9 January 1952, RG 59 611.41/1-1152 (NARA).
[152] Eden to Tehran, 4 December 1951, FO 428/1514 (TNA).
[153] 'MAN OF THE YEAR: Challenge of the East', *TIME Magazine*, 7 January 1952.
[154] Memorandum of Conversation at Dinner at British Embassy, 6 January 1952, RG 59 611.41/1-1452; Talks Between the President and Prime Minister Churchill, 9 January 1952, RG 59 611/41/1-1152 (NARA).
[155] Ibid.

Majlis and halt the ransacking of opposition newspaper offices. In the disorder up to twenty-two people were rumoured to have killed and scores more injured, including a Greek journalist and Tehran's acting chief of police.[156] In a report for Eden, Middleton suggested that the government had used 'private gangs' to attack its opponents and force anti-nationalist journalists to seek sanctuary in the Majlis. In contrast, National Front newspapers, the Toilers and Ayatollah Kashani attacked the Anglo-Iranian Oil Company for organizing thugs to create disorder.[157] It is likely that both sides' accusations contained at least a kernel of truth.

Sensing an opportunity, opposition deputies scrambled to ensure the Majlis was quorate, so a motion of interpellation could be laid against the prime minister.[158] In discussions with Oriental Counsellor Lancelot Pyman, anti-nationalist leaders suggested that economic and social disorder had undermined Mossadegh's parliamentary support, and he could no longer count on a majority of deputies. Instead, they believed he would attempt to rig the forthcoming election to protect his majority.[159] British contacts warned that the nationalist movement would go on the offensive during the campaign and had planned populist attacks on the forces of imperialism to buoy their supporters and silence opponents.[160] The response to the World Bank's attempts to mediate a settlement to the dispute illustrated deepening political division. Talks led by the bank's Vice President Robert Garner took place between November 1951 and April 1952 and produced a proposal to appoint a temporary management board to oversee the sale of Iranian oil to the AIOC, the profits from which would be held in escrow pending final settlement. With oil flowing, Garner and his colleagues hoped that both parties may be more amenable to reaching a settlement.[161] However, in a furious response, Ayatollah Kashani condemned World Bank officials for 'preserving the privileges of the large powers' and accused the United States of acting on behalf of their British allies.[162] From the left, the Tudeh attacked Mossadegh's leadership on similar grounds, arguing that Iranian nationalism

---

[156] Middleton to Foreign Office, 6 December 1951; Middleton to Foreign Office, 7 December 1951, FO 248/1514 (TNA).
[157] Middleton to Foreign Office, 8 December 1951; Middleton to Eden, 10 December 1951, FO 248/1514 (TNA).
[158] Pyman Minutes, 31 December 1951, FO 248/1514 (TNA).
[159] Pyman Minutes, 21 January 1952, FO 248/1514 (TNA).
[160] Middleton Minutes, 10 January 1952, FO 28/1531 (TNA).
[161] Press Release No. 285: Review of the International Bank's Negotiations Concerning the Iranian Oil Problem, 3 April 1952 (WBGA).
[162] Despatch From the Station in Iran to the Central Intelligence Agency, 10 January 1952, *FRUS, 1952-1954, Iran - 2018*.

must define itself by its anti-imperialism and ability to provide for the country's workers.[163]

Such hard-line opposition made further talks untenable, and the Iranian government announced its intention to ease financial pressures by selling oil to whoever wished to purchase it. On 22 January 1952, the day the Majlis motion of interpellation was due to be debated, Mossadegh outflanked his opponents in the nationalist movement by ordering the closure of Britain's Iranian consulates. The 'jovial' prime minister told Middleton that this decision was a direct response to continued interference in Iranian politics and suggested that British agents needed to be eradicated. Once achieved 'the nation would be united and strong as never before'.[164]

Already sceptical that Mossadegh could be reasoned with, the CIA warned that there was 'no prospect' of a settlement with the AIOC. Instead, the agency believed that the Iranian government would now attempt to sell its oil to the Soviet Union. Given Iran's limited export capacity, doing so would provide few immediate solutions to their economic crisis. However, it would inevitably see them drift further from the West's orbit and facilitate the Tudeh.[165] British estimates were similarly bleak. As early as November, Middleton warned his American counterparts that there was now a 'real danger' of a Soviet-backed coup being launched, adding that 'Communists and fellow-travellers' had penetrated the state's civilian and military apparatus.[166] Although not a communist himself, Mossadegh was repeatedly identified by British officials as offering little resistance to their march through Iran's institutions.[167]

The first coup

On 15 February, Hossein Fatimi, a close ally of Mossadegh, was shot and wounded by a member of Fada'iyan-e Islam.[168] The following month 'scuffles' between the Tudeh and right-wing groups linked to the Rashidians left multiple

---

[163] Declaration of the Tudeh Party Central Committee, 25 December 1951, FO 248/1517; Chancery to Foreign Office, 14 February 1952, FO 248/1531 (TNA).
[164] Middleton Minutes, 11 February 1952, FO 248/1531 (TNA).
[165] Security Information, 21 February 1952, CIA-RDP79R01012A001400010010-3 (CIA).
[166] Document 56: Telegram From the Embassy in Iran to the Department of State, 28 November 1951, FRUS, 1952-1954, Iran - 2018.
[167] Middleton to Foreign Office, 4 December 1951, FO 371/91465; Shepherd to Strang, 21 January 1952; Middleton to Ross, 25 February 1952, FO 371/98596 (TNA).
[168] Middleton to Foreign Office, 16 February 1952, FO 371/98596 (TNA).

people dead.[169] With anarchy on the streets and widespread accusations of ballot-rigging, elections in some areas were halted and martial law imposed. Where voting went ahead, there were signs that the nationalist movement was fracturing and that with it extreme fringes were gaining ground.[170] Once again, alternative prime ministerial candidates jostled for position and to win the backing of foreign diplomatic and security services. Sayyid Zia had long been the preferred British candidate, but with little popular support he could easily be depicted as London's stooge by his enemies and was eyed suspiciously in Washington.[171] Conscious that his candidacy may help to keep Mossadegh in post, Zia withdrew but continued to serve as a go-between and intriguer for the British. Aware of the rivalries within the National Front, he reached out to Ayatollah Kashani and attempted to identify a candidate who may be agreeable to the firebrand cleric and the British.[172] Similar steps had been taken by the Rashidians and it was hoped that appeals to the ayatollah's vanity could overcome his anti-imperialism.[173]

With their preferred candidate withdrawn, the British placed their hope in Ahmad Qavam. Introduced to Robin Zaehner by Assadollah Rashidian, the former prime minister had been in regular contact with the professor throughout 1951.[174] Qavam possessed a sizeable parliamentary following, name recognition and support within the AIOC.[175] Known for his cunning, suspicions lingered as to Qavam's reliability as an ally. He was, however, available and able, traits that Middleton acknowledged were in short supply.[176] British confidence was boosted by Qavam's suggestion that he would lead Iran as a dictator and take radical steps to restore order, including arresting Mossadegh and Kashani, and guaranteeing AIOC management of the oil industry.[177] To prop up the new government, tentative proposals were drawn up to offer Qavam a package of financial support and agree a mutually beneficial oil concession.[178]

---

[169] Middleton to Ross, 31 March 1952, FO 248/1531 (TNA).
[170] Middleton to Bowker, 31 December 1951; Middleton to Ross, 14 February 1952, FO 371/98595; Pyman Minutes, 19 March 1952, FO 248/1531 (TNA).
[171] Foreign Office to Tehran, 11 September 1951, FO 248/1514 (TNA).
[172] Pyman Minutes, 21 October 1951, FO 248/1514 (TNA).
[173] Zaehner Minutes, 15 May FO 248/1531 (TNA).
[174] Minutes: Lunch with the Shah, 16 March 1951; Tehran to Foreign Office, 21 March 1951; Zaehner Minutes, 7 November 1951, FO 248/1514 (TNA).
[175] Information Report: Leading Prime Ministerial Candidates, 28 March 1951, CIA-RDP82-00457R007300570016-6 (CIA).
[176] Middleton to Foreign Office, 28 November 1951, FO 371/91465 (TNA).
[177] Falle Minutes, 28 April 1952; Middleton Minutes, 16 June 1952, FO 248/1531 (TNA).
[178] Persian Oil, 7 June 1952; Ross Minutes, 14 June 1952; The Form of a Settlement of the Dispute over the Persian Oil Industry, 19 June 1952, FO 371/98690 (TNA).

British agents were conscious that the public should not view Qavam as London's preferred nominee. Instead, they hoped that Mossadegh could be dislodged 'without creating an impression of "supporting" X and "opposing" Y'.[179] The shah, they believed, could facilitate a stable transition of power, but despite repeated efforts from British agents and assets, he was hesitant to throw his support behind any operation.[180] Coordinated action was taken to stiffen his resolve, including representations by anti-nationalist clerics.[181] To Mossadegh's fury, Assadollah Rashidian helped persuade the shah's mother and ambitious, well-connected twin sister, Ashraf, to offer their support to Qavam.[182] The British were further encouraged by Henderson's discussions with the monarch. Although unwilling to endorse the prime minister's removal, the ambassador set out Iran's myriad socio-economic challenges and considered alternative candidates for high office.[183] However, despite rising hopes, the shah remained unwilling to take decisive action against the prime minister. Having failed to dismiss Mossadegh, opposition deputies warned that the moment may have passed and Qavam himself was reported to be 'cowed and discouraged' by opportunities missed.[184] Frustrated by political inertia, Sam Falle fell back on orientalist tropes of the kind so frequently employed by Shepherd and suggested that it was 'difficult for the western mind to understand the motives that have actuated the shah in the last few days'.[185]

Aware of the plots against him but convinced the Iranian people were behind him, Mossadegh retaliated and presented the shah with an ultimatum: either he be given the executive powers needed to deal with unconstitutional machinations and foreign intrigue, including control of the War Ministry, or he would resign.[186] Under enormous pressure the shah refused and, true to his word, Mossadegh resigned from office on 16 July 1952.[187] An inquorate Majlis met immediately

---

[179] Zaehner Minutes, 15 June 1952, FO 248/1531 (TNA).
[180] Falle Minutes, 16 May 1952; Zaehner Minutes, 14 June 1952, FO 248/1531 (TNA); Document 79: Telegram From the Embassy in Iran to the Department of State, 13 June 1952, *FRUS, 1952-1954, Iran - 2018*.
[181] Abrahamian, *Oil Crisis in Iran*, 31.
[182] Document 65: Despatch From the Embassy in Iran to the Department of State, 16 February 1952, *FRUS, 1952-1954, Iran - 2018*; Zaehner Minutes, 13 May 1952, FO 248/1541; Middleton to Eden, 8 July 1952, FO 371/98600 (TNA).
[183] Zaehner Minutes, 23 June 1952; Falle Minutes, 30 June 1952, FO 248/1531 (TNA); Document 79: Telegram From the Embassy in Iran to the Department of State, 13 June 1952; Document 80: Telegram From the Embassy in Iran to the Department of State, 20 June 1952 *FRUS, 1952-1954, Iran - 2018*.
[184] Falle Minutes, 13 July 1952, FO 248/1531 (TNA).
[185] Falle Minutes, 8 July 1952, FO 248/1541 (TNA).
[186] Talking Points, 10 June 1952, FO 371/98691; Middleton to Eden, 17 July 1952, FO 371/98600 (TNA).
[187] Middleton to Foreign Office, 17 July 1952, FO 248/1539 (TNA).

Figure 5.4 Security forces attempt to disperse crowds that have rallied in Mossadegh's defence, July 1952. Courtesy of Getty Images Bettmann/Contributor.

and the votes of just forty deputies returned Qavam to office for a fifth time.[188] In a public statement, Mossadegh laid the blame for this resignation firmly at the shah's feet.[189] A coup of sorts had been carried out, but its choreography left much to be desired. Far from appearing decisive, the shah seemed weak and was now directly at odds with the nationalist movement. Although the situation was imperfect, the British government was determined to support *their* man. Officials began discussions with their American counterparts on the kind of financial aid that Qavam could be offered and held exploratory meetings with William Fraser and Neville Gass to consider how quickly a new oil concession could feasibly be agreed.[190] In correspondence with Middleton, Eden expressed hope that the oil crisis could be resolved without leading to the kind of social foment that fuelled Iranian nationalism.[191] In a public address, Qavam

---

[188] Middleton to Eden, 28 July 1952, FO 248/1541 (TNA).
[189] Middleton to Foreign Office, 17 July 1952; Middleton to Foreign Office, 18 July 1952, FO 248/1539 (TNA).
[190] Document 85: Telegram From the Embassy in Iran to the Department of State, 18 July 1952; Document 86: Telegram From the Department of State to the Embassy in the United Kingdom, 18 July 1952; Document 88: Telegram From the Embassy in Iran to the Department of State, 19 July 1952, *FRUS, 1952-1954, Iran - 2018*; Falle Minutes, 19 July 1952, FO 248/1539; Bowker Minutes, 19 July 1952; Makins Minutes, 19 July 1952; Makins Minutes, 21 July 1952, FO 371/98691 (TNA).
[191] Eden to Middleton, 19 July 1952, FO 371/98601 (TNA).

announced that reaching an agreement with the AIOC was his first priority and warned his opponents that any unrest would be met with military force.[192] To Middleton's delight, the new prime minister appeared ready to return Iran to 'orderly and rational government' and willing to restore some facets of British hegemony there.[193]

British diplomatic cables send in the hours following Qavam's appointment suggested that Mossadegh had made an unnecessary error and inadvertently disbarred himself from power. This was, however, a clear miscalculation. Despite the prime minister's promise to use security forces to crush dissent, thousands took to the street in Mossadegh's defence. Nationalists branded Qavam a British puppet and appealed to the police and army to turn against his government. A temporary *entente* between the National Front and Tudeh developed with both groups taking part in protests against imperialism.[194] Despite his liaisons with Zia and the Rashidians, Ayatollah Kashani called for 'holy struggle' against the British and nationalist trade unions demanded that workers strike in Mossadegh's defence. Outside the Majlis crowds chanted not only 'death to Anglo-American imperialists!' but also 'down with the shah'. Likely orchestrated by Tudeh factions, the spectre of republicanism deeply disturbed the monarch. As the crowd descended on parliament, soldiers opened fire killing some twenty civilians and injuring hundreds more. According to Middleton, the rioting and bloodshed destroyed the shah's already fragile confidence and he refused to cede any new powers to the prime minister or agree to the Majlis' dissolution. Reportedly 'broken' by the strength of public opposition he faced, Qavam had little choice but to resign.[195] Unable to resist the wave of support for Mossadegh, he was invited to return to office.[196] On royal instruction, soldiers withdrew and ceded control of the street to now jubilant crowds. Less than a week after his resignation, a private Majlis session confirmed Mossadegh as prime minister, and the shah accepted to his demands for additional powers.[197] Surveying the scenes before him, Middleton reported that the words 'death to the British' and 'death to the shah' had been daubed over the embassy's walls.[198]

---

[192] Middleton to Foreign Office, 18 July 1952; Middleton to Foreign Office, 19 July 1952, FO 248/1539 (TNA).
[193] Middleton to Eden, 28 July 1952, FO 248/1541 (TNA).
[194] Falle Minutes, 20 July 1952; Tehran to Foreign Office, 20 July 1952, FO 248/1539; Middleton to Ross, 28 July 1951, FO 371/98603 (TNA).
[195] Chancery to Foreign Office, 21 July 1952, FO 248/1531; Middleton to Foreign Office, 21 July 1952, FO 248/1539 (TNA).
[196] Middleton to Eden, 28 July 1952, FO 248/1541 (TNA); 'The Mob in Iran', *The Washington Star*, 25 July 1952.
[197] Middleton to Foreign Office, 22 July 1952, FO 248/1539 (TNA).
[198] Middleton to Foreign Office, 23 July 1952, FO 248/1539 (TNA).

As if to compound British misery, Mossadegh's return to office coincided with the International Court of Justice's decision on the Anglo-Iranian dispute. The court found that it did not have jurisdiction to deal with the dispute, suggesting that the agreement reached between Iran and AIOC in 1933 did not constitute a treaty between the British and Iranian governments. Although not a ruling in Iran's favour per se, it was by no means a defeat and afforded Mossadegh's supporters yet another reason to celebrate. In a dour message to the foreign secretary, Oliver Franks reported that with the prime minister's position secure, the Truman administration felt it was 'most critical' that steps be taken to arrest Iran's slide into ruin and was considering an offer of financial support to Mossadegh's government.[199] This was an endorsement of convenience and a recognition that having defeated his anti-nationalist rivals, the biggest threat to the prime minister now came from extremist tendencies within his movement.[200]

Despite the surge of popularity that had propelled Mossadegh back into office, Middleton did not believe that all was lost and continued to question the nationalist movement's sustainability given its inherent contradictions. Although the prime minister had temporarily united Iran's far left and Islamist tendencies, he had exacerbated division between his government and the shah, potentially alienating sizeable numbers of moderate Iranians and, crucially, the Iranian armed forces. While Mossadegh's return to office was clearly a setback, the chargé d'affaires reiterated the deep networks of British influence that persisted in Iran and insisted that there was 'still the possibility of a military coup d'état if it is not too long delayed'.[201] Crucially, his assessment was shared by many in the American intelligence services and the CIA confirmed its intention to continue to explore 'every possible alternative on our part to save Iran'.[202]

---

[199] Franks to Foreign Office, 26 July 1952, FO 371/98691; Franks to Eden, 31 July 1952, FO 416/105 (TNA).
[200] Document 103: Telegram From the Department of State to the Embassy in Iran, 29 July 1952, *FRUS, 1952-1954, Iran - 2018*.
[201] Middleton to Foreign Office, 27 July 1952, FO 248/1531 (TNA).
[202] Document 101: Byroade to Acheson, 29 July 1952; Document 102: Minutes of Director of Central Intelligence Smith's Meeting, 29 July 1952, *FRUS, 1952-1954, Iran - 2018*.

6

Countdown to midnight

With Tehran's streets cleared and Mossadegh back in office, British officials surveyed the situation before them. The prime minister appeared to be in a stronger position than ever, his authority proven by an outpouring of popular support. At the same time, the International Court's refusal to consider the British case against Iran was considered by his supporters to be yet another reason to celebrate. However, the contradictions inherent to the heterogeneous nationalist movement had not been resolved. Mossadegh had faced down his internal and external opponents but remained under pressure from Kashani and the Tudeh. Little more than two weeks after Mossadegh returned to office, Chargé d'Affaires George Middleton hopefully reported that 'although there is no immediate likelihood of Musaddiq falling, he is beset by many difficulties'.[1]

Determined to prevent Iran sliding into chaos, the American government considered the steps that may be taken to preserve political stability including financial assistance. One of the few constants in Iranian politics, the British government remained convinced that Mossadegh was beyond reason and persisted in convincing the United States that he needed to be removed. As 1952 progressed into 1953, the threat of communism and risk Iranian nationalism posed to international economic stability were vital means of jockeying the Americans into action.

Barely a year after his return to office, Mossadegh had been forced from power and was awaiting trial for rebellion against the shah. The prime minister's defenestration was the crescendo of years of political chaos as foreign powers struggled to reconcile their economic and strategic interests with the Iranian people's desires. The Anglo-American coup was not, however, necessarily a victory for the British. Instead, it illuminated their declining power vis-à-vis the United States and inability to independently uphold their informal empire in Iran.

[1] Middleton to Eden, 11 August 1952, FO 371/98603 (TNA).

A very British coup

Having failed to topple Mossadegh, the British government reluctantly reconsidered a diplomatic resolution to the oil crisis. Convinced that 'getting some oil moving' was essential, Head of the Eastern Department Archibald Ross recommended that the government should seize any opportunity for fresh negotiations.[2] Following tentative discussions with George Middleton, the now-secure prime minister issued a note inviting the British to open tentative discussions on 7 August.[3] As a sign of good will, Foreign Office officials agreed that the Iranian government could claim this invitation had been instigated at Britain's request.[4] The return to arbitration was welcomed by the Americans albeit with caveats. Although sceptical that Mossadegh could act a bulwark to communism, Loy Henderson accepted that British policy needed to undergo 'radical changes' given new political conditions.[5] A similar assessment was made by Secretary of State Dean Acheson who advised that rapprochement with Mossadegh was 'unfortunately' the best option now available.[6] In correspondence with Whitehall, British Ambassador Oliver Franks warned that while the Americans remained sympathetic to arguments concerning compensation the Iranian government owed, their patience was limited and priorities divergent. In particular, they 'did not trust the statesmanship of the AIOC' and questioned whether a figure from outside the company should lead any future negotiations.[7]

An American aide memoire set out a proposed joint strategy to settle the oil dispute, including an immediate $10 million grant to the Iranian government and new arbitration commission to consider compensation levels.[8] Determined to 'gallop together' with the United States and concerned that their allies could offer yet more 'bright ideas', the British agreed to loosen export and currency restrictions and formally return to the negotiating table.[9] Mossadegh, Churchill believed, stood 'at the very edge of bankruptcy, revolution and death'. Although

---

[2] Ross Minutes, 28 July 1952, FO 371/98691 (TNA).
[3] Middleton to Foreign Office, 25 July 1952, FO 371/98691; Middleton to Eden, 11 August 1952, FO 371/98603 (TNA).
[4] Foreign Office Minutes, 18 August 1952, FO 371/98694 (TNA).
[5] Document 98: Embassy in Iran to the Department of State, 24 July 1952, *FRUS, 1952-1954, Iran -* 2018.
[6] Document 188: Secretary of State to the Embassy in the United Kingdom, 26 July 1952, *FRUS, 1952-1954, Iran - Vol. X*.
[7] Franks to Strang, 15 August 1952, FO 371/98694 (TNA).
[8] Document 194: Acheson to the Embassy in Iran, 31 July 1952, *FRUS, 1952-1954, Iran - Vol. X*.
[9] Foreign Office Minutes, 20 August 1952; Foreign Office to Washington, 20 August 1952; Foreign Office to Washington, 23 August 1952; Bowker Memorandum, 23 August 1952, FO 371/98694 (TNA).

his grip on power was assured, his country's perilous economic conditions were impossible to ignore and necessitated some kind of settlement.[10] On the British prime minister's suggestion, the White House and Downing Street prepared a joint statement to bring about an 'early and equitable solution' to the protracted dispute.[11] Initial signs from Tehran were positive and Middleton reported that he had enjoyed his 'most hopeful and productive' meeting with Mossadegh to date.[12]

Despite the resumption of negotiations, British officials in Whitehall and Tehran continued to assess how Mossadegh could be replaced. His government had not only expropriated British assets without due process or compensation but – whether by naivety or design – had given succour to the combined forces of domestic chaos and communism.[13] Although denied by both parties, the links between the National Front and the Tudeh were widely rumoured and expressed most clearly during Qavam's removal.[14] More important than any formal links was a shared style of politics in which authority was derived not through parliament or the royal palace, but on the street. Middleton argued that Mossadegh's return to power relied on the forces of extremism and the mob in its basest form.[15] For his part, the prime minister was identified as suffering from 'megalomania' and was willing to sacrifice his nation's material interests in pursuit of ideological vanity.[16] It was highly unlikely, the chargé d'affaires reported, that he could be removed through 'normal constitutional methods' and a coup remained the most effective option available.[17]

Successfully executing such an operation would be extremely difficult. First, although the coalition Mossadegh had assembled was riddled with contradictions, in resisting Qavam, the nationalist movement had demonstrated its collective strength. There was, quite simply, no political alternative with such broad appeal. Second, the shah, already unconfident in his own decision-making abilities, was dismayed by July's events and had fallen into a deep depression. Following a visit to the royal palace, Middleton recorded that he was 'likely to

---

[10] Document 203: The Acting Secretary of State to the Embassy in Iran, 22 August 1952, FRUS, 1952-1954, Iran - Vol. X; Foreign Office to Washington, 20 August 1952, FO 371/98694 (TNA).
[11] Churchill to Franks, 20 August 1952, FO 416/105; Foreign Office to Tehran 26 August 1952, FO 371/98684 (TNA); Henderson to the Department of State, 30 August 1952, RG 59 888.2553/8–3052 (NARA).
[12] Middleton to Eden, 14 August 1952, FO 416/105 (TNA).
[13] Middleton to Ross, 4 August 1952, FO 371/98603; Foreign Office to Washington, 25 August 1952, FO 371/98694 (TNA).
[14] Ross Memorandum, 24 July 1952, FO 371/98602 (TNA).
[15] Middleton to Eden, 28 July 1952, FO 248/1541 (TNA).
[16] Middleton to Bowker, 28 July 1952, FO 248/1531 (TNA).
[17] Middleton to Eden, 28 July 1952, FO 248/1541; Middleton to Bowker, 28 July 1952, FO 248/1531 (TNA).

bow his head before any political storm' and could not be relied upon to support Mossadegh's dismissal again.[18] Third, with Qavam defeated there was no obvious pro-British candidate.[19] Sayyid Zia remained the most high-profile Anglophile but suffered from a narrow support base and myriad enemies.[20] Pointing to the recent Arab nationalist coup in Egypt, Foreign Secretary Anthony Eden told Julius Holmes, a minister at the American Embassy in London, that he 'did not consider that we should give up hope that a local Naguib could be found' in Iran.[21] However, although British intelligence networks had cultivated strong links with royal courtesans and thugs, they had done little to develop new political leaders.

Although the American government prioritized a negotiated settlement, officials continued to evaluate the circumstances under which they would support an alternative candidate to Mossadegh and developed guidance for operations should his government come under threat from communist forces, including unspecified 'unconventional activities' and arming anti-government tribal groups.[22] Despite State Department reticence, the CIA continued to press for a more active, anti-communist strategy in Iran. Engaged by the Psychological Strategy Board – the body tasked with developing American information warfare – to advise on the situation, Max Thornburg argued that the conditional support offered to Mossadegh by Islamic fundamentalists and doctrinaire Marxists demonstrated the nationalist movement's dysfunctionality. To 'save the rest of the Middle East from going the same route as Persia', it was vital that the American government strengthen alternative power bases and assume some of the responsibilities the British had proven incapable of fulfilling.[23] Particularly important, Thornburg argued, was the shah who, despite his personal defects, could count on sizeable public support and the army's backing.[24] Well experienced in Iranian politics, Thornburg outlined nine steps the monarch would need to take in the twenty-four hours following any coup including declaring martial law, dissolving the Majlis and invoking the royal prerogative to secure a new government.[25] Shared with the CIA's Tehran Station, Deputy Director Allen

---

[18] Middleton to Foreign Office, 28 August 1952, FO 371/98603 (TNA).
[19] Ross Minutes, 6 August 1952, FO 371/98602 (TNA).
[20] Falle Minutes, 28 July 1952, FO 248/1531 (TNA).
[21] Eden to Franks, 6 August 1952, FO 371/98602(TNA).
[22] Document 104: Minutes of Director of Central Intelligence Smith's Meeting, 30 July 1952; Document 109: State Guidance on Emergency Operations in Iran, 31 July 1952; Document 101: Byroade to Acheson, 29 July 1952, *FRUS, 1952-1954, Iran - 2018*.
[23] Document 116: Memorandum of Conversation between Max Thornburg and Ray Allen, 20 August 1952, *FRUS, 1952-1954, Iran - 2018*.
[24] Document 118: Thornburg Memorandum, 22 August 1952, *FRUS, 1952-1954, Iran - 2018*.
[25] Ibid.

Dulles suggested Thornburg's recommendations should be the basis for future discussions on the agency's strategy in Iran.[26]

British antipathy towards Mossadegh was given fresh credence when his government broke off from discussions in a manner Middleton described as 'not only negative but to an extent hostile'.[27] Declaring the 1933 concession invalid, Mossadegh refused to countenance it as a basis for any new settlement, and demanded that the British make a £50 million payment in compensation for past underpayments and what the AIOC's 'balance sheet showed to be due to Persia'.[28] The prime minister made clear his anger towards political interference in Iran and intimated that British officials were responsible for whipping up unrest. Although his claim that a Ministry of Works employee had distributed munitions was refuted as 'absurd', the prime minister's more general accusations were undeniable.[29] Mossadegh also complained bitterly that previous correspondence had been ignored and suggested that this was part of a conscious British effort to delay a settlement and damage Iran's economy. In a sign of his anger, he even threatened to break off all diplomatic relations with the UK.[30]

Granted additional plenary powers when he returned to office, American officials in Tehran warned that Mossadegh's government had begun to 'resemble a classic one-man dictatorship'.[31] In a snub to the shah, the prime minister excluded monarchists from his cabinet and prioritized populist reforms to minimize taxes for the peasantry and extend the electoral franchise. Described as vague and inconclusive in British reports, these steps may be interpreted either as an exercise in expanding Iranian democracy or diluting entrenched political powers.[32] The army, a conservative bulwark that Middleton reported was already 'in a state of complete bewilderment', was gutted of senior officers and its budget slashed.[33] Appealing to the nationalist movement's basest elements, Razmara's assassin, Khalil Tahmasebi, was freed from prison and legal action was pursued against Qavam.[34] As Mossadegh implemented his

---

[26] Document 119: Wisner to Roosevelt, undated, *FRUS, 1952-1954, Iran - 2018*.
[27] Middleton to Foreign Office, 27 August 1952 (TNA).
[28] Ibid.; Middleton to Foreign Office, 30 August 1952, FO 800/813 (TNA).
[29] Middleton to Foreign Office, 28 August 1952, FO 800/813 (TNA).
[30] Middleton to Foreign Office, 25 August 1952, FO 371/ 98694 (TNA).
[31] Summary of a Report by the First Secretary of the United States Embassy in Tehran, 22 November 1952, FO 371/98606 (TNA).
[32] Middleton to Foreign Office, 27 July 1952, FO 248/1531; Middleton to Eden, 25 August 1952, FO 371/98603; Middleton to Foreign Office, 31 July 1952, FO 371/98602 (TNA).
[33] Middleton to Foreign Office, 21 August 1952, FO 371/98603; Bowker Minutes, 18 June 1952, FO 371/98694 (TNA).
[34] Middleton to Eden, 11 August 1952, FO 371/98603 (TNA).

programme at pace, the increasingly prostrate and depressed shah could do nothing to resist.

George Middleton advised Eden that Mossadegh's legislative agenda was a response to pressure from extremist elements within the National Front and demonstrated the prime minister's desire to safeguard his position.[35] Ambitious hardliners, particularly Ayatollah Kashani who had recently been elected Majlis president, were not deferential to prime ministerial authority and derived power from mosques, bazaars and the mob. Increasingly, British and American intelligence reported that Kashani and Mossadegh were at 'loggerheads' and found that ayatollah was attempting to unite disparate nationalist opponents of the prime minister, including the Tudeh.[36] A vehement anti-communist, a coalition, even of temporary convenience, between Kashani and the Tudeh appears unlikely. However, there is strong evidence to suggest that Kashani sought support from figures and groups as diverse as Sayyid Zia and the Rashidians, the shah's sister Princess Ashraf and the American Embassy.[37] Now described in the British Embassy as 'up to no good and causing Musaddiq trouble', Kashani's behaviour reflects not only his Machiavellian ambitions, but the fluidity and fragility of Iranian political coalitions.[38] By mid-September, senior British informants suggested that Kashani was on the verge of making his move against the prime minister.[39] For British officials, it may have been tempting to see Mossadegh vanquished by a nominal ally; however, this was unlikely to be in their immediate interests and could precipitate Iran's wholesale socio-economic collapse.

Iran was awash with rumours that foreign powers were again engineering disturbances to preserve Britain's power.[40] Among the most baffling was that Denis Healey, now a Labour MP, had used his position as secretary of

---

[35] Ibid.
[36] Middleton to Foreign Office, 8 August 1952, FO 371/98602; Foreign Office to Washington, 9 August 1952, FO 371/98691; Foreign Office to Amman, 27 August 1952, FO 371/98603; Burrows Memorandum, 29 September 1952, FO 371/98604 (TNA); Document 124: Embassy in Iran to the Department of State, 28 September 1952; Document 125: Monthly Report Prepared in the Office of Policy Coordination, Directorate of Plans, CIA, undated – September 1952, *FRUS, 1952-1954, Iran - 2018*; Kashani's Threat to Mossadegh, 8 September 1952, CIA-RDP82-00457R013800350003-2 (CIA).
[37] Zaehner Minutes, 1 October 1951; Pyman Minutes, 14 October 1951; Pyman Minutes, 21 October 1951; Middleton to Foreign Office, 14 November 1951, FO 248/1514 (TNA).
[38] Falle Minutes, 25 August 1952, FO 248/1531; Middleton to Foreign Office, 13 October 1952, FO 371/98604; Fateh Report, 22 December 1952, FO 371/104561 (TNA).
[39] Logan Memorandum, 15 September 1952, FO 371/98604 (TNA).
[40] Document 138: Study of CIA Capabilities in Iran, undated, *FRUS, 1952-1954, Iran - 2018*.

the party's International Department to order Mossadegh's assassination.[41] Brushed off by Healey as an elaborate hoax by mischief-making Trotskyists in London, it remained clear that, in Middleton's words, 'all kinds of small anti Musaddiq plots' were afoot, including from within the British intelligence network.[42] Although 'deeply depressed' by the failure to topple Mossadegh in July, Assadollah Rashidian continued to plot the prime minister's downfall.[43] He encouraged the British government to lend its support to General Fazlollah Zahedi, a veteran conservative senator who had been in contact with the Tehran Embassy since at least late 1951.[44] In his early sixties, Zahedi was a former Cossack who had served as Iran's chief of police first under Reza Shah and again in 1949. A National Front supporter, he followed this with a stint as minister of the interior under Mossadegh, a position he lost after failing to quell spiralling political violence between the Tudeh and its opponents. Described in British intelligence reports as 'more of a politician than a soldier', until 1952 Zahedi was most notable for supplying German agents with information during the Second World War.[45] Such indiscretions were easily forgotten after he suggested that the prime minister was a 'dictator' who was incapable of preventing Iran's slide towards economic ruin and communism.[46]

Facing dismemberment under Mossadegh, Middleton reported that agitation within Iran's army was growing, adding that while other military figures were more popular than Zahedi, the general was the most willing to galvanize and direct discontent.[47] In early October, Sam Falle noted in an uptick in Zahedi's activity and reported that a cadre of retired military leaders had taken an oath against the government.[48] Now in regular contact with the Rashidians, Zahedi worked enthusiastically to organize 'disgruntled elements' within the National Front and across Iranian society.[49] Known to be 'very friendly' with senior members of the Iranian Trades Union Congress, Zahedi made fresh attempts to 'woo the trade union movement' and establish an alternative working-class

---

[41] Mossadegh to British Embassy, Tehran, 14 May 1952; Walker to Foreign Office, 16 May 1952, FO 371/98599 (TNA).
[42] Killick to Foreign Office, 29 May 1952, FO 371/98599; Middleton to Foreign Office, 28 August 1952, FO 800/813 (TNA).
[43] Falle Minutes, 28 July 1952, FO 248/1531 (TNA).
[44] Middleton Minutes, 20 December 1951, FO 248/1531 (TNA).
[45] Leading Personalities in Persia, 11 August 1952, FO 416/105 (TNA).
[46] Falle, *My Lucky Life*, 82; Middleton to Foreign Office, 7 August 1952, FO 371/98602 (TNA).
[47] Middleton to Foreign Office, 4 August 1952, FO 371/98602 (TNA).
[48] Falle Minutes, 2 October 1952, FO 248/1532 (TNA).
[49] Middleton to Foreign Office, 6 August 1952, FO 371/98602 (TNA); Middleton to Foreign Office, 13 October 1952, FO 371/98604 (TNA); Central Intelligence Bulletin, 4 October 1952, 05973633 (CIA).

power base to the communist Tudeh and nationalist Toilers.[50] Recognizing the National Front's fragmentation, he also reached out to its Islamist factions. According to Sayyid Zia, Kashani had offered Zahedi his tacit endorsement, a suggestion the general appeared to confirm in subsequent discussions with Middleton.[51] The diversity of Zahedi's support meant it was difficult to frame the general as a mere 'imperialist stooge'.[52] Unlike the Rashidians and Zia, he was not an Anglophile but rather hoped that British patronage could help him to fulfil his personal ambitions.

In response to the plots against him, Mossadegh took steps to shore up his support within the National Front and the security services.[53] He publicly accused the British government and the AIOC – 'the avaristic foreign company' – of subverting Iranian democracy and reprimanded them for abrogating international law.[54] On 13 October, police arrested Habibollah, Qodratollah and Assadollah Rashidian and former Military Governor of Tehran General Abdul Hejazi on charges of trying to overthrow the government. Accused of treason, Zahedi responded with a speech that not only professed his innocence but also claimed that Mossadegh was responsible for the 'disunity, rebellion and insecurity' endured by the Iranian people and relied on 'empty lies and propaganda' to preserve his power.[55] The extraordinary claims marked Zahedi out as the most visible figurehead around whom Iran's anti-Mossadegh factions could organize but enraged the prime minister. As a senate member, Zahedi enjoyed parliamentary immunity and took *bast* under Ayatollah Kashani's protection to avoid arrest. In return National Front deputies voted to dissolve Iran's second chamber, dismissing it as 'a creation of the British'.[56] Zahedi was forced into hiding, taking refuge in safehouses arranged by the Rashidians' network to evade capture.[57] Eight days later, Mossadegh, determined to crush the conspiracy against him, ordered the closure of the British Embassy in Tehran and demanded that Middleton and his staff evacuate the premises. Having warned

[50] Labour Attaché's Report, April to June 1951, 27 July 1951; Diack Minutes, 26 July 1951, FO 371/91628; Rothnie Minutes, 5 October 1951, FO 371/91464; Leading Personalities in Persia, 11 August 1952, FO 416/105 (TNA).
[51] Middleton to Foreign Office, 7 August 1952, FO 371/98602; Middleton to Eden, 30 September 1952, FO 371/98604; Falle Minutes, 12 October 1952, FO 247/1531 (TNA).
[52] Falle, *My Lucky Life*, 83; Ross Memorandum, 29 July 1952, FO 371/95603 (TNA).
[53] Central Intelligence Bulletin, 4 October 1952, 05973633 (CIA).
[54] Middleton to Foreign Office, 17 October 1952, FO 371/98605 (TNA).
[55] Middleton to Foreign Office, 13 October 1952; Middleton to Foreign Office, 14 October 1952; FO 371/98604; Text of General Zahedi's Declaration, 15 October 1952, FO 248/1531 (TNA).
[56] Middleton to Foreign Office, 22 October 1952, FO 371/98605 (TNA); Summary of a Report by the First Secretary of the United States Embassy in Tehran, 22 November 1952, FO 371/98606 (TNA).
[57] Transcript: Interview with Norman Darbyshire for End of Empire (NSA).

that a diplomatic rupture was imminent, the chargé d'affaires bemoaned the failure of his time in Iran. He suggested an inability to make headway in resolving the oil dispute had left British officials demoralized and claimed that some had 'mentally evacuated' their posts even before their eviction. Most substantively, Middleton described the collapse of Anglo-Iranian diplomacy as evidence of Mossadegh's obstinacy and the impossibility of a negotiated outcome. He hoped that the United States would finally come 'into line' and recognize that the prime minister was a threat to Western interests and Iranian stability.[58]

On 23 October, Anglo-American officials, including senior intelligence staff, met at the soon-to-be-closed British Embassy.[59] Central to discussions was the British paper 'The Communist Danger in Persia', which set out possible responses should Iran fall to communism through constitutional or unconstitutional means and was written with concerted Anglo-American action in mind.[60] Coinciding with the rise in McCarthyism, the language employed in the report was designed to appeal to the United States' preoccupation with communism and link Iran to wider patterns of revolutionary subversion.[61] Heavily influenced by Middleton's reportage and previous suggestion that Mossadegh 'would not hesitate to cooperate with the Communists if it served his anti British purposes', the report intimated that the Tudeh had benefited from a deterioration in social, economic and political conditions and were likely to enjoy further opportunities as the Iranian state's capacities deteriorated.[62] Although American officials considered the paper to be 'generally factually correct' they questioned whether it truly reflected the challenge in Iran and if its proposed solutions were realistic.[63] A coup d'état was discussed in abstract terms and 'overt outside intervention' cited as a possible response to communist revolution.[64] In such circumstances, the feasibility of any intervention was likely to rely on the continued presence of 'a legitimate Iranian authority', most likely the shah, around whom opposition forces could rally.[65] Although a four-page annex entitled 'Covert Activities'

---

[58] Middleton to Ross, 20 October 1952, FO 371/98605 (TNA).
[59] Burrows to Ross, 25 October 1952, FO 371/98605 (TNA); Document 133: Byroade to Matthews, 15 October 1952; Document 134: Jernegan to Matthews, 23 October 1952, *FRUS, 1952-1954, Iran - 2018*.
[60] Ross Memorandum, 21 August 1952; Gandy Memorandum, 3 September 1952; Bowker Memorandum, 19 September 1952 FO 371/98604; The Communist Danger in Persia, 31 October 1952, FO 371/98605 (TNA).
[61] Burrows to Bowker, 11 October 1952, FO 371/98605 (TNA).
[62] Middleton to Foreign Office, 28 August 1952, FO 800/813 (TNA); Document 133: Byroade to Matthews, 15 October 1952; Document 134: Jernegan to Matthews, 23 October 1952, *FRUS, 1952-1954, Iran - 2018*.
[63] Ibid.
[64] Burrows to Ross, 23 October 1952, FO 371/98605 (TNA).
[65] Document 134: Jernegan to Matthews, 23 October 1952, *FRUS, 1952-1954, Iran - 2018*.

remains classified, it is clear that other possible responses included launching a covert propaganda campaign, encouraging tribal unrest and Iran's partition into defined spheres of influence.

Although inconclusive, the discussions stiffened British resolve and convinced officials that the United States' 'complete capitulation' in Iran was unlikely.[66] However, points of Anglo-American disagreement remained obvious. The British government continued to insist that Mossadegh was an uncompromising fanatic who had opened the door to socio-economic dislocation and political extremism. In contrast, American policy makers feared that if the prime minister were removed there was no candidate capable of preventing their country from collapsing into anarchy.[67] Keenly aware that the United States was now the sole arbiter of Western interests in Iran, British diplomatic and intelligence officials made concerted efforts to cajole their allies towards a harder position. Before leaving Iran, Monty Woodhouse made arrangement to preserve the Rashidians' network and maintain contact with the brothers through MI6 agents based at Nicosia in Cyprus led by Norman Darbyshire. He then returned to the UK for discussions with senior diplomats and Anthony Eden. The foreign secretary acknowledged that covert action could not succeed without Washington's support, which Woodhouse took as an implicit instruction 'to pursue the idea further with the Americans'. Along with Sam Falle, he travelled to the United States to lobby officials from the diplomatic and intelligence services on the continued necessity of removing Mossadegh from office.[68] They received a 'sympathetic hearing' from the CIA having emphasized the growth threat of communism and the prime minister's inability to restrain the Tudeh.[69] Stressing Mossadegh's poor health and many rivals, architectural history expert turned intelligence agent Donald Wilber argued that the United States should begin succession planning and alliance building along lines not dissimilar to the British.[70] Following meetings with Woodhouse and Falle, Wilber's senior colleague Kermit Roosevelt commended MI6's 'already sketched out plan for battle'.[71] Although diplomatic staff remained cool towards British proposals, the Foreign Office believed that Loy Henderson privately favoured an operation

---

[66] Ross to Burrows, 10 November 1952, FO 371/98605 (TNA).
[67] The Communist Danger in Persia, 31 October 1952; Ross to Burrows, 10 November 1952, FO 371/98605 (TNA).
[68] Woodhouse, *Something Ventured*, 116–17; Falle, *My Lucky Life*, 83–4; Koch, *Zendebad, Shah!*, 15; Transcript: Interview with Norman Darbyshire for End of Empire (NSA); Transcript: Interview with Sam Falle, 'Iran', *End of Empire*.
[69] Ibid.
[70] Document 123: Wilber Memorandum, 23 September 1952, *FRUS, 1952-1954, Iran - 2018*.
[71] Roosevelt, *Countercoup*, 108.

against Mossadegh and was convinced that the Tudeh would 'inevitably gain power' under his leadership.[72]

In late November, the British opened more formal but still exploratory discussions concerning a coup against Mossadegh in favour of a more 'reliable' prime minister.[73] Foreign Office records on these discussions are heavily redacted or unavailable, but it is clear that British diplomats were undertaking a concerted effort to create an 'anti-Communist mood', supposedly with Ambassador Henderson's endorsement.[74] In discussions with their State Department counterparts, British officials again warned that they saw 'virtually no prospect of an oil settlement with Mosadeq' and had 'little hope that his government will be able to prevent a Communist takeover'.[75] Like Woodhouse and Falle, the Foreign Office used the threat of communism as a rhetorical stick to prod the Americans towards intervention. Still non-committal, State Department officials acknowledged that covert operations were not only feasible but also 'could probably be handled in such a way that British and American connection with it could never be proven'. However, the political consequences of Mossadegh's removal – both in Iran and across the Middle East – were too difficult to predict and no consensus for intervention yet existed. Instead, the American government chose to review options as diverse as financial support for Mossadegh's government to 'softening (it) up', so it could be toppled.[76]

British Minister to the United States Christopher Steel was subsequently invited for follow-up talks attended by Director of Policy Planning Paul Nitze. These discussions focused on the three scenarios the State Department believed were most likely. First, that Mossadegh remained in power and took steps against the Tudeh. Second, that he fell and his replacement was more inclined to oppose communism. And, finally, that there was no change of government policy and the Tudeh were gradually able to take control. Referring to the prime minister's alleged tendency for vacillation, Steel argued that Mossadegh was unlikely to act decisively against the Tudeh. Deputy Assistant Secretary of State John Jernegan disputed this point and suggested, in contrast to recent British intelligence reports, that Ambassador Henderson had advised Washington that if Mossadegh 'were able to effect an oil settlement or otherwise strengthen the

---

[72] The Danger of Communism in Persia, 22 November 1952, FO 371/98605 (TNA).
[73] Proposal to Organize a Coup d'état in Iran and Oil Problem, 26 November 1952, RG 59 788.00/11-2652 (NSA).
[74] Burrows to Ross, 22 November 1952, FO 371/98606 (TNA).
[75] Proposal to Organize a Coup d'état in Iran and Oil Problem, 26 November 1952, RG 59 788.00/11-2652 (NSA).
[76] Ibid.; Document 147: Statement of Policy Proposed by the National Security Council, 20 November 1952, *FRUS, 1952-1954, Iran - 2018*.

financial position of his government, he would take a firmer position against the Tudeh'. Concerning a coup, British representatives acknowledged that while it was certainly not risk free 'it might be less dangerous than continued reliance upon the Mosadeq government as a barrier against Communism'.[77]

This claim continued to divide American officials. The CIA remained hawkish and claimed that social, economic and political conditions in Iran were 'developing favorably' for the Soviet Union. The agency also warned that further negotiations with Mossadegh were unlikely to be successful and the Tudeh would gradually assume greater influence throughout the Iranian state apparatus.[78] However, the agency's analysis was nuanced and acknowledged that without an armed wing, a successful revolt was unlikely to take place immediately.[79] State Department officials, meanwhile, remained insistent that Mossadegh could still choose to act against the Tudeh on his own volition, particularly if doing so would guarantee his government's security.[80] In a reiteration of their expressed commitment to negotiation, the National Security Council agreed to 'continue to assist in every practicable way to effect an early and equitable liquidation of the oil controversy' and refused to offer Britain the support they craved.[81] According to Acheson, the American government's policy was 'to save Iran without unnecessarily damaging our relations with the United Kingdom'.[82] This did not, however, mean adopting a course that may be detrimental to their own interests or regional security. In his discussions with Steel, Nitze refused to rule out a coup at some point in future, but also insisted that no action would be authorized at this stage. In light of Britain's failure to convince their allies to join them in launching a covert operation against Mossadegh, further negotiations were suspended.[83]

The Iranian government's decision to expel Britain's diplomatic mission had hardened the Truman administration's position towards Iran, but it remained

---

[77] British Proposals to Organize a Coup d'état in Iran, 3 December 1952, RG 59 788.00/12-352 (NSA).
[78] Probable Developments in Iran Through 1953, 13 November 1952, CIA-RDP79R01012A002500030001-2 (CIA).
[79] Document 134: Memorandum From the Deputy Assistant Secretary of State for Near Eastern, South Asian, and African Affairs (Jernegan) to the Deputy Under-Secretary of State (Matthews), 23 October 1952, *FRUS, 1952-1954, Iran - 2018*; Communism in the Free World, 1 January 1953, CIA-RDP86B00269R000800080001-4 (CIA); Abrahamian, *Oil Crisis in Iran*, 67-70.
[80] Document 152: National Intelligence Estimate, 9 January 1953, *FRUS, 1952-1954, Iran - 2018*.
[81] NSC 136/1: United States Policy Regarding the Present Situation in Iran, 20 November 1952 (GWA); Document 180: Progress Report to the National Security Council, 20 March 1953, *FRUS, 1952-1954, Iran - 2018*.
[82] Secretary of State to Secretary of Defense, 4 November 1952, *History of the Joint Chiefs of Staff: The Joint Chiefs of Staff and National Policy Vol. IV 1950 - 1952.* (Washington, DC: Office of the Chairman of the Joint Chiefs of Staff, 1998), 188-9.
[83] British Proposals to Organize a Coup d'état in Iran, 3 December 1952, RG 59 788.00/12-352 (NSA).

reluctant to enter into action that could tip Iran, and perhaps even the Middle East, into chaos. Unconvinced by British claims concerning the Tudeh's immediate revolutionary potential, the State Department reluctantly believed that keeping Mossadegh in office was the best means of holding the Iranian state together. Certain that continued unilateral espionage operations would not succeed and constituted a reputational risk, Deputy Under-Secretary of State Pierson Dixon called for the Rashidians' network to be disbanded.[84] Although the brothers emphatically refused, Woodhouse later recorded that without American support plans to topple Mossadegh – now known within MI6 as Operation Boot – were 'practically extinct'.[85] However, despite growing British pessimism, two events revived their hope that Mossadegh could be removed. First, in January 1953, Dwight Eisenhower was inaugurated, establishing an administration that was more belligerent towards communism in Iran than its predecessor. Second, with a negotiated settlement still unforthcoming, Mossadegh threatened to slash the price of Iranian oil, undercutting the Anglo-American oil giants and threatening market stability.

Mossadegh's last opportunity

Upon taking office, President Eisenhower appointed a number of figures who were not only hawkish towards communism but already ill-disposed towards Mossadegh. Chief among these was the new CIA director Allen Dulles, who had forcefully advocated for the prime minister's removal as early as May 1951.[86] His elder brother, John Foster, was appointed Secretary of State and kept the president informed of developments through informal, unminuted briefings over cocktails in the Oval Office.[87] According to Nasrollah Fatemi, Iran's delegate to the United Nations, the elder Dulles brother was implacably opposed to anything that might disturb Western investments overseas and promised that Mossadegh would 'not get away with' nationalizing the oil industry.[88] Meanwhile, Walter Bedell Smith, previously CIA director and another advocate for intervention, was appointed Under-Secretary of State. Kermit Roosevelt later recalled that even before Eisenhower's inauguration, Smith demanded to know when 'our

[84] William Roger Louis, 'Britain and the Overthrow of the Mosaddeq Government', in *Mohammad Mosaddeq and the 1953 Coup in Iran*, ed. Gasiorowski and Byrne, 166-7.
[85] Woodhouse, *Something Ventured*, 122.
[86] Document 25: Minutes of Director of Central Intelligence Smith's Meeting, 9 May 1951, *FRUS, 1952-1954, Iran - 2018*.
[87] Stephen E. Ambrose, *Eisenhower: Soldier and President* (Riverside: Simon & Schuster, 2014), 32.
[88] Transcript: Interview with Nasrollah Fatemi, 'Iran', *End of Empire*.

goddam operation' was going to begin.[89] The hardening of attitudes towards Iran was accompanied by a broad reconsideration of national security policy and increased emphasis on covert operations to restrain Soviet expansionism.[90]

Having failed to win American support for a coup in December the British government had reluctantly returned to diplomatic engagement with their Iranian counterparts. With the AIOC's consent, an offer was extended to Mossadegh that included impartial arbitration, commercial negotiations and American aid in a bid to entice him back to formal negotiations.[91] This was, however, almost immediately rejected.[92] Despite American pressure, the prime minister refused to countenance any agreement that would leave Iran in 'bondage forever' and demanded that the British offer be rewritten entirely.[93] After almost two years of disjointed negotiations, accusations and counter-accusations, it was clear that what little goodwill existed between London and Tehran had been exhausted. In discussions with Henderson, Mossadegh insisted that the British were at fault and claimed that they were 'using fanatical religious groups, Communist-front organizations, and the tribes' to overthrow him.[94] Unlike his predecessors, John Foster Dulles refused to countenance asking London for further concessions and instead demanded rapprochement from the Iranians.[95] Mossadegh declined to back down and suggested that there was 'no hope' of reaching a mutually acceptable arrangement with the British. The Iranian government intended to manage its oil industry independently and, recognizing that exporting to Europe and North American would be impossible, planned to seek new buyers, including behind the Iron Curtain, and would cut prices to attract them.[96] This was an alarming new development. Not only would his plans lead to closer

---

[89] Roosevelt, *Countercoup*, 115.
[90] Document 80: Memorandum to the National Security Council by the Executive Secretary, 22 July 1953; Document 93: Report to the National Security Council by the National Security Council Planning Board, 30 September 1953, *Foreign Relations of the United States: Diplomatic Papers, 1952-1954, National Security Affairs*, Vol. II, Pt. I (Washington, DC: United States Government Printing Office, 1984).
[91] Cabinet Conclusions, 6 January 1953; Cabinet Conclusions, 20 January 1953, CAB 128/26; Foreign Office to Gifford, 14 January 1953; United States Embassy to Foreign Office; 18 January 1953, FO 371/104609; Fraser to Foreign Office, 15 January 1953, FO 371/104610 (TNA).
[92] Eden to Makins, 23 January 1953, FO 371/104610 (TNA).
[93] Document 296: The Secretary of State to the Embassy in the United Kingdom, 10 February 1953, *FRUS, 1952-1954, Iran - Vol. X*.
[94] Document 153: Briefing Notes Prepared in the Central Intelligence Agency for Acting Director of Central Intelligence Dulles, 18 February 1953, *FRUS, 1952-1954, Iran - 2018*.
[95] Document 298: Secretary of State to the Embassy in Iran, 18 February 1953, *FRUS, 1952-1954, Iran - Vol. X*.
[96] Document 153: Briefing Notes Prepared in the Central Intelligence Agency for Acting Director of Central Intelligence Dulles, 18 February 1953, *FRUS, 1952-1954, Iran - 2018*; Document 296: The Secretary of State to the Embassy in the United Kingdom, 10 February 1953; Document 297: Henderson to Department of State, 14 February, 1953, *FRUS, 1952-1954, Iran - Vol. X*.

Soviet-Iranian relations, but they would also undermine international oil pricing structure and adversely affect significant American investments.[97] In Cabinet, Eden briefed his colleagues on American fears that 'a substantial quantity' of Iranian oil could soon flood the market and suggested that Washington would not allow this to happen uncontested.[98] To date, American policy towards Iran has prioritized stability and Mossadegh's latest gambit appeared to be a significant threat to it.

The Iranian press continued to be dominated by rumours that foreign agents were planning coups and countercoups and nationalist deputies denounced 'imperialistic machinations' from the Majlis' floor.[99] As negotiations with the British collapsed, Mossadegh took steps to protect his position and settle old scores. Almost 300 new military officers were appointed, limits on public demonstrations extended and media reporting restrictions introduced.[100] When civil servants began to protest against delayed salary payments they were described by a government spokesperson as engaging in 'provocative activities' and banned from industrial action.[101] Despite a bout of poor health, Kashani remained a thorn in the prime minister's side and attacked socio-economic reforms, including a bill to enfranchise women and national ownership of industry at the expense of the bazaar. The ayatollah also criticized Mossadegh's failure to arrest sliding living standards, drawing support from across the opposition spectrum.[102] Kashani was backed by a growing number of religious leaders, including Ayatollah Borujerdi, the supreme cleric who had studiously avoided being drawn on matters political. Concerned by Mossadegh's rumoured 'indifference' to religion, strained relationship with the shah and alliance with the Tudeh, Borujerdi feared that Iran was drifting towards a spiritual abyss. Detached from foreign intelligence agencies, the cleric's independent network of influence was undeniable and included the Prelate of Tehran Ayatollah Behbahani.[103]

---

[97] Foreign Office to Makins, 18 February 1953, FO 371/104612; Refusal of Dr Musaddiq to Face Up to Our Proposals, 21 February 1953, FO 416/106 (TNA).
[98] Cabinet Conclusions, 17 March 1953, CAB 128/26 (TNA).
[99] Rothnie Minutes, 10 January 1953, FO 371/104561 (TNA).
[100] BBC Monitoring: Mossadegh's Report to the Majlis, 14 December 1952, FO 371/104561; Washington to Foreign Office, 8 December 1952; Rothnie Minutes, 15 December 1952, FO 371/98606 (TNA).
[101] American Embassy Tehran to American Embassy London, 26 February 1953; 'Punishment of Government Employees Going on Strike', Etela'at, 23 February 1953, FO 371/104564; Commonwealth Relations Office to Rothnie, 20 February 1953, FO 371/104562 (TNA).
[102] Henderson to the Department of State, 20 February 1953, FRUS, 1952-1954, Iran - 2018; Foreign Office to Eden, 3 March 1953, FO 416/106 (TNA); Masoud Kazemzadeh, The Iran National Front and the Struggle for Democracy: 1949-Present (Boston: De Gruyter, 2022), 16-17.
[103] Darioush Bayandor, Iran and the CIA: The Fall of Mosaddeq Revisited (Basingstoke: Palgrave Macmillan, 2010), 150-4.

Alongside religious opposition, groups of what the Foreign Office dubbed 'Young Turks' were emerging to the prime minister's left and right.[104] In October 1952, the Toilers, effectively the nationalist movement's labour wing, split over a dispute concerning their relationship with the Tudeh, complaints from religious members associated with Kashani and allegations of foreign infiltration, and Mozaffar Baghai became its undisputed leader. Previously an ally of Mossadegh, Baghai had grown disillusioned with the prime minister and formed a united front with Kashani's Society of Muslim Warriors, an explicitly Islamist street gang. In receipt of foreign funding, the Toilers now attacked Mossadegh in the Majlis and in the press.[105] On the far right, a number of violent parties emerged. The most important of these was the neo-Nazi SUMKA led by Davud Monshizadeh, an Iranian-born antisemite who had spent the Second World War in Germany. With a membership of just a few hundred in 1953, the SUMKA had an outsized influence thanks to the presence of around 100 trained 'shock troops' capable of bringing disorder to the street and meting out political violence to Tudeh supporters and nationalists. Monshizadeh was not only rumoured to be in contact with Zahedi and the royal court but received guidance from Assadollah Rashidian and financial support from the British and American governments.[106] It appeared that foreign efforts to sow political discord in Iran were beginning to bear fruit.

The political atmosphere was so fraught that Deputy Prime Minister Hassibi Kazemi alleged that a change of government could come 'within (a) few weeks' as even supposed allies turned against the prime minister.[107] Indicative of growing unrest, members of the Supreme Oil Council – the body responsible for the NIOC's management – resigned.[108] Unbowed by pressure, Mossadegh took to the airwaves, declaring that he had proved his loyalty to Iran's constitution and his authority rested solely with the Iranian people.[109] Attacking continued foreign operations against him, the prime minister demanded that his plenary powers

---

[104] Foreign Office to New York, 19 November 1952; Rothnie Minutes, 22 December 1952, FO 371/98606; Rift in the National Front, 22 December 1952; Ward to Rothnie, 23 January 1953, FO 371/104561 (TNA).
[105] Middleton to Ross, 13 October 1952, FO 371/98605; American Embassy Tehran to American Embassy London, 5 June 1953, FO 371/104567 (TNA); CSH: Overthrow of Premier Mossadeq of Iran, Appendix B 'London' Draft of the TPAJAX Operational Plan, 20.
[106] The National Socialist Party of Iran, 3 May 1952, RG 59 788.00/5-532 (NARA); Document 192: Waller to Roosevelt, 16 April 1953; Document 344: Despatch from the Embassy in Iran to the Department of State, 5 November 1953, *FRUS, 1952-1954, Iran - 2018*; CIA Information Report, December 1953, CIA-RDP81-01036R000100120031-4 (CIA); Abrahamian, *Oil Crisis in Iran*, 44; Rahnema, *Behind the 1953 Coup in Iran*, 56–7.
[107] Document 155: Henderson to State Department, 20 February 1953, *FRUS 1941 Vol. III*, 20.
[108] Commonwealth Relations Office to Rothnie, 20 February 1953, FO 371/104562 (TNA).
[109] American Embassy Tehran to American Embassy London, 23 January 1953, FO 371/104561 (TNA).

be extended for another year.¹¹⁰ Outraged, Kashani resigned as Majlis speaker, paralysing parliament until a replacement could be elected.¹¹¹ The National Front had fallen apart and Mossadegh was forced to rely on a diminishing hardcore of loyal deputies in parliament.¹¹² The opposition's fragmentation created a state of political inertia with no single faction strong enough to topple the prime minister. The British saw this volatility as an opportunity and a threat. While it might be possible to funnel cash to dissidents to provoke a 'showdown' with Mossadegh, there was an obvious risk that the Soviet Union would do likewise.¹¹³

As in 1952, British officials described the shah as a font of 'passive resistance' to Mossadegh. He refused to publicly oppose the prime minister but did nothing to discourage sectarian attacks against him.¹¹⁴ Aware that the monarch's institutional strength could be used to rally opponents, Mossadegh attacked the palace's 'interference' in Iranian politics and ordered Zahedi's arrest for sedition, forcing the general to once again seek refuge in the Majlis.¹¹⁵ The prime minister also demanded that the shah surrender crown lands, 'desist from seeing persons known to be critical of Mosadeq' and surrender control of the army.¹¹⁶ To increase pressure on him, Mossadegh allegedly produced a dossier that detailed the royal family's 'financial irregularities'.¹¹⁷ Reported to be on the verge of a nervous breakdown, the monarch threatened to leave the country rather than cede any more powers to the prime minister.¹¹⁸ On 28 February, news of the shah's imminent departure began to spread. In an act of defiance, shah loyalists, hired thugs and retired officers linked to Zahedi began to muster in the bazaar, outside the royal palace and in front of Mossadegh's home. Many of those present were members of the Committee for Saving the Motherland and Devotees of the Shah, shadowy military-adjacent organizations with overlapping memberships

---

¹¹⁰ Text of Prime Minister Mosadeq's Latter to the Majlis Requesting Extension of Plenary Powers, 8 January 1953; American Embassy Tehran to American Embassy London, 22 January 1953, FO 371/104562 (TNA).
¹¹¹ Koch, *Zendebad, Shah!*, 6–7.
¹¹² Rothnie Minutes, 7 February 1953, FO 371/104562 (TNA).
¹¹³ Rothnie Minutes, 22 December 1952, FO 371/98606; Rift in the National Front, 22 December 1952, FO 371/104561 (TNA).
¹¹⁴ Rothnie Memorandum, 19 March 1953, FO 371/104564 (TNA).
¹¹⁵ Ross to Dixon, 26 February 1953, FO 371/104562; American Embassy Tehran to American Embassy London, 27 February 1953, FO 371/104563 (TNA); The Situation in Iran, 10 March 1953, CIA-RDP80R01443R000100080016-7 (CIA).
¹¹⁶ Document 304: Henderson to the Department of State, 24 February 1953, *FRUS, 1952-1954, Iran - Vol. X*.
¹¹⁷ Quarrel Between Musaddiq and the Shah, 26 February 1953; Rothnie Minutes, 27 February 1953, FO 371/104562 (TNA).
¹¹⁸ Ross Minutes, 27 February 1953, FO 371/104562 (TNA).

and a shared objective to remove the prime minister from office.¹¹⁹ Rapidly assembled, the mob included groups that were in close contact with Anglo-American intelligence operatives and others linked to Kashani and Behbahani.¹²⁰ Following sporadic outbreaks of violence, Mossadegh was forced to take refuge in the Majlis while the crowds were dispersed.

American ascendancy

Iran appeared to be spiralling towards anarchy and Mossadegh's threat to export cut-price oil had spooked the American government.¹²¹ In a strongly worded letter to President Eisenhower, Allen Dulles attempted to map out the chaotic situation and list the Western assets available to remedy it. Recognized to be insufficient, Dulles suggested that options for their supplementation were under consideration. He also commented on the growing 'street machine' facing Mossadegh and suggested that the unrest offered the shah an opportunity to seize the initiative and wrestle control from the prime minister. However, the CIA director acknowledged that 'his past record does not suggest that he will act'.¹²² Dismissing residual opposition within the American government, the CIA director rejected analytical expertise that did not correspond with his hawkish perspective.¹²³

While there is no single document detailing the moment the American government committed itself to removing Mossadegh, the chaos engulfing Iran and decisions made by the prime minister in early 1953 were the trigger. As noted by a CIA internal history written in the mid-1970s, the decision, and subsequent American action, was 'conceived and approved at the highest levels of government'.¹²⁴ It is likely that over drinks in the Oval Office the president acquiesced to the Dulles brothers' insistence that Mossadegh's leadership was

---

[119] Rahnema, *Behind the 1953 Coup in Iran*, 49–52; Ray Takeyh, *The Last Shah: America, Iran, and the Fall of the Pahlavi Dynasty* (New Haven: Yale University Press, 2021), 97.
[120] Foreign Office to Washington, 27 February 1953, FO 371/104562 (TNA); Transcript: Interview with Sam Falle, 'Iran', *End of Empire*; Document 166: Telegram From the Embassy in Iran to the Department of State, 28 February 1953, *FRUS, 1952-1954, Iran - 2018*; Bayandor, *Iran and the CIA*, 74–8.
[121] Koch, *Zendebad, Shah!*, 16; Probable Developments in Iran Through 1953, 13 November 1952, CIA-RDP79R01012A002500030001-2 (CIA).
[122] Document 169: Memorandum From Director of Central Intelligence Dulles to President Eisenhower, 1 March 1953, *FRUS, 1952-1954, Iran - 2018*.
[123] Koch, *Zendebad, Shah!*, 118–20.
[124] CIAHS: The Battle for Iran, undated (NSA), 26.

a threat to the fight against communism and international economic stability. Although minutes remain unavailable, British Foreign Secretary Anthony Eden discussed Mossadegh's future when he visited Washington, DC in early March with notes subsequently relayed to CIA operative Kermit Roosevelt.[125] After almost two years of British advocacy, the American government had reached the same conclusion as their allies: incapable of reaching an acceptable settlement on the oil question and a danger to Western interests, Mossadegh needed to be removed. Although London and Washington now had a shared goal, their rationales remained divergent. For the British, a change of government was critical to safeguarding their oil interests, a position unchanged since 1951. In contrast, the Eisenhower administration hoped to prevent Iran from undermining oil price stability and glissading towards the Soviet Union. By choosing to intervene in Iran, the United States clearly supplanted its ally as the most influential foreign power there. In freefall since the AIOC's nationalization, Britain's inability to execute its preferred policy without American support illustrates the decline of its informal empire in Iran.

Operational planning for Mossadegh's removal, still referred to in Britain as Boot and as the TPAJAX Project or Operation Ajax in the United States, demonstrated this new preponderance of power. At CIA headquarters a Special Iran Task Force was set up headed by Roosevelt with support from Donald Wilber and £1 million was made available 'to bring about the fall of Mossadeq'.[126] On 16 April, Wilber circulated a comprehensive report on the conditions facing operatives.[127] It analysed both the likelihood of removing Mossadegh and securing a favourable replacement, singling out Zahedi as the most suitable candidate. Wilber stressed that the shah's 'active support and moral leadership' was indispensable to operational viability.[128] Royal involvement would give the operation the veneer of legality and help create a sense that Mossadegh's government was illegitimate and unconstitutional.[129] The shah's character deficiencies were well known, but he remained one of the few alternative power bases to the prime minister and could count on widespread clerical support thanks to Ayatollah Borujerdi.

Talks with MI6 agent Norman Darbyshire opened at the British Station in Nicosia, Cyprus on 13 May and closed a little of two weeks later. Discussions

---

[125] Document 179: Memorandum for the Record, 18 March 1953, *FRUS, 1952-1954, Iran - 2018*.
[126] CSH: Overthrow of Premier Mossadeq of Iran, 3.
[127] Document 192: Waller to Roosevelt, 16 April 1953, *FRUS, 1952-1954, Iran - 2018*.
[128] CSH: Overthrow of Premier Mossadeq of Iran, 3.
[129] Ibid., 8–9.

were wide-ranging but began by stress testing conditions in Iran, not least determining whether Zahedi really was the most effective figurehead for the Anglo-American operation. There was, Wilber reported, 'no friction or marked differences of opinion' between MI6 and CIA, and British agents were allegedly 'perfectly content' to follow the line set by the United States.[130] This claim is difficult to verify; however, Darbyshire subsequently acknowledged that organizational primacy was ceded to the Americans and that 'we, on instruction, were more forthcoming than the CIA were with us'.[131] MI6 offered the Americans access to the Rashidian network for the first time, but CIA headquarters and the Tehran Station agreed that the identities of key American assets would not be disclosed.[132] Dubbed the 'Boscoe Brothers' by Roosevelt, recent scholarship suggests that Ali Jalali and Farrokh Keyvani were the American government's main points of contact in Iran. CIA trained journalists with a deep antipathy towards communism; the Boscoes were well connected to the Iranian neo-Nazi movement and the royal court through Princess Ashraf.[133] Illustrating the small intelligence pool from which agents were drawing, until the British revealed their network, there was a degree of suspicion that the Rashidians – known as Nossey and Cafron by the CIA – and the Boscoes were in fact one and the same.

Agents developed a joint operational plan, which suggested that in the face of Mossadegh's popularity 'public opinion must be fanned to fever pitch' against the prime minister.[134] The shah would be crucial in securing the new government's legitimacy and guaranteeing the army's support. Once agreed, the proposals were shared with the Rashidians, who remained in contact with Darbyshire via triweekly wireless discussions and in-person meetings in Geneva, and circulated to MI6 and CIA headquarters, the Foreign Office and the State Department.[135] On 15 June, intelligence representatives met at the British agency's headquarters in Westminster to thrash out further amendments to the operational plan, the so-called London draft. As in Nicosia, the British representatives let the Americans take the lead and confirmed that the Rashidians and their network would be made available to the CIA operatives in Iran. In general terms, the London draft adopted a phased approach with funds channelled through pre-existing channels to strengthen Zahedi's political and military coalition

---

[130] Ibid., 6.
[131] Transcript: Interview with Norman Darbyshire for End of Empire (NSA).
[132] CSH: Overthrow of Premier Mossadeq of Iran, 7–8.
[133] Rahnema, *Behind the 1953 Coup in Iran*, 80–5; Abrahamian, *Oil Crisis in Iran*, 127; Roosevelt, *Countercoup*, 68–9.
[134] CSH: Overthrow of Premier Mossadeq of Iran, 9.
[135] Ibid., 10.

and undermine Mossadegh's popularity. Agents would use the 'forceful and scheming' Princess Ashraf to lean on the shah and secure his acquiescence for Mossadegh's removal. He would then sign three firmans: an open letter calling on military officers to cooperate with the bearer; a decree naming Zahedi chief of staff; and a further decree calling on the army to follow the chief of staff's direction. The Rashidians' network, meanwhile, would launch a wave of demonstrations against Mossadegh and organize gangs of thugs to create chaos in Tehran and attack National Front and Tudeh supporters. The draft suggested total British expenditure of £137,500 with a further £147,500 provided by the CIA.[136] Although the plan's specific details, particularly concerning the number of firmans issued, changed in the field, its broad thrust remained consistent.[137]

The Foreign Office approved the plan on 1 July and the State Department followed 10 days later. In agreeing to the coup, the State Department insisted on two conditions. First, that the American government would provide aid in the region of $60 million in the first year to stabilize the new Iranian government. Second, that the British government provide assurances that they would be 'flexible' in future oil negotiations and would not attempt to force upon Zahedi terms that could 'alienate' the Iranian public.[138] British Ambassador to the United States Roger Makins confirmed British acceptance of the terms in a note to Walter Bedell Smith on 23 July 1953.[139] Talks between MI6 and CIA officials were also held to agree which military and government leaders, Tudeh members and civilians would be arrested in post-Mossadegh clean-up operations.[140] Even as intelligence officers met, new information was shared suggesting that the Soviet Union was prepared to offer Mossadegh the support required to overcome his government's immediate financial difficulties.[141]

The Rashidian's network was crucial in disseminating a torrent of anti-Mossadegh propaganda prepared by the CIA Art Group in the Iranian press and bribing newspaper owners and editors.[142] As per the operational plan drafted in Nicosia, grey propaganda was used to depict the prime minister as anti-religious, 'leading the country into complete economic collapse' and part of a Tudeh/Soviet

---

[136] Ibid., Appendix B, 1.
[137] CIAHS: The Battle for Iran, 52.
[138] Koch, *Zendebad, Shah!*, 39–40.
[139] Document 250: Makins to Smith, 23 July 1953, *FRUS, 1952-1954, Iran - 2018*.
[140] CSH: Overthrow of Premier Mossadeq of Iran, Appendix D: Report on Military Planning Aspect of TPAJAX, 6–7.
[141] Document 247: Soviet Union Offers to Settle Iranian Financial Crisis, 22 July 1953, *FRUS, 1952-1954, Iran - 2018*.
[142] CSH: Overthrow of Premier Mossadeq of Iran, 20–1; Transcript: Interview with Richard Cottam, 'Iran', *End of Empire*.

conspiracy.¹⁴³ Playing on long-standing local prejudices, black propaganda alleging that Mossadegh had Jewish ancestry and employed homosexual advisers was also widely distributed.¹⁴⁴ Meanwhile, at least $60,000, and likely much more, was passed onto Zahedi to help him 'win additional friends and to influence key people'.¹⁴⁵ Without plans of his own, Zahedi relied on British and American agents and their contacts. According to Wilber, the CIA and MI6 'approached and purchased' Majlis deputies and clerics to oppose Mossadegh in parliament and before their congregations.¹⁴⁶ Despite his long record of Islamic fundamentalism and xenophobia, Ayatollah Kashani was one of those recruited to support the operation.¹⁴⁷ The ayatollah's ideological deficiencies were well known, but his network of influence was rivalled only by his 'cupidity' and 'fantastic delusions of grandeur'.¹⁴⁸ Although Kashani was believed to be perhaps the only individual less suitable to hold office than Mossadegh, MI6 agreed that he could be an asset in the coalition to topple the prime minister.¹⁴⁹ In particular, the ayatollah offered British and American intelligence links to a clerical network that opposed Mossadegh and yet another pool of hardened street fighters.¹⁵⁰

Anglo-American operatives did not shy away from violent in action or threat. Even before Boot/Ajax's approval, Iran's most senior police officer, Brigadier-General Mahmoud Afshartous, was abducted and murdered by a cabal of retired army officers linked to the Rashidians.¹⁵¹ Having maintained the capacity to 'stir up tribal revolts', the British were widely suspected to have had a hand in the ambush of an Iranian military column in February.¹⁵² To sow further confusion, operatives posed as Tudeh members and threatened Islamic leaders with 'savage punishment' should they oppose Mossadegh.¹⁵³ At least one false flag attack –

---

¹⁴³ Ibid., Appendix A Initial Operational Plan for TPAJAX as cabled from Nicosia to Headquarters on 1 June 1953, 7.
¹⁴⁴ Abrahamian, *The Coup*, 178.
¹⁴⁵ CSH: Overthrow of Premier Mossadeq of Iran, Appendix B, 2.
¹⁴⁶ Ibid., 18–22.
¹⁴⁷ Document 187: Memorandum Prepared in the Embassy in the United Kingdom, 7 April 1953, *FRUS, 1952-1954, Iran - 2018*; Transcript: Interview with Norman Darbyshire for End of Empire (NSA).
¹⁴⁸ Assessment of the Position and Potentialities of Kashani, undated; FO 371/104566 (TNA); Document 43: Despatch From the Embassy in Iran to the Department of State, 20 August 1951, *FRUS, 1952-1954, Iran - 2018*.
¹⁴⁹ Office of Intelligence Research: Potential Character of a Kashani-Dominated Government, 31 March 1953, FO 371/104565; Makins to Foreign Office, 13 April 1953, FO 371/104564; Ross to Beeley, 16 April 1953, FO 371/104566 (TNA).
¹⁵⁰ Foreign Office, Persia: Political Review of the Recent Crisis, 2 September 1953, RG 59 788.00/9-253 (NSA).
¹⁵¹ Bayandor, *Iran and the CIA*, 84.
¹⁵² CSH: Overthrow of Premier Mossadeq of Iran, 27; Abrahamian, *Oil Crisis in Iran*, 42; 'Persian Tribal Clash Near Oil Region', *The Times*, 16 February 1953.
¹⁵³ Ibid., 37.

the 'sham bombing' of a prominent local Muslim leader's home – was carried out and contact was made with a 'terrorist gang' – likely Fada'iyan-e Islam or the Society of Muslim Warriors – via unnamed clerical contacts.[154] Iranian sources indicate that in the months preceding the coup against Mossadegh, CIA cash was funnelled to the SUMKA and other neo-Nazi groups through Keyvani and Jalali, and the Rashidians continued to orchestrate the swelling ranks of thugs.[155]

By the summer of 1953, preparations for Boot/Ajax were believed to be making good progress. In the Majlis, the opposition was increasingly gaining momentum and socio-economic conditions continued to turn against Mossadegh. However, Anglo-American intelligence agents still faced persistent challenges. Although they attempted to work behind a veil of secrecy, rumours that Mossadegh was under threat from foreign agents were constant. Alert to the machinations against him, the prime minister called for those deputies who still backed his government to resign with twenty-eight doing so.[156] The nationalist press turned on those who remained and castigated them as agents of the hated British. Mossadegh had, according to the Foreign Office, completed his lurch into 'mobocracy'.[157] Attacking his opponents for creating a stalemate that left his government 'in no position to do anything', Mossadegh demanded parliament's dissolution, a power that rested solely with the shah. In an audacious move, the prime minister attempted to circumvent the royal prerogative by staging a yes/no referendum on 'the expression of the will of the people' towards the Majlis' dissolution.[158] Corruption in the hastily arranged poll was rife, and opponents like Kashani called on 'patriotic Moslems' to boycott it.[159] Mossadegh's popularity had clearly fallen since he came to office, but he still commanded significant support, access to nationwide media outlets, including Radio Tehran, and the apparatus of the state.[160] Even in these circumstances, the prime minister's victory was of impossible proportions. He reportedly won the referendum by a margin of over 99.9 per cent, some two million votes for and barely 1,200 against.[161] *The New*

---

[154] CSH: Overthrow of Premier Mossadeq of Iran, vi–vii; Appendix B, B21.
[155] Bayandor, *Iran and the CIA*, 127; Rahnema, *Behind the 1953 Coup in Iran*, 56–7.
[156] Houghton Memorandum, 21 July 1953, FO 371/104569 (TNA).
[157] Dissolution of the Majlis, 14 August 1953, FO 371/104569 (TNA).
[158] Events in Iran, 17 July 1953; American Embassy, Tehran to American Embassy, London, 14 August 1953; Untitled Memorandum, 14 August 1953; FO 371/104569; Gandy Minutes, 31 July 1953, FO 371/104568 (TNA); Document 242: Roosevelt to Mitchell, 17 July 1953, *FRUS, 1952-1954, Iran - 2018*.
[159] Document 242: Roosevelt to Mitchell, 17 July 1953, *FRUS, 1952-1954, Iran - 2018*; American Embassy Tehran to American Embassy London, 2 August 1953, FO 371/104569 (TNA).
[160] Houghton Memorandum, 21 July 1953, FO 371/104569; Gandy Minutes, 31 July 1953, FO 371/104568 (TNA).
[161] American Embassy Tehran to American Embassy London, 14 August 1953, FO 371/104569 (TNA); Rahnema, *Behind the 1953 Coup in Iran*, 287.

York Times reported that the referendum was 'a plebiscite more fantastic and farcical than any ever held under Hitler or Stalin' and evidence that Mossadegh was attempting to 'make himself unchallenged dictator of the country'.[162] The prime minister defended his action on the basis that popular will superseded all constitutional restraints.[163]

Many elements of the tainted referendum alienated moderate nationalists, particularly reported collaboration with the Tudeh. Watching from a distance, the Foreign Office suggested that without a political machine of his own, Mossadegh 'intended to depend on the Communists' and would attempt to 'blackmail the West' by threatening to align his government with the Soviet Union.[164] Throughout the summer, the Tudeh had flexed its muscle and regularly organized thousands of supporters on Tehran's streets leading to violent clashes with police and their opponents. For American diplomatic and intelligence officials, the Tudeh's disciplined adherents were as concerning as their increasingly militant attacks on the shah and the Western powers.[165] Despite the threats against him and mounting disorder, the shah remained mulishly uncommitted to the coup and Zahedi's candidacy.[166] Although the Americans had assumed operational primacy, British figures, particularly Norman Darbyshire, continued to play a vital supporting role. Accompanied by CIA counterpart Stephen Meade, Darbyshire travelled to Paris for meetings with Princess Ashraf. Initially cool on the Anglo-American plans, Darbyshire's promise to meet her expenses, which included 'a great wad of notes' and a first-class ticket to Nice, quickly won her over. The British agent impressed upon the princess that her brother must understand his vital contribution to the operation and the role Assadollah Rashidian would play as a mediator between MI6 officers in Cyprus and the palace. Darbyshire also maintained contact with the shah's inner circle, particularly through Ernest Perron, his private secretary and confidant, and Soleiman Behboudi, the head of the imperial household.[167]

---

[162] 'Iranian Fantasy', *The New York Times*, 4 August 1953.
[163] Koch, *Zendebad, Shah!*, 8–9.
[164] Gandy Minutes, 27 July 1953; American Embassy Tehran to American Embassy London, 2 August 1953; Gandy Minutes, 19 August 1953, FO 371/104569 (TNA); Document 259: Draft National Intelligence Estimate, 12 August 1953, *FRUS, 1952-1954, Iran - 2018*.
[165] Document 231: Monthly Report Prepared in the Directorate of Plans, CIA, undated; Document 246: Mattison to the Department of State, 22 July 1953, *FRUS, 1952-1954, Iran - 2018*.
[166] Document 212: Memorandum of Conversation, 30 May 1953, *FRUS, 1952-1954, Iran - 2018*.
[167] CSH: Overthrow of Premier Mossadeq of Iran, 22–4, 36; Transcript: Interview with Norman Darbyshire for End of Empire (NSA).

To stiffen the shah's resolve and demonstrate the shared Western commitment to Operation Boot/Ajax, the United States despatched Brigadier General H. Norman Schwarzkopf to Tehran.[168] Posted to Iran to advise on police reform over a decade previously, Schwarzkopf was liked and respected by the shah and seen as the ideal candidate to secure his signature on the already-drafted firmans dismissing Mossadegh and appointing Zahedi.[169] The general's visit stoked further rumours of foreign plots, and pro-government newspapers pointedly reported that there was 'no doubt he (is) not here on (a) sightseeing tour'. Blunter still was the Tudeh press, which attacked Schwarzkopf as an 'arch spy of imperialism'.[170] Finding the young monarch to be aloof and distrusting, Schwarzkopf recommended that intelligence agents engage with him directly, a risky manoeuvre that risk blowing their cover.[171]

Indecisive by nature, the shah sought clarity as to who exactly was behind the operation and assurance that the British and American governments would not abandon him should events go awry. Assadollah Rashidian met with him at least six times in late July and early August to explain the operation and cajole him into endorsing it. To prove the plan had been approved at the highest levels of government, Darbyshire arranged for the BBC to broadcast a phrase selected by the shah during their Persian-language programming. Rather than 'it is now midnight', the BBC's presenter instead said, 'it is now *exactly* midnight.' However, despite hearing this signal, the shah remained non-committal and requested more time to consider the situation.[172] To encourage him, Roosevelt travelled to the royal palace under a blanket in the back of a car for a midnight rendezvous. Recognizing the shah's nervousness, the CIA agent emphasized President Eisenhower and Prime Minister Churchill's commitment to the operation and promised that they would defend him should things go wrong. To demonstrate his government's commitment, Eisenhower used a speech at the Governor's Conference in Seattle to condemn Mossadegh as undemocratic and opening the door to communism.[173] In the days that followed the address, Roosevelt and Rashidian visited the shah and shared with him a list of officers who were committed to taking in the operation. Following this final round of persuasion, and on the condition that he would be helped to leave Iran should the coup fail, the shah agreed to sign the firmans prepared by the CIA before travelling to his

---

[168] Document 227: Memorandum of Conversation, 26 June 1953, *FRUS, 1952-1954, Iran - 2018*.
[169] CSH: Overthrow of Premier Mossadeq of Iran, viii.
[170] American Embassy Tehran to American Embassy London, 6 August 1953, FO 371/104569 (TNA).
[171] Roosevelt, *Countercoup*, 147–9.
[172] Ibid., 156–7; CSH: Overthrow of Premier Mossadeq of Iran, 24–6.
[173] *Dwight D. Eisenhower: 1953: Containing the Public Messages, Speeches, and Statements of the President, January 20 to December 31, 1953*, Public Papers of the Presidents of the United States (Washington, DC: Office of the Federal Register, 1960), 156.

palace at Ramsar on the Caspian Sea.[174] In a final twist, Roosevelt, at the tail end of a late-night drinking binge, found that the Rashidian brothers' courier had failed to deliver the firmans before the shah travelled north. He called on Colonel Nassiry, the chief imperial bodyguard, to deliver them and finally received the signed documents at close to midnight on 12 August.[175]

Countercoup

Time was of the essence. His coalition fractured, Mossadegh appeared to be 'playing for the support of the Tudeh' and looked as though he may use the authority he believed the referendum had given him to strike against the shah. To rally his supporters, he took to the air waves and linked the referendum result with a wider campaign to revive Iran's 'ancient glories and independence' and drive out malignant foreign influence.[176] On 15 August, having met with a cabal of officers, Zahedi retired to a safehouse while truckloads of monarchist soldiers were sent to arrest senior nationalists, including Foreign Minister Hossein Fatemi and the prime minister himself.[177] However, it quickly became clear that details of the coup had been leaked and Mossadegh was aware of the operation against his government.[178] When soldiers arrived at the prime minister's home to issue the firman dismissing him from office they found that he had fled and were arrested by well-armed guards. Loyalist army units subsequently seized key positions across Tehran and disarmed members of the shah's Imperial Guard.[179] At 05.45 on 16 August, Radio Tehran broadcast a special report on the failed coup. Messages soon flooded the CIA Station advising that Iranian officers had abandoned their posts and were fleeing.[180] The American Embassy enquired as to whether a firman naming Zahedi as prime minister had been received by the Iranian government, but this was denied as a forgery by Mossadegh's staff.[181] At midday Radio Tehran issued another statement, this time on behalf of the prime minister's office. It claimed that the referendum result demonstrated the people's will and again

---

[174] Roosevelt, *Countercoup*, 158–61; CSH: Overthrow of Premier Mossadeq of Iran, 35–6.
[175] Ibid., 169–71; Foreign Office, Persia: Political Review of the Recent Crisis, 2 September 1953, RG 59 788.00/9-253 (NSA); CIAHS: The Battle for Iran, 52–4.
[176] Woodhouse, *Something Ventured*, 127; American Embassy, Tehran to American Embassy, London, 14 August 1953; Gandy Minutes, 19 August 1953, FO 371/104569 (TNA).
[177] Political Events in Persia since July 1953, 2 November 1953, FO 371/104572 (TNA).
[178] Gandy Minutes, 17 August 1953, FO 371/104569 (TNA).
[179] CSH: Overthrow of Premier Mossadeq of Iran, 41–2.
[180] Ibid., 44.
[181] Ibid., 46.

called for the Majlis to be dissolved.[182] Suspected plotters, including Perron and a score of officers, were arrested and a manhunt to find General Zahedi began.[183]

With a 100,000 rial bounty on his head, the general found shelter alongside the Rashidians in the American Embassy. The coup had not only failed, but the forces opposed to Mossadegh seemed to have imploded. CIA headquarters advised the Tehran Station to prepare evacuation plans but not before Roosevelt threatened to kill any American assets who withdrew their support for Zahedi and the shah.[184] Released from custody, Fatemi held a press conference, denouncing the shah as a traitor and proclaiming that the Iranian people 'want to drag you from behind your desk to the gallows'.[185] Without informing Zahedi, Western intelligence agents or the American Embassy, the shah fled Iran and travelled to Rome via Baghdad.[186] On the evening of 16 August crowds gathered in Majlis Square for a pro-government rally that was broadcast by Radio Tehran. Successive speakers lauded Mossadegh's bravery in the face of foreign aggression and attacked the shah for his treachery and cowardice. The rally was followed by rioting and outbreaks of sporadic violence between the Tudeh and the army. Reports that soldiers had beaten communists until they shouted 'long live the shah!' buoyed spirits at the American Embassy and stiffened the plotters' collective resolve. Despite their initial failure, Wilber hoped the 'project was not quite dead' and Roosevelt, having conferred with Zahedi, agreed.[187] In contrast, CIA headquarters believed that the coup had failed and ordered that any further action against Mossadegh 'should be discontinued'.[188] It is unclear whether this instruction was intentionally disobeyed or, as per Roosevelt's account, had not been received.[189]

As American agents attempted to resuscitate their mission, the Tudeh's Tehran Provincial Committee called for the monarchy's elimination. The party's national executive instructed its members to demand a 'democratic republic' and the end of the Pahlavi dynasty.[190] At the same time, they issued an extraordinary statement, which claimed that the 'time for talking has ended' and urged

---

[182] Ibid., 48; Roosevelt, *Countercoup*, 172–5; CIAHS: The Battle for Iran, 59.
[183] Gandy Minutes, 17 August 1953, FO 371/104569 (TNA).
[184] CSH: Overthrow of Premier Mossadeq of Iran, 50, 60–1; Mark J Gasiorowski, 'The 1953 Coup d'État Against Mossadeq', in *Mohammad Mosaddeq and the 1953 Coup in Iran*, ed. Gasiorowski and Byrne, 250.
[185] CSH: Overthrow of Premier Mossadeq of Iran, 55.
[186] Document 348: Henderson to State Department, 20 August 1953, *FRUS, 1952-1954, Iran - Vol. X*.
[187] CSH: Overthrow of Premier Mossadeq of Iran, 52–8.
[188] Ibid., 64.
[189] Roosevelt, *Countercoup*, 190.
[190] Maziar Behrooz, 'The 1953 Coup in Iran and the Legacy of the Tudeh', in *Mohammad Mosaddeq and the 1953 Coup in Iran*, ed. Gasiorowski and Byrne, 120.

members with access to firearms to report to the party.[191] In subsequent talks with Mossadegh, the Tudeh urged the prime minister to supply them with 10,000 rifles and small arms and to unilaterally declare a republic, requests he rejected out of hand. Demonstrating their power and growing confidence, the party's supporters rallied in Tehran but protests quickly descended into rioting. Armed gangs roamed the streets attacking the premises of monarchist newspapers and political opponents and tearing down statues of the shah.[192] British intelligence claimed some credit for the disorder; Norman Darbyshire later insisted that the Rashidians had 'provided people to infiltrate the demonstrations' and instigate unrest.[193] The MI6 agent hoped that mobs so nakedly threatening the shah would help associate Mossadegh with lawlessness and turn the public against him. To preserve order, the government arrested up to 600 Tudeh activists, severely diluting the party's presence on the street.

The CIA agreed with Darbyshire's analysis and identified the public's fear of the Tudeh as a key means of undermining the prime minister.[194] Rather than a legitimate response to unconstitutional behaviour and foreign interference, Roosevelt and his colleagues framed Mossadegh's refusal to accept the firman dismissing him from office as a challenge to royal authority and Iran's constitutional norms. In doing so they hoped to force the Iranian public into a choice between a nationalist movement that had led their country into anarchy with communist assistance and the monarchy, an institution that promised stability and investment from abroad. Escorted by CIA Station Chief Joe Goodwin, journalists Kennett Love of *The New York Times* and Don Schwind of the Associated Press met with General Zahedi's son, Ardeshir, who handed them photocopies of the signed firmans dismissing Mossadegh from office.[195] *The New York Times* published the documents in full and CIA agents distributed them to journalists at Tehran's Park Hotel to undermine the prime minister's legitimacy. On 17 August, American intelligence officers, their assets, Zahedi and the Rashidians held a four-hour 'council of war' and agreed that they would

---

[191] Document 262: Mattison to the Department of State, 16 August 1953; Document 276: Telegram From the Station in Iran to the Central Intelligence Agency, 18 August 1953, *FRUS, 1952-1954, Iran - 2018*.

[192] Foreign Office, Persia: Political Review of the Recent Crisis, 2 September 1953, RG 59 788.00/9-253 (NSA); Document 348: Henderson to the Department of State, 20 August 1953, *FRUS, 1952-1954, Iran - Vol. X*.

[193] Transcript: Interview with Norman Darbyshire for End of Empire (NSA).

[194] Document 275: Memorandum Prepared in the Office of National Estimates, Central Intelligence Agency, 17 August 1953, *FRUS, 1952-1954, Iran - 2018*.

[195] Document 266: Mattison to the Department of State, 16 August 1953, *FRUS, 1952-1954, Iran - 2018*; Gandy Minutes, 17 August 1953, FO 371/104569 (TNA).

launch a second coup two days later.¹⁹⁶ The revised operation was multifaceted and designed to fully utilize the networks built up by British and American agents over the previous two years. Playing on fears of communist insurrection among the country's Muslim leadership, Ayatollah Behbahani would be despatched to Qum to request that Ayatollah Borujerdi, the supreme cleric, issue a fatwa against communism.¹⁹⁷ Meanwhile, in exchange for $10,000 delivered via a CIA intermediary, Ayatollah Kashani offered use of his followers.¹⁹⁸ In a show of support for the monarchy, Anglo-American assets in Tehran planned a demonstration euphemistically described by Wilber as an opportunity for 'loyal army officers and soldiers and the people to rally to the support of religion and the throne'.¹⁹⁹ Darbyshire was far more blunt, suggesting that agents had 'decided to bring the boys out onto the streets' and unleash the thugs organized by the Rashidians and the Boscoe Brothers.²⁰⁰

Ambassador Henderson visited the prime minister on the evening of 18 August and warned him that by clinging on to power he was damaging Iran's stability and credibility. Mossadegh unsurprisingly refuted this analysis and advised the ambassador not to interfere in Iran's internal affairs. Henderson raised the shah's firman dismissing him from office, but Mossadegh insisted the monarch had no authority to demand a change of government.²⁰¹ Within hours of this final meeting, a crowd reported to be around 3,000 strong had assembled in southern Tehran. Well armed with sticks and clubs, the Foreign Office acknowledged that they 'had obviously been hired for the purpose'.²⁰² Alongside the mob was a coterie of weightlifters, wrestlers and gymnasts who tumbled, bent iron bars and flexed their muscles to draw a crowd.²⁰³ Initially, only one newspaper, *Shahed*, had published the firman naming Zahedi as prime minister. However, on the morning of 19 October, typeset copies were

---

[196] CSH: Overthrow of Premier Mossadeq of Iran, 56–7.
[197] Document 273: Telegram From the Station in Iran to the Central Intelligence Agency, 17 August 1953; Document 285: Telegram from the Station in Iran to the Central Intelligence Agency, 19 August 1953, *FRUS, 1952-1954, Iran - 2018*; CSH: Overthrow of Premier Mossadeq of Iran, 57.
[198] Gasiorowski, 'The 1953 Coup d'État Against Mossadeq', 254; Azimi, *Iran*, 332.
[199] CSH: Overthrow of Premier Mossadeq of Iran, 56–7.
[200] Transcript: Interview with Norman Darbyshire for End of Empire (NSA).
[201] Document 280: Henderson to the State Department, 18 August 1953, *FRUS, 1952-1954, Iran - 2018*.
[202] Foreign Office, Persia: Political Review of the Recent Crisis, 2 September 1953, RG 59 788.00/9-253 (NSA).
[203] Woodhouse, *Something Ventured*, 129; CIAHS: The Battle for Iran, Appendix C: The Legend: How the Press Viewed TPAJAX, 6.

Figure 6.1 With Anglo-American backing, mobs rally in Tehran. Courtesy of Getty Images.

distributed across Tehran alongside a statement which stressed that the general was Iran's legitimate prime minister.[204]

Although aware of the first plot against him, Mossadegh now found himself taken by surprise and undermined by subordination. As the demonstrators marched north chanting 'death to Mossadegh' and 'long live the shah,' Tehran's Zahedi-supporting police chief Brigadier Nasrollah Modabber ordered his officers to stand down. Buses and trucks were organized to ferry shah loyalists into central Tehran, and their crowds' numbers were swelled by Imperial Guards in civilian garb, police officers, members of numerous far-right organizations and even 'well-to-do people' who resented Mossadegh's supposed dalliance with the Tudeh. Although Ayatollah Behbahani's attempt to raise a fatwa was unsuccessful, the cleric instructed his supporters to join the mob and provided logistical support.[205] Having dismissed Modabber, Mossadegh ordered the army to disperse the crowd, but officers ignored his instructions. When soldiers were finally deployed most chose to join the demonstrators in support of the shah. By midday, thugs had looted and torched the headquarters of three pro-government parties and half a dozen nationalist newspapers. In previous months, members of the Tudeh had regularly taken part in hand-to-

---

[204] CSH: Overthrow of Premier Mossadeq of Iran, 65.
[205] Foreign Office, Persia: Political Review of the Recent Crisis, 2 September 1953, RG 59 788.00/9-253 (NSA).

hand combat with their political opponents and it is likely that they would have offered some resistance. However, with hundreds of members under arrest, the party was impotent to resist. Although a handful of Marxists and republicans joined pro-Mossadegh soldiers in opening fire on the mob, they were easily overcome.

At 14.30, under CIA direction, the crowd seized Radio Tehran and the royal firman appointing Zahedi was read on air. By 15.30, they had taken the General Staff Headquarters and other government offices with little resistance. In a cable to CIA headquarters, Roosevelt reported that the 'overthrow of Mossadeq appears on verge of success' and Zahedi was escorted from a safehouse to the radio station.[206] Moving quickly to shore up his power base, he broadcast a statement that included an appeal for the military to drive out 'subversive elements' and invited those officers forcibly retired under the previous prime minister to apply for reinstatement. A desperate defence of Mossadegh's home lasted until 18.00 but ceased when tanks began shelling the premises. In hiding nearby, Mossadegh was arrested on 20 August and taken to the Officers' Club for detention before being transferred to a military prison.[207] In the days that followed the coup, Zahedi appealed for law and order to prevail and despatched military units to stamp out any resistance. The new government ordered taxi drivers not to take passengers beyond Tehran's city limits as Mossadegh's allies were rounded up and arrested. His position secure, the shah returned and Henderson reported that a wave of 'spontaneous joy' was sweeping across the country.[208]

In some respects, the success of Operation Boot/Ajax was a victory for the intelligence networks developed and policies advocated since Herbert Morrison was foreign secretary. However, although Britain's Iranian assets had played a key role in removing Mossadegh from office, the operation also illustrated the cessation of their power in Iran. From the records available, it appears that Whitehall was in the dark throughout the affair and relied on a drip feed of information from Washington and BBC news monitoring reports.[209] In a sign

---

[206] Document 286. Telegram From the Station in Iran to the Central Intelligence Agency, 19 August 1953, *FRUS, 1952-1954, Iran - 2018*.

[207] Foreign Office, Persia: Political Review of the Recent Crisis, 2 September 1953, RG 59 788.00/9-253 (NSA); Gandy Minutes, 20 August 1953; Tehran Situation Report, 22 August 1953, FO 371/104570 (TNA); Document 348: Henderson to the Department of State, 20 August 1953, *FRUS, 1952-1954, Iran - Vol. X*; Kennett Love, 'Royalists Oust Mossadegh; Army Seizes Helm', *The New York Times*, 20 August 1953.

[208] Document 350: Henderson to the State Department, 21 August 1953, *FRUS, 1952-1954, Iran - Vol. X*.

[209] Gandy Minutes, 16 August 1953; American Embassy Tehran to American Embassy London, 16 August 1953, FO 371/104569 (TNA).

of how distant the Foreign Office was from events, minutes from 19 August, as crowds rallied in support for the shah, refer to not only the 'failure of the military coup' but also the likelihood of American rapprochement with Mossadegh.[210] The situation was only marginally better for MI6 agents in Cyprus who relayed messages between London, Washington and Tehran. Although the British network was fundamental in laying the groundwork for the abortive coup and in facilitating the successful second attempt, Norman Darbyshire could only communicate with the CIA's Tehran Station and the Rashidians via intermittent radio broadcasts and was largely resigned to the role of operational spectator rather than active participant. Similarly, while the British government applauded the 'authenticity' of the countercoup narrative constructed by Roosevelt and his CIA colleagues, there is no evidence to suggest that they were involved in its creation.[211]

Defenestrated, Mossadegh cut a lonely figure as he awaited trial. As prime minister he had undoubtedly made mistakes and failed to recognize the limits of popular legitimacy. His commitment to delivering the will of the people he had at times been inflexible and struggled to translate his lofty principles into viable policy solutions. By threatening to sell cut-price oil on the open market he offered the Eisenhower government, already determined to see him replaced, the pretext necessary to launch a coup against him. Operation Boot/Ajax was a bitter full stop in the campaign to liberate Iran's most valuable commodity and expunge the informal empire that had dominated Iran throughout its recent history. Sentenced to three years in solitary confinement on 21 December 1953, Mossadegh rose to sarcastically tell the court that the verdict 'increased my historical glories. I am extremely grateful you convicted me. Truly tonight the Iranian nation understood the meaning of constitutionalism.'[212]

---

[210] Gandy Minutes, 19 August 1953, FO 371/104569 (TNA).
[211] Summary of Political & Economic Developments in Iran for the Period 20 August–2 September 1953, 20 October 1953, FO 371/104572 (TNA).
[212] Welles Hangen, 'Mossadegh Gets 3-Year Jail Term', *The New York Times*, 22 December 1953.

Reflecting on the end of empire in Iran

Mossadegh had been removed, but General Zahedi's position was far from certain. Without any democratic legitimacy, the new prime minister relied on the power of the army and looked for emergency financial support from Britain and the United States to restore his country's crumbling economy. Assessing the situation, CIA officials suggested that stability could only be achieved through 'a rapid improvement of the country's finances and economy'. Revitalizing the Seven Year Plan and launching a nationwide propaganda campaign would, they hoped, reduce the twin threats of 'extreme nationalism and communism'.

The CIA's self-described 'paramilitary operations' were wound down, and responsibility for containing Zahedi's opponents was handed over to the Iranian government and army.[1] This task was executed with vigilance and hundreds of suspected Tudeh members were hunted down. An unknown number of activists were executed and many others exiled.[2] The Tudeh's threat to Iran was routinely cited by British officials as evidence that intervention in Iran was required. In retrospect, the communist menace appears to have largely been a convenient foil for efforts to win American support for a coup against Mossadegh. Now out of power, the former prime minister was tried and found guilty of treason. Despite Zahedi's hopes that he would be executed, Mossadegh received the lighter sentence of three years in solitary confinement.[3]

In February 1954, British Chargé d'Affaires Denis Wright reported that Mossadegh still enjoyed the 'latent support' of many Iranians and 'no Persian government in foreseeable future can afford to ignore the nationalism which he stirred up'. According to Wright, the Zahedi government, although in control, lacked anything by way of popular support.[4] In a swift turnaround, the CIA judged that by the end of 1954 authority in Iran had 'reverted to the shah and

---

[1] Document 308: Monthly Report Prepared in the Directorate of Plans, Central Intelligence Agency, undated, *FRUS, 1952-1954, Iran - 2018*.
[2] Tehran Situation Report, 29 September 1953, FO 371/104571 (TNA); Behrooz, 'The 1953 Coup in Iran and the Legacy of the Tudeh', 124.
[3] Document 353: Memorandum of Conversation, 22 December 1953, *FRUS, 1952-1954, Iran - 2018*.
[4] Wright to Eden, 7 January 1954, FO 416/107 (TNA).

the conservative traditional ruling group'.[5] Mossadegh had at times displayed stubbornness, callousness and authoritarianism. He had, however, been able to command significant public and parliamentary support. With his removal, Iran's experiment in popular, if imperfect, democracy ended.

The agreement eventually made with Prime Minister Zahedi was a final full stop in the decline of British power in Iran. Under pressure from the United States, the Anglo-Iranian Oil Company, now rechristened BP, was forced to accept membership in a consortium – Iranian Oil Participants (IOP) – that took Iranian oil back into the international market. Its founding members were BP (40 per cent), Gulf Oil (8 per cent), Royal Dutch Shell (14 per cent) and Compagnie Française des Pétroles (later Total S.A., 6 per cent). The final 22 per cent was divided equally between the American firms that made up Aramco: Standard Oil of California (Chevron), Standard Oil of New Jersey (Exxon), Standard Oil Co. of New York (Mobil and later, ExxonMobil) and Texaco. As in Saudi Arabia, the new consortium adopted a fifty-fifty profit-sharing formula with Tehran. Framed as a joint undertaking between Iran and the West, equity had limitations and the IOP refused to open its books to Iranian auditors or to appoint Iranians to its board of directors.

Alive to suggestions that opponents may accuse Zahedi of collaborationism, British officials made a conscious effort not to 'hustle' the new prime minister.[6] However, from a cool start, relations failed to significantly recover. Sensing shifts in diplomatic power, the shah increasingly rejected British overtures and was 'quick to resent any suggestion of advice' offered by the British Embassy.[7] In the coup's aftermath the indecisiveness that had plagued him throughout the oil crisis was gradually replaced with assertiveness concerning his role in Iranian politics and relations with the West. American and British sources acknowledge that with no support base of his own Zahedi relied on the shah's patronage, a situation he found difficult to accept.[8] The prime minister's shortcomings were manifest and he became a vessel for long-standing concerns about political corruption and Iran's sluggish development.[9] In April 1955, after less than two

---

[5] Document 375: National Intelligence Estimate, 7 December 1954, *FRUS, 1952-1954, Iran - 2018*.

[6] Note for Use by Sir Frank Roberts, 8 October 1953, FO 371/104571 (TNA).

[7] Document 393: Despatch From the Embassy in Iran to the Department of State, 11 March 1957, *Foreign Relations of the United States: Diplomatic Papers, 1955-1957, Near East Region, Iran, Iraq, Volume XII*, Second Edition (Washington DC: United States Government Printing Office, 1991).

[8] Document 374: Quarterly Report Prepared in the Directorate of Plans, Central Intelligence Agency, 12 October 1954, *FRUS, 1952-1954, Iran - 2018*.

[9] Document 367: Information Report Prepared in the Central Intelligence Agency, 14 June 1954, *FRUS, 1952-1954, Iran - 2018*.

years in power, the shah ordered Zahedi's resignation and replaced him with Mossadegh's predecessor and long-time court favourite, Hossein Ala.[10]

This decision crystallized the shah's new approach to governance, and the American government praised him for his 'growing maturity'.[11] Having resisted a coup against him in 1958, he increasingly came to rely on authoritarianism to demonstrate his control, occasionally with the support of arms purchased from the UK. Parliaments continued to sit, but their role was effectively ceremonial, packed as they were with deputies the British described as 'the king's men'.[12] For the rest of his life, Mossadegh's legacy haunted the shah. In helping to remove the popular prime minister, he had undermined his legitimacy in the eyes of the people and perhaps guaranteed that he would always be feared more than loved. In helping to crush Iraniandemocracy in favour of authoritarianism tainted with persistent foreign influence, the shah shares some responsibility with Britain and the United States for helping to usher in an age of polarized political and, eventually, fundamentalism. He remained in power until 1979 when revolution saw him exiled and an Islamic Republic established under Ayatollah Khomeini, a one-time follower of Ayatollah Kashani. One of the most visible symbols of discontent towards the shah and his rule was a strike by tens of thousands of oil workers, which paralysed the state and lowered international production by as much as 7 per cent.

Ann Lambton, the revered orientalist scholar who was among the first figures to openly advocate for a coup against Mossadegh, would later present lectures on the prime minister's time in office and the relationship between state power, the Iranian public and oil. Pointing to the joint occupation of Iran and Reza Shah's deposition as a moment of liberation, Lambton charts the course of new political movements, the ebbs and flows of Marxism and nationalism in particular. Mossadegh subsequently emerged as the most popular and cogent voice in support of a nationally owned and operated oil industry delivering for the Iranian people alone. From this relatively measured analysis, however, Lambton veers into orientalist conjecture. Far from providing a realistic solution to Iran's economic and social ills, Mossadegh's advocacy of nationalization was an emotional spasm that failed to comprehend the oil industry's complexities or the necessity of British management. The prime minister, she argues, became

---

[10] Document 304: Telegram From the Embassy in Iran to the Department of State, 8 April 1955, *FRUS, 1955-1957, Vol. XII, Near East Region, Iran, Iraq*.
[11] Document 393. Despatch From the Embassy in Iran to the Department of State, 11 March 1957, *FRUS, 1955-1957, Vol. XII, Near East Region, Iran, Iraq*.
[12] Iran: Annual Review for 1956, 18 January 1957, FO 416/110 (TNA).

'emotional to the point of hysteria, spoiled by power and adulation' and in need of removal to safeguard Iran from communism.[13]

Lambton's account does not, however, acknowledge the British or American role in the events that occurred in August 1953, and wholly ignores the rumours of foreign interference that swept Tehran in the days after Zahedi became prime minister. Lambton's attitude is mirrored by the British government, which continues to deny researchers access to crucial documents concerning the coup against Mossadegh. It is only possible to speculate as to why successive administrations, whether Labour or Conservative, have been so determined to maintain a veil of secrecy and whether this reflects a modicum of collective regret if not shame. Sources that explain the collapse of British power in Iran and MI6's role in Operation Boot/Ajax can be pieced together, but our understanding remains incomplete.

In retrospect, it is clear that the British fundamentally misunderstood Mossadegh and the nationalist movement. Viewed as erratic, demagogic and, eventually, beyond reproach, there is a certain irony in the fact that the prime minister's upper class background and liberal nationalist ideology were broadly in line with accepted Anglo-American norms. Treated solely as a contractual and diplomatic disagreement, the moral fundamentalism that sat beneath Iranian claims to *their* oil was generally ignored. Myopia concerning Anglo-Iranian relations was a collective, rather than individual failure. It is possible to point to myriad examples of individual official's misunderstanding and even bigotry, but these reflected a wider institutional cultural and British imperialism. After Mossadegh became prime minister, the Foreign Office's perceived threat of Soviet expansionism – as embodied by the Tudeh – was undeniable; however, it was of secondary importance to maintaining control over a profitable foreign asset. British acceptance, following American probing, of the 'principle of nationalization' is demonstrative of the limited concessions that London was willing to make. Accepting nominal Iranian ownership of oil reserves while Britain maintained a monopoly over extraction, refinement and export was a rhetorical fix rather than a substantive response to Iranian demands. As with British attitudes towards Mossadegh, the Foreign Office and Anglo-Iranian Oil Company failed to acknowledge the legitimacy of the arguments being made by Tehran or adequately respond to them.

'What argument can I advance against anyone claiming the right to nationalize the resources of their country?' Foreign Secretary Ernest Bevin asked in 1946 in one of the few attempts to tackle the paradox between Labour's policy

---

[13] Mussadeq and the Persian Oil Problem, undated - 1969, Ann Lambton Papers – Box 55/7 (DUA).

of nationalization at home and continued exploitation abroad.[14] However, while Bevin may have wrestled with this contradiction, he refused to countenance the prospect of Iranian oil being controlled by the Iranian government. Instead, his preferred, though ineffective policy, was to try and minimize local discontent while exporting wealth to support Britain's post-war reconstruction. In Bevin's socialism any notions of international solidarity were a distant second to improving the material conditions of the British working classes.

The foreign secretary had been particularly keen to repurpose and redeploy the Iranian labour movement in support of British interests. In 1946 and 1951, Iranian workers and their trade unions were key to reshaping Anglo-Iranian relations and providing a vocal, visible outlet for popular discontent. In turn, the British had attempted to develop the labour movement's anti-communist elements and redeploy them in defence of British interests. Although this had failed, trade unions remained sites of resistance to state power. In November 1953, workers launched a solidarity strike as Mossadegh went on trial. In response, security forces broke up pickets with gunfire.[15] Quelled by force, the relationship between government and labour returned to a similar status as under Reza Shah. Although Zahedi had forged alliances with the Iranian Trades Union Congress, his interest in Iran's anti-communist labour movement quickly diminished and they were subsumed into a wider state apparatus. The 1959 Labour Law codified Iran's trade unions' relationship with government and management along corporatist lines and prevented them from freely organizing.

When welfare imperialism proved too costly and too difficult to implement, a diversity of alternative methods were used to safeguard British interests, particularly public relations and propaganda, political interference and, most successfully, espionage. Through the Tehran Embassy and the Anglo-Iranian Oil Company, money was funnelled to client journalists, Anglophile politicians and anti-communist trade unionists with varying degrees of success. In the elevation of figures like Sayyid Zia and Amir Keivan, it is possible to trace the sinews of British imperialism in Iran and understand its diversity and malleability. It is most stark, however, in the networks established by the Rashidian brothers with the instruction and support of operatives like Robin Zaehner, Norman Darbyshire and Monty Woodhouse. By 1953 the British could call on a sprawling web of informants and thugs that ran from the Royal Palace to the armed forces via Tehran's backstreet gyms. The mob that was so crucial to Mossadegh's removal

---

[14] Bevin Minutes, 20 July 1946, FO 800/484 (TNA).
[15] Tehran Situation Report, 3 November 1953, FO 371/104571; Gandy Minutes, 13 November 1953, FO 371/104572 (TNA).

from office was in large part a British construction and its lead operatives, according to the CIA's Richard Cottam, were 'true agents in the sense that they worked for the British Government and knew they did'.[16]

The transition from monopoly to oligopoly punctuated the end of informal empire in Iran and illustrated Britain's declining power. Informal imperialism had benefited London for decades but was unsustainable as Cold War tensions deepened and nationalist pressures stretched already threadbare resources. As Lambton acknowledged, British predominance in the Persian Gulf had historically been challenged by Russia from the north but for the first time had been 'taken' by another foreign power, in this case the United States.[17] In replacing Mossadegh with Zahedi, the Eisenhower administration had acted not only to safeguard Iran from possible Soviet intrigue but also to preserve the normal operations of the international oil business and stave off the dangerous precedent of Western investments overseas falling to nationalization. American investment in Iran followed and major brands like General Motors and DuPont launched operations there.

In 1951 Labour's minister of defence, the gruff Clydesider, Manny Shinwell warned that a failure to meet the challenge Mossadegh posed with force would precipitate a domino effect across the Middle East including the Suez Canal's nationalization. In some respects, his prediction proved accurate when, on 26 July 1956, Gamal Abdel Nasser's government took control of the canal. The logic that sat behind Shinwell's argument was, however, faulty. Lusty demands for gunfire to protect overseas interests were attractive but ill-conceived and owed much to an age that had passed. Ultimately, the period between 1941 and 1953 was one of British international decline regardless of protests to the contrary. Scarred and impoverished by war, international conditions were inhospitable to the British conception of empire. The Labour government experimented with welfare imperialism, but this proved to be an expensive mistake, which their successors chose not to repeat. Instead, as in Iran and Suez, Britain retreated or was removed from all but a handful of the empire's outposts. The challenge Mossadegh presented did not trigger this process but rather illustrates it. With the legacies of British imperialism under continued scrutiny, considering the prelude to nationalization and the events that followed presents a valuable opportunity to reflect on the empire's diverse forms and the varied means by which it was upheld.

---

[16] Transcript: Interview with Richard Cottam, 'Iran', *End of Empire*.
[17] Mussadeq and the Persian Oil Problem, undated - 1969, Ann Lambton Papers – Box 55/7 (DUA).

Bibliography

Archival sources

The British Library
BP Archives
CIA Electronic Reading Room
Churchill Archives Centre
Durham University Archives
Hansard
Harry S. Truman Presidential Library
House of Commons Library
International Court of Justice Library
Iranian Oral History Collection
Labour History Archives
London School of Economics Archives
National Archives and Records Administration
National Security Archives
The National Archives
United Nations Treaty Collection
University of Oxford Middle East Centre
Wilson Center Digital Archives

Document collections

Andrews, F. David, ed. *The Lost Peoples of the Middle East: Documents of the Struggle for Survival and Independence of the Kurds, Assyrians, and Other Minority Races in the Middle East*. Salisbury: Documentary Publications, 1982.

Dwight D. Eisenhower: 1953: Containing the Public Messages, Speeches, and Statements of the President, January 20 to December 31, 1953. Public Papers of the Presidents of the United States. Washington, DC: Office of the Federal Register, 1960.

Foreign Relations of the United States: Diplomatic Papers, 1941, The British Commonwealth; The Near East and Africa Vol. III. Washington, DC: United States Government Printing Office, 1959.

Foreign Relations of the United States: Diplomatic Papers, 1942, The Near East and Africa Vol. IV. Washington, DC: United States Government Printing Office, 1963.

Foreign Relations of the United States: Diplomatic Papers, 1944, The Near East, South Asia, and Africa, The Far East Vol. V. Washington, DC: United States Government Printing Office, 1965.
Foreign Relations of the United States: Diplomatic Papers, 1945, The British Commonwealth, The Far East Vol. VI. Washington, DC: United States Government Printing Office, 1969.
Foreign Relations of the United States: Diplomatic Papers, 1945, The Near East and Africa Vol. VIII. Washington, DC: United States Government Printing Office, 1969.
Foreign Relations of the United States: Diplomatic Papers, 1946, The Near East and Africa Vol. VII. Washington, DC: United States Government Printing Office, 1969.
Foreign Relations of the United States: Diplomatic Papers, 1947, The Near East and Africa Vol. VI. Washington, DC: United States Government Printing Office, 1971.
Foreign Relations of the United States: Diplomatic Papers, 1949, The Near East, South Asia and Africa Vol. VI. Washington, DC: United States Government Printing Office, 1977.
Foreign Relations of the United States: Diplomatic Papers, 1950, The Near East, South Asia and Africa Vol. V. Washington, DC: United States Government Printing Office, 1978.
Foreign Relations of the United States: Diplomatic Papers, 1950, Western Europe Vol. III. Washington, DC: United States Government Printing Office, 1978.
Foreign Relations of the United States: Diplomatic Papers, 1951, The Near East, and Africa Vol. V. Washington, DC: United States Government Printing Office, 1982.
Foreign Relations of the United States: Diplomatic Papers, 1952-1954, Iran, 1951–1954. Second Edition. Washington, DC: United States Government Printing Office, 2018.
Foreign Relations of the United States: Diplomatic Papers, 1952-1954, Iran, 1951–1954, Vol. X. Washington, DC: United States Government Printing Office, 1989.
Foreign Relations of the United States: Diplomatic Papers, 1952-1954, National Security Affairs, Vol. II, Pt. I. Washington, DC: United States Government Printing Office, 1984.
Foreign Relations of the United States: Diplomatic Papers, 1955-1957, Near East Region, Iran, Iraq, Volume XII. Second Edition. Washington, DC: United States Government Printing Office, 1991.
Harry S. Truman, *Containing the Public Messages, Speeches, and Statements of the President, April 12 to December 31, 1945.* Public Papers of the Presidents of the United States. Washington, DC: United States Government Printing Office, 1961.
History of the Joint Chiefs of Staff: The Joint Chiefs of Staff and National Policy Vol. IV 1950-1952. Washington, DC: Office of the Chairman of the Joint Chiefs of Staff, 1998.
Labour Party: *Report of the 44th Annual Conference.* London: The Labour Party, 1945.
Labour Party: *Report of the 45th Annual Conference.* London: The Labour Party, 1946.
Labour Party: *Report of the 49th Annual Conference.* London: The Labour Party, 1950.

Peace or War? Full Report of the Momentous Debate at the Margate Trades Union Congress on the Present International Crisis. London: Trades Union Congress, 1937.

Report of Proceedings at the 67th Annual Trades Union Congress. London: Co-Operative Printing Society, 1935.

Summary of the Labor Situation in Iran. Washington, DC: United States Government Department of Labor, 1955.

Books

Abrahamian, Ervand. *Iran between Two Revolutions.* Princeton Studies on the Near East. Princeton: Princeton University Press, 1983.

Abrahamian, Ervand. *Oil Crisis in Iran: From Nationalism to Coup D'etat.* Cambridge: Cambridge University Press, 2021.

Abrahamian, Ervand. *The Coup: 1953, the CIA, and the Roots of Modern U.S.-Iranian Relations.* New York: New Press, 2015.

Abrahamian, Ervand. *Tortured Confessions: Prisons and Public Recantations in Modern Iran.* Berkeley: University of California Press, 1999.

Acheson, Dean. *Present at the Creation: My Years in the State Department.* New York: Norton, 1987.

Ambrose, Stephen E. *Eisenhower: Soldier and President.* Riverside: Simon & Schuster, 2014.

Amineh, Mehdi Parvizi and Mehdi Parvizi Amineh. *Die Globale Kapitalistische Expansion Und Iran: Eine Studie Der Iranischen Politischen Ökonomie, 1500–1980.* Münster: Lit, 1999.

Ansari, Ali M. *Modern Iran Since 1921: The Pahlavis and After.* London: Longman, 2003.

Asgharzadeh, A. *Iran and the Challenge of Diversity: Islamic Fundamentalism, Aryanist Racism, and Democratic Struggles.* New York: Palgrave Macmillan, 2007.

Atabaki, Touraj, Elisabetta Bini and Kaveh Ehsani, eds. *Working for Oil: Comparative Social Histories of Labor in the Global Oil Industry.* Cham: Springer International, 2018.

Attlee, C. R. *As It Happened.* London: Heinemann, 1954.

Azimi, Fakhreddin. *Iran: The Crisis of Democracy.* London: I.B. Tauris, 1989.

Bamberg, J. H. *The History of the British Petroleum Company Vol. II: The Anglo-Iranian Years, 1928–1954.* Cambridge: Cambridge University Press, 2000.

Barnett, Correlli. *The Lost Victory: British Dreams, British Realities, 1945–1950.* London: Macmillan, 1995.

Bayandor, Darioush. *Iran and the CIA: The Fall of Mosaddeq Revisited.* Basingstoke: Palgrave Macmillan, 2010.

Beisner, Robert L. *Dean Acheson: A Life in the Cold War*. New York: Oxford University Press, 2009.

Biglari, Mattin. *Refining Knowledge: Labour, Expertise and Oil Nationalisation in Iran, 1933–51*. Edinburgh: Edinburgh University Press, 2023.

Bill, James A. *The Eagle and the Lion: The Tragedy of American-Iranian Relations*. New Haven: Yale University Press, 1988.

Brown, George. *In My Way: The Political Memoirs of Lord George-Brown*. London: Gollancz, 1971.

Bryant, Arthur. *The Turn of the Tide: A History of the War Years Based on the Diaries of Field Marshall Lord Alan Brooke, Chief of the Imperial General Staff*. New York: Doubleday & Company, 1957.

Bullard, Reader and E. C. Hodgkin. *Letters from Tehran: A British Ambassador in World War II, Persia*. London: I.B. Tauris, 1991.

Bullock, Alan. *Ernest Bevin, Foreign Secretary: 1945-1951*. The Life and Times of Ernest Bevin. London: Heinemann, 1983.

Bullock, Alan. *Ernest Bevin, Trade Union Leader, 1881-1940*. The Life and Times of Ernest Bevin. London: Heinemann, 1960.

Cable, James. *Intervention at Abadan: Plan Buccaneer*. London: Palgrave Macmillan, 1991.

Chaqueri, Cosroe. *The Left in Iran: 1941-1957*. London: Merlin Press, 2011.

Churchill, Winston. *The Grand Alliance*. The Second World War Vol. III. Boston: Houghton Mifflin, 1986.

Citrine, Walter. *Men and Work: An Autobiography*. London: Hutchinson, 1964.

Cook, Chris and John Stevenson. *A History of British Elections since 1689*. London: Taylor & Francis, 2016.

Curzon, George N. *Persia and the Persian Question: Vol. II*. London: Longman, Green & Co, 1892.

Dalton, Hugh. *High Tide and After: Memoirs 1945-1960*. London: Muller, 1962.

De Bellaigue, Christopher. *Patriot of Persia: Muhammad Mossadegh and a Very British Coup*. London: Vintage, 2013.

Defty, Andrew. *Britain, America, and Anti-Communist Propaganda, 1945-53: The Information Research Department*. London and New York: Routledge, 2004.

Dixon, Piers. *Double Diploma: The Life of Sir Pierson Dixon, Don and Diplomat*. London: Hutchinson, 1968.

Dorril, Stephen. *Mi6: Fifty Years of Special Operations*. London: Fourth Estate, 2001.

Elm, Mostafa. *Oil, Power, and Principle: Iran's Oil Nationalization and Its Aftermath*. Syracuse: Syracuse University Press, 1994.

Falle, Sam. *My Lucky Life: In War, Revolution, Peace and Diplomacy*. Lewes: Book Guild, 1996.

Fawcett, Louise L'Estrange. *Iran and the Cold War: The Azerbaijan Crisis of 1946*. Cambridge: Cambridge University Press, 2009.

Ferrier, R. W. *The History of the British Petroleum Company Vol. I: The Developing Years, 1901-1932*. Cambridge: Cambridge University Press, 2000.

Foot, Michael, Richard Crossman and Ian Mikardo. *Keep Left*. London: The New Statesman, 1947.
Gaitskell, Hugh and Philip Maynard Williams. *The Diary of Hugh Gaitskell, 1945-1956*. London: Cape, 1983.
Gelvin, James L. *The Modern Middle East: A History*. Oxford: Oxford University Press, 2005.
Ghoreichi, Ahmad. *The External Relations of Iran under Reza Shah*. Berkeley: University of California Press, 1960.
Godley, John. *Living Like a Lord*. London: Gollancz, 1955.
Heinlein, Frank. *British Government Policy and Decolonisation, 1945-63: Scrutinising the Official Mind*. London: Routledge, 2002.
Heiss, Mary Ann. *Empire and Nationhood: The United States, Great Britain, and Iranian Oil, 1950-1954*. New York: Columbia University Press, 1997.
Hyam, Ronald. *Understanding the British Empire*. Cambridge: Cambridge University Press, 2010.
Jackson, Ashley. *Persian Gulf Command: A History of the Second World War in Iran and Iraq*. New Haven: Yale University Press, 2018.
Kamrava, Mehran. *A Dynastic History of Iran: From the Qajars to the Pahlavis*. Cambridge: Cambridge University Press, 2022.
Katouzian, Homa. *Musaddiq and the Struggle for Power in Iran*. London: I.B. Tauris, 2009.
Kazemzadeh, Masoud. *The Iran National Front and the Struggle for Democracy: 1949-Present*. Boston: De Gruyter, 2022.
Kemp, Norman. *Abadan: A First-Hand Account of the Persian Oil Crisis*. London: Wingate, 1953.
Kinzer, Stephen. *All the Shah's Men: An American Coup and the Roots of Middle East Terror*. Hoboken: J. Wiley & Sons, 2003.
Ladjevardi, Habib. *Labor Unions and Autocracy in Iran*. Syracuse: Syracuse University Press, 1985.
Lansbury, George. *Labour's Way with the Commonwealth*. London: Methuen & Co, 1935.
Louis, William Roger. *The British Empire in the Middle East: 1945-1951; Arab Nationalism, the United States and Postwar Imperialism*. Oxford: Oxford University Press, 1998.
Marsh, Steve. *Anglo-American Relations and Cold War Oil: Crisis in Iran*. New York: Palgrave Macmillan, 2003.
McGhee, George Crews. *Envoy to the Middle World: Adventures in Diplomacy*. New York: Harper & Row, 1983.
Millspaugh, Arthur C. *Americans in Persia*. Washington, DC: The Brookings Institute, 1946.
Mitchell, Timothy. *Carbon Democracy: Political Power in the Age of Oil*. London: Verso, 2013.
Morgan, Kenneth O. *Keir Hardie: Radical and Socialist*. Radical Men, Movements, and Ideas. London: Weidenfeld & Nicolson, 1975.

Morgan, Kenneth O. *Labour in Power, 1945-1951*. Oxford: Oxford University Press, 1985.

Motter, Thomas Hubbard Vail. *The Persian Corridor and Aid to Russia*. Washington, DC: Office of the Chief of Military History, Department of the Army, 1952.

Naficy, Hamid. *A Social History of Iranian Cinema, Volume II: The Industrializing Years, 1941-1978*. Durham: Duke University Press, 2011.

Ovendale, Ritchie, ed. *The Foreign Policy of the British Labour Governments, 1945-1951*. Leicester: Leicester University Press, 1984.

Pahlavi, Mohammad Reza. *Answer to History*. New York: Stein and Day, 1980.

Pelling, Henry. *The Labour Governments, 1945-51*. London: Palgrave Macmillan, 1984.

Pope, Rex. *The British Economy since 1914: A Study in Decline?* Seminar Studies in History. London: Routledge, 2013.

Rahnema, Ali. *Behind the 1953 Coup in Iran: Thugs, Turncoats, Soldiers, Spooks*. New York: Cambridge University Press, 2015.

Rezun, Miron. *The Iranian Crisis of 1941: The Actors, Britain, Germany, and the Soviet Union*. Cologne: Böhlau, 1982.

Roosevelt, Kermit. *Countercoup: The Struggle for the Control of Iran*. New York: McGraw Hill, 1979.

Saville, John. *The Politics of Continuity: British Foreign Policy and the Labour Government, 1945-46*. London and New York: Verso, 1993.

Shafiee, Katayoun. *Machineries of Oil: An Infrastructural History of BP in Iran*. Infrastructures Series. Cambridge: The MIT Press, 2018.

Shaw, George Bernard. *Fabianism and the Empire: A Manifesto by the Fabian Society*. London: Grant Richards, 1900.

Sreberny, Annabelle and Massoumeh Torfeh. *Persian Service: The BBC and British Interests in Iran*. London: I.B.Tauris, 2014.

Stannard, Julian. *Basil Bunting*. Tavistock: Liverpool University Press, 2018.

Straw, Jack. *The English Job: Understanding Iran and Why It Distrusts Britain*. London: Biteback Publishing, 2020.

Takeyh, Ray. *The Last Shah: America, Iran, and the Fall of the Pahlavi Dynasty*. New Haven: Yale University Press, 2021.

Tarikhi, Parviz. *The Iranian Space Endeavor: Ambitions and Reality*. New York: Springer, 2014.

Thomas, Dylan and Paul Ferris. *The Collected Letters*. London: J. M. Dent, 2000.

Thorpe, Andrew. *A History of the British Labour Party*. Basingstoke: Palgrave Macmillan, 2015.

Vaughan, James R. *The Failure of American and British Propaganda in the Arab Middle East, 1945-57: Unconquerable Minds*. Basingstoke: Palgrave Macmillan, 2005.

Vickers, Rhiannon. *The Labour Party and the World, Volume 1: Evolution of Labour's Foreign Policy, 1900-51*. Manchester and New York: Manchester University Press; Palgrave, 2011.

Wainwright, Darius. *American and British Soft Power in Iran, 1953-1960: A 'Special Relationship'?* London: Palgrave Macmillan, 2021.
Ward, Steven R. *Immortal: A Military History of Iran and Its Armed Forces.* Washington, DC: Georgetown University Press, 2014.
Weiler, Peter. *Ernest Bevin.* Lives of the Left. Manchester and New York: Manchester University Press, 1993.
Wilber, Donald. *Iran, Past and Present: From Monarchy to Islamic Republic.* Princeton: Princeton University Press, 2014.
Williams, Francis. *A Prime Minister Remembers: The War and Post-War Memoirs of the Rt. Hon. Earl Attlee.* London: Heinemann, 1961.
Williams, Francis. *Ernest Bevin: Portrait of a Great Englishman.* London: Hutchinson, 1952.
Woodhouse, C. M. *Something Ventured: An Autobiography.* London: Granada, 1982.
Younger, Kenneth Gilmour and Geoffrey Warner. *In the Midst of Events: The Foreign Office Diaries and Papers of Kenneth Younger, February 1950-October 1951.* London: Routledge, 2005.
Zabih, Sepehr. *The Mossadegh Era: Roots of the Iranian Revolution.* Chicago: Lake View Press, 1982.
Zāhidī, Ardashīr and Aḥmad Aḥrār. *The Memoirs of Ardeshir Zahedi: Volume I - From Childhood to the End of My Father's Premiership (1928-1954).* Bethesda: Ibex Publishers, 2012.

Articles, chapters and theses

Abrahamian, Ervand. 'Factionalism in Iran: Political Groups in the 14th Parliament (1944-46)'. *Middle Eastern Studies* 14, no. 1 (January 1978).
Abrahamian, Ervand. 'May Day in the Islamic Republic'. In *Khomeinism: Essays on the Islamic Republic.* Berkeley: University of California Press, 1993.
Azimi, Fakhreddin. 'Unseating Mosaddeq: The Configuration and Role of Domestic Forces'. In *Mohammad Mosaddeq and the 1953 Coup in Iran*, edited by Mark J. Gasiorowski and Malcolm Byrne. Syracuse: Syracuse University Press, 2017.
Behrooz, Maziar. 'The 1953 Coup in Iran and the Legacy of the Tudeh'. In *Mohammad Mosaddeq and the 1953 Coup in Iran*, edited by Mark J. Gasiorowski and Malcolm Byrne. Syracuse: Syracuse University Press, 2017.
Blackburn, Raymond. 'Bevin and His Critics'. *Foreign Affairs* 25, no. 5 (January 1947).
Callaghan, John. 'In Search of Eldorado: Labour's Colonial Economic Policy'. In *Labour's High Noon: The Government and the Economy, 1945-51*, edited by Jim Fyrth. London: Lawrence & Wishart, 1993.
Chaqueri, Cosroe. 'Did the Soviets Play a Role in Founding the Tudeh Party in Iran?' *Cahiers Du Monde Russe* 40, no. 3 (1999).

Cotton, C. M. M. 'Labour, European Integration and the Post-Imperial Mind, 1960-75'. In *The British Labour Movement and Imperialism*, edited by Billy Frank, Craig Horner and David Stewart. Newcastle upon Tyne: Cambridge Scholars, 2010.

Crinson, Mark. 'Abadan: Planning and Architecture under the Anglo-Iranian Oil Company'. *Planning Perspectives* 12, no. 3 (January 1997).

Elling, Rasmus Christian. 'War of Clubs: Struggle for Space in Abadan and the 1946 Oil Strike'. In *Violence and the City in the Modern Middle East*, edited by Nelida Fuccaro. Stanford: Stanford University Press, 2016.

Eshraghi, F. 'The Immediate Aftermath of Anglo-Soviet Occupation of Iran in August 1941'. *Middle Eastern Studies* 20, no. 3 (1984).

Feis, Herbert. 'The Anglo-American Oil Agreement'. *Yale Law Journal* 55, no. 5 (August 1946).

Fieldhouse, David K. 'The Labour Governments and the Empire-Commonwealth'. In *The Foreign Policy of the British Labour Governments, 1945-1951*, edited by Ritchie Ovendale. Leicester: Leicester University Press, 1984.

Gasiorowski, Mark J. 'The 1953 Coup d'État Against Mossadeq'. In *Mohammad Mosaddeq and the 1953 Coup in Iran*, edited by Mark J. Gasiorowski and Malcolm Byrne. Syracuse: Syracuse University Press, 2017.

Heiss, Mary Ann. 'The International Boycott of Iranian Oil and the Anti-Mosaddeq Coup of 1953'. In *Mohammad Mosaddeq and the 1953 Coup in Iran*, edited by Mark J. Gasiorowski and Malcolm Byrne. Syracuse: Syracuse University Press, 2017.

Hinden, Rita. 'Socialism and the Colonial World'. In *New Fabian Colonial Essays*, edited by Arthur Creech Jones. London: Hogarth Press, 1959.

Javadzadeh, Abdolrahim. 'Marxists into Muslims: An Iranian Irony'. Florida International University, 2007.

Jones, Jack H. 'My Visit to the Persian Oilfields'. *Journal of the Royal Central Asian Society* 34, no. 1 (January 1947).

Lambton, A. K. S. 'Some of the Problems Facing Persia'. *International Affairs* 22, no. 2 (1946).

Louis, William Roger. 'Britain and the Overthrow of the Mosaddeq Government'. In *Mohammad Mosaddeq and the 1953 Coup in Iran*, edited by Mark J Gasiorowski and Malcolm Byrne. Syracuse: Syracuse University Press, 2017.

Louis, William Roger. 'Musaddiq, Oil and the Dilemmas of British Imperialism'. In *Ends of British Imperialism: The Scramble for Empire, Suez and Decolonization: Collected Essays*, edited by William Roger. London: I.B. Tauris, 2006.

McFarland, Stephen L. 'Anatomy of an Iranian Political Crowd: The Tehran Bread Riot of December 1942'. *International Journal of Middle East Studies* 17, no. 1 (1985).

Qaimmaqami, Linda. 'The Catalyst of Nationalization: Max Thornburg and the Failure of Private Sector Developmentalism in Iran, 1947–1951'. *Diplomatic History* 19, no. 1 (1995).

Roberts, Frank K. 'Ernest Bevin as Foreign Secretary'. In *The Foreign Policy of the British Labour Governments, 1945-1951*, edited by Ritchie Ovendale. Leicester: Leicester University Press, 1984.

Saville, John. 'C. R. Attlee: An Assessment'. *The Socialist Register* 20 (1983).

Seccombe, I. and R. Lawless. 'Work Camps and Company Towns: Settlement Patterns and the Gulf Oil Industry'. University of Durham, Centre for Middle Eastern and Islamic Studies Working Paper, 1987.

Speller, Ian. 'A Splutter of Musketry? The British Military Response to the Anglo-Iranian Oil Dispute, 1951'. *Contemporary British History* 17, no. 1 (March 2003).

Sreberny, Annabelle and Massoumeh Torfeh. 'The BBC Persian Service, 1941-1979'. *Historical Journal of Film, Radio and Television* 28, no. 4 (October 2008).

Sreberny, Annabelle and Massoumeh Torfeh. 'The BBC World Service – From Wartime Propaganda to Public Diplomacy: The Case of Iran'. In *Diasporas and Diplomacy Cosmopolitan Contact Zones at the BBC World Service (1932–2012)*, edited by Marie Gillespie and Alban Webb. London: Routledge, 2013.

Stoff, Michael B. 'The Anglo-American Oil Agreement and the Wartime Search for Foreign Oil Policy'. *The Business History Review* 55, no. 1 (1981).

Taylor, Jack. 'Oil, Scots and the Great Game in Iran'. *Nutmeg: The Scottish Football Periodical*, no. 25 (September 2022).

Vaughan, James R. '"A Certain Idea of Britain": British Cultural Diplomacy in the Middle East, 1945-57'. *Contemporary British History* 19, no. 2 (June 2005).

Vaughan, James R. '"Cloak without Dagger": How the Information Research Department Fought Britain's Cold War in the Middle East, 1948-56'. *Cold War History* 4, no. 3 (August 2006).

Zirinsky, Michael P. 'Imperial Power and Dictatorship: Britain and the Rise of Reza Shah, 1921–1926'. *International Journal of Middle East Studies* 24, no. 4 (November 1992).

Webpages and television programmes

Azimi, Fakhreddin. 'British Influence in Persia, 1941-47'. Encyclopaedia Iranica, 2003. https://www.iranicaonline.org/articles/great-britain-vi

Chaqueri, Cosroe. 'Eskandari Solayman Mirza'. Encyclopaedia Iranica, 1997. https://www.iranicaonline.org/articles/eskandari-solayman-mohsen-mirza

'Remarks before the American-Iranian Council', 17 March 2000. https://1997-2001.state.gov/statements/2000/000317.html

'Remarks by the President on a New Beginning', 4 June 2009. https://obamawhitehouse.archives.gov/the-press-office/remarks-president-cairo-university-6-04-09

Safiri, F. and H. Shahidi. 'The British Broadcasting Corporation'. Encyclopaedia Iranica, 2003. https://www.iranicaonline.org/articles/great-britain-xiii.

'The End of Empire'. Iran. Granada Television, 1985.

Newspapers and magazines

Life
The Economist
The Guardian
The LA Times
The New York Times
The Spectator
The Times
The Times of India
The Washington Star
Time

Index

Abadan
  British withdrawal from   144, 146–8, 154–5
  city of   6–7, 16, 83, 90, 113
  political unrest   63, 66, 112, 136–7
  refinery capacity   5–6, 32, 51–2, 136, 147
Acheson, Dean   96, 135, 147, 155, 167, 176, 186
  Anglo-Iranian negotiations   117, 123, 125–6, 128, 138, 152
Ala, Hossein   96, 132–3, 137, 209
Albright, Madeleine   2
Allen, George   74, 83, 96
Anglo-Iranian Oil Company (AIOC)   9–11, 14, 16, 31, 32, 39, 42, 62, 118, 142, 146, 162, 147, 158, 208, 210
  formation and operations before 1945   5–6, 8, 52
  intervention in Iranian politics   35, 36, 64–5, 90–5, 158, 168, 170, 173, 182, 211
  labour relations   64–73, 75, 77–8, 80–1, 82–4, 112–13, 119, 135–6, 157
  nationalization   133–7, 149
  negotiations with Mossadegh   140, 142–4, 149–56, 161, 168–9, 174, 176, 179, 188
  relations with the British Government   67–70, 78, 84–6, 88, 95, 110, 164
  service provision   6–7, 67, 82–3, 107
  Supplemental Agreement negotiations   99–106, 110–11, 117, 119, 122–6, 128–32
Anglo-Persian Institute   89, 92
Attlee, Clement   10, 43, 44, 50, 67, 87–8, 115
  foreign policy development   48–9, 55–7, 127, 131

  responding to nationalization   138, 140, 146–7, 149, 153, 157, 164
Azerbaijan   17, 21, 25, 30, 31, 40
  People's Government   57–62
  reincorporation   74–5

Berthoud, Eric   131, 163
Bevan, Aneurin   87, 113
Bevin, Ernest
  on Azerbaijan   56–7
  background and ideology   45–6, 48–9, 51–5, 127, 210–11
  disagreements with Clement Attlee   56–7
  health   87, 130–2
  labour reform   66, 69–72, 74–5, 78, 81, 112
  propaganda and black operations   81, 93, 114
  relationship with the AIOC   71–2, 78, 84–5
  Supplemental Agreement   100–1, 105–6, 124–9
Boscoe Brothers   194, 197, 203
Bowker, James   157
Briance, John   114
British Broadcasting Corporation (BBC)   34, 89, 90, 94, 127, 149, 199, 205
British Council   35, 89, 91
Bullard, Reader
  Azerbaijan   40–2
  political analysis   15–16, 18, 20–2, 24, 31, 119
  recommendations for intervention in Iran   36–8, 58–61
  xenophobia   23–4, 62
Bunting, Basil   85

Central Intelligence Agency (CIA)   2, 160, 162, 207
  anti-communism   163, 178, 186

assessment of Mossadegh 162, 169, 174, 187, 192
    coup planning 178–9, 187, 192–5
    early cooperation with Britain 163, 184
    the first coup 195–200
    the second coup 200–6
Churchill, Winston 164, 165, 167, 176, 199
    in opposition 140, 149, 154
    wartime prime minister 24, 35, 43
Conservative Party 139–41, 154, 155, 164, 210
Cottam, Richard 160, 212
Cripps, Stafford 16, 88, 100–1, 127
Cuthbert, William 70–1

Dalton Hugh 33, 50, 87–8, 127, 149
Darbyshire, Norman 9, 159–61, 184, 193–4, 198, 199, 202–3, 206, 211
Davies, Ernest 131
Democrats 73, 74, 97–8
Dixon, Pierson 52, 87, 187
Dreyfus, Louis 22, 24
Dulles, Allen 11, 162, 178–9, 187, 192
Dulles, John Foster 11, 187, 188, 192

Eden, Anthony 36, 40, 52, 165, 167, 168, 172, 178, 184, 189, 193
Eisenhower, Dwight 187, 192, 193, 199, 206
Elkington, E. H. O. 112

Fada'iyan-e Islam 108, 115, 135, 169, 197
Falle, Sam 9, 159–61, 171, 181, 184, 185
Fateh, Mostafa 78
Foroughi, Mohammad Ali 20–1
Forouhar, Gholam Hossein 129
Franks, Oliver 123–4, 128, 134–5, 149–50, 152, 174, 176
Fraser, William 66, 67, 69, 78, 83–4, 104, 130, 134, 172

Gaitskell, Hugh 87, 127, 145
Gandy, Christopher 84
Gass, Neville 99–100, 102, 172
Germany 13–16, 18, 21, 26, 27, 30, 33, 34, 43
Grady, Henry 117–18, 122–3, 125, 130, 165

Hakimi, Ebrahim 58–61, 64, 99
Haldane Porter, David 114
Harries, Edgar 79–80, 112
Harriman, Averell 151–2, 166
Hazhir, Abdolhossein 108
Healey, Denis 54, 85–7, 140, 141, 180–1
Hedayat, Khosrow 80–1
Henderson, Loy 96, 165–6, 171, 176, 184–5, 188, 203, 205
Hinden, Rita 45, 47
Hird, Kenneth 63, 79, 82
House of Commons 2, 50, 61, 131, 140
Hurley, Patrick 33, 39

Information Research Department (IRD) 93

Jackson, Basil 113, 123, 125, 150–3
Jernegan, John 185
Jones, Jack 70–1

Kashani, Ayatollah Sayyid Abul Qasim 115, 132, 155, 168, 170, 173, 175, 180, 182, 189–92, 196, 197, 203, 209
Keivan, Amir 120, 157–8, 211

Labour Party
    electoral performance 45, 63, 87, 127, 164
    history 45–9, 133
    internal discontent 54–7, 127–8, 148
    International Department 48, 54, 85–7, 140, 145, 180–1
    policy in Iran 9, 49–54, 75–6, 81, 98, 141, 152, 164, 167, 210
Lambton, Ann 4, 18, 19, 23, 27, 34, 85, 109, 111, 158–60, 165, 209–10, 212
Lawford, Valentine 110, 113
Le Rougetel, John 69, 83, 89, 97, 109, 110, 114
    assessment of the Tudeh 64–7, 74, 81
    labour reform 71–3
    the Seven Year Plan 95–6, 98
    the Supplemental Agreement 99, 101–6
Lee, Frederick 70–1, 157
Liddell, Guy 114, 148, 163
Lindon, A. C. V. 78

Index

McGhee, George   116–17, 124–5, 130, 134, 149–50, 156
McNeil, Hector   79
MacNeill, M. A. C.   157–8
Majlis   13, 18–19
   elections   28, 30, 81, 97, 108, 110, 167–8
   legislative terms
      Thirteenth   20–5, 36
      Fourteenth   31, 38, 40–1, 46, 61–2
      Fifteenth   91, 98, 101–4, 106, 107
      Sixteenth   111, 115–16, 118–21, 123–5, 127, 129, 132, 135, 142, 158, 160, 162, 168–9
      Seventeenth   171–3, 178, 180, 189–92, 196, 197, 201
   Oil Committee   116, 128–9, 131–3, 137
Mansur, Ali   115, 118, 120
MI5   113, 114
MI6   88, 113, 159, 165, 184, 187, 193–6, 198, 202, 206, 210
Middleton, George   118, 159, 161, 163, 168–70, 172–5, 181, 182
   Relationship with Mohammad Mossadegh   176–80, 183
Millspaugh, Arthur   22, 24, 27, 37, 38
Ministry of Information   33, 55
Mohammad Reza Shah   1–3, 10–12, 24, 26, 40, 61, 101, 103, 107–8, 113, 115, 118–20, 129, 132, 173, 174, 198, 207–9
   background and status in Iranian politics   18–22, 32, 37–8
   relationship with Mohammad Mossadegh   116, 137, 138, 157, 173, 179, 180, 189
   role in Operation Boot/Ajax   160–2, 166, 171, 172, 175, 177–8, 180, 183–4, 191–5, 197–206
   socio-economic reform   95–6, 99, 104–6, 110–11, 123
Morrison, Herbert   48, 89
   as foreign secretary   133–4, 140, 152–3, 205
   support for military action   146–9
Mossadegh, Mohammad   1–3, 9–12, 97, 103, 109
   background and ideology   25–8

   British reaction to   139–41
   first attempted coup   157–67, 169–74
   first oil crisis   38, 41–3
   National Front's formation   107–8
   Operation Boot/Ajax   177–206
   as prime minister   137–8, 141–2, 145, 147–8, 150–7, 168–9, 175–7, 179–80, 197–8
   return to the Majlis   115–17, 119, 121–2, 128, 129, 131–2, 134, 135

National Front   108, 110, 115–16, 118–22, 128–34, 136–7, 140, 142–3, 154, 155, 158, 160, 162–3, 165, 168, 170, 173, 177, 180–2, 191, 195
Nitze, Paul   185, 186
Noel-Baker, Philip   112–13
Northcroft, Ernest   100

Oakshot, Ronald   85
Obama, Barack   2
Official Committee on Communism (Overseas)   93, 113
Oil Workers Union   78–9

Pahlavi, Ashraf   171, 180, 194, 195, 198
Perron, Ernest   160–1, 198, 201
Pirnia, Hossein   99–100
Public Relations Bureau   34–6, 93–4
Pyman, Lancelot   168

Qavam, Ahmad
   prime minister, 1942–3   21–4
   prime minister, 1946–7   61–2, 64, 66, 67, 73–5, 79–81, 97–8, 95–6
   prime minister, 1952   158, 170–3, 177–8
   relationship with the Tudeh and the Soviet Union   58, 62, 64, 66

Rashidian brothers   159–61, 165, 169–71, 180–2, 184, 187, 190, 194–203, 206, 211
Razmara, Ali
   assassination   131–2, 161–2, 179
   cooperation with British intelligence   114–15

as prime minister   118–30
Reza Shah   7, 10, 13–14, 16–19, 21, 23, 25–6, 28, 31, 37, 42, 43, 159, 181, 209, 211
Roosevelt, Franklin   16, 33, 35
Roosevelt, Kermit   184, 187, 193, 194, 199–202, 205, 206
Rousta, Reza   77, 79, 98

Sa'ed, Mohammad   101
Sargent, Orme   73, 84
Schwarzkopf, Norman   199
Seven Year Plan   95–6, 98, 99, 107, 115, 118, 125, 162, 207
Shawcross, Hartley   147
Shepherd, Francis   115, 118–20, 124, 128, 135–6, 138, 150, 154–5, 165
  analysis of Iranian politics   110, 121–2, 129–3, 136, 137, 139–40, 162–4
Shinwell, Manny   146–7, 212
Smith, Walter Bedell   75, 187–8, 195
Soheily, Ali   20–1, 24–5, 140
Soviet Union   9, 127, 136–7, 159
  American perceptions of   116–17, 126, 134, 162, 165–6, 169, 186, 188, 193
  British opposition to   88, 91, 93, 94, 127, 146–8, 153, 191, 195–6, 198, 210
  British perceptions of   52–4, 57
  cooperation with the Tudeh   63–4, 66, 68, 70–2, 74–7, 79, 80, 87
  demand for an oil concession   38–43
  invasion and occupation of Iran   13–17, 21, 26, 28, 30–4
  occupation of Azerbaijan   57–62
  relations with Mossadegh   151, 188–9, 195
Steel, Christopher   185–6
Stokes, Richard   152–4, 166
Straw, Jack   3
SUMKA   190, 197
Supplemental Agreement   99, 102–8, 110–11, 115–20, 122–6, 128–34, 150

Tewson, Vincent   112–13
Thomas, Dylan   7
Thornburg, Max   96, 104, 118, 123, 162, 178–9
Toilers   158, 167–8, 182, 190
Trades Union Congress (Iran)   81, 211
Trades Union Congress (UK)   46, 53, 55, 77, 79, 112–13, 127
Transport and General Workers' Union   48, 53, 84
Truman, Harry   50, 151, 152, 155
Tudeh   28–31, 37–8, 40–2, 62, 111, 135–6, 160, 175, 189, 199
  political unrest   63–7, 77–8, 80, 113, 137, 142, 167–9, 173, 177, 180–2, 184–7, 190, 195–6, 198, 200–2
  Rahbar   30, 40, 64, 65, 68, 81
  relationship with Britain   31–2, 68, 70–3
  suppression of   67, 74, 81–2, 103, 114, 120, 202, 207

Wagner, Joseph   123
Wheeler, Geoffrey   88, 93–4, 163
Wilber, Donald   160, 184, 193, 194, 201, 203
Willoughby, Vere   83
Woodhouse, Christopher Montague ('Monty')   9, 165–6, 184–5, 187, 211
World Federation of Trade Unions (WFTU)   77–9
Wright, Denis   3, 207
Wright, Michael   108

Younger, Kenneth   114, 118–19, 130, 133–4, 164

Zaehner, Robin Charles   9, 159–61, 165, 166, 170, 211
Zahedi, Fazlollah   1, 157, 181–2, 190, 191, 193–6, 198–205, 207–12
Zia, Sayyid   36–8, 40, 42, 62, 115, 120, 132, 158, 159–60, 163–4, 170, 178, 180, 182, 211

www.ingramcontent.com/pod-product-compliance
Lightning Source LLC
Chambersburg PA
CBHW071834300426
44116CB00009B/1543